# A Common Worship Year A Miscellany

## A bumper resource for the principal seasons

Compiled by
# NICK FAWCETT

kevin
**mayhew**

First published in 2004 by
KEVIN MAYHEW LTD
Buxhall, Stowmarket, Suffolk, IP14 3BW
E-mail: info@kevinmayhewltd.com

© 2004 Kevin Mayhew Ltd

For a list of sources from which this book was compiled
see page 471.

9 8 7 6 5 4 3 2 1 0

ISBN  1 84417 290 2
Catalogue No.  1500719

Cover design by Angela Selfe
Typesetting by Richard Weaver

Printed and bound in Great Britain

# Contents

## HOLY WEEK

## EASTER

## ASCENSION

## PENTECOST

## TRINITY

## ALL SAINTS

# Foreword

It's been another busy week, and once again Sunday looms large on the horizon, yet you've barely had time to think about the services you're due to lead, let alone to prepare an address, family talk, prayers and so forth. Worse still, you've somehow found time, only to find your mind a blank, the wellspring of inspiration having run dry. Anyone who has been involved in the ministry or the leading of public worship will empathise with such scenarios all too well. Such moments of crisis can strike at any time, but perhaps most commonly during the great festivals and seasons of the Christian Year. Christmas, Holy Week and Easter, in particular, can be frenetic times with a host of extra events and services to organise, yet, as the years pass we can find it increasingly difficult to find new ways of approaching passages and stories from Scripture that we have already explored countless times before.

This miscellany of material has been put together as a tool for all those entrusted with the responsibility of leading worship. Drawing from such writers as Susan Sayers, Michael Forster, Katie Thompson, Peter Dainty, Pete Townsend, Stuart Thomas and Gerald O'Mahony, among many others and from my own books, it offers a resource book covering the principal seasons of the Church calendar, starting with Advent and progressing through to All Saints' Day. Beginning with an up-to-date translation of the recommended Gospel reading for Year A of *Common Worship* (generally taken from the Katie Thompson resource book *Hear the Good News*), it provides a variety of prayers, all-age-talk suggestions, service outlines, poems, meditations, sketches and other reflective material, together with introductory comments concerning key festivals and practical suggestions as to how these might be celebrated.

Most of the material can be used as it stands, though some – the all-age-talk material in particular – will require further thought and preparation. Nobody can provide a complete off-the-shelf package, and of course we would not want that, for we need to make worship our own, prayerfully seeking God's guidance as we weave diverse threads into a single tapestry. My hope, though, is that this book will help provide some of these threads, and so serve as a tool to all given the responsibility and privilege of leading the worship of God's people.

NICK FAWCETT

# Advent

Advent

# The First Sunday of Advent

*The return of Christ – be ready to welcome him*

## Matthew 24:36-44

*(also Isaiah 2:1-5; Psalm 122; Romans 13:11-14)*

### A reading from the Gospel of Matthew (24:37-44)

Jesus said to his disciples:

> Just as the flood in Noah's time took people by surprise, so too will the Son of Man come when no one expects him. You must stay alert and be ready, because you do not know when your master will return. If the owner of a house knew when the burglar planned to visit, then he would stay awake and keep guard. So you must always keep yourselves ready to welcome the Son of Man at an unexpected time.

This is the Gospel of the Lord
**Praise to you, Lord Jesus Christ**                          Katie Thompson

# Introductory material

We are here to celebrate the first Sunday in Advent; a day which is almost unique in the Christian calendar, for it calls us, in a way few other days can, to consider both past, present and future. It looks back to the coming of Jesus Christ; not just his birth in Bethlehem, but the promises of God made long before to Abraham and his people across the centuries. It looks forward to his coming again; that day when he will return in glory to establish his kingdom and reign victorious. And in the light of both these perspectives, it urges us to reflect on the present moment; to examine the life we are living, and then to ask ourselves, quite simply: have we received the joy Christ offers, and are we ready to welcome him should he return here and now? Hear then the words of Scripture and consider what God is saying about *your* past, *your* present and *your* future – in other words, what Advent is saying to *you*.

Nick Fawcett

# Prayers

## Advent thanksgiving

Loving God,
    we thank you for this glad time of year,
        this Advent season which reminds us of so much,
        and which reveals so wonderfully the extent of your love.
    For your coming and coming again in Christ,
        **we thank you.**

This is a time for looking back
    and remembering the birth of your Son,
    light into our darkness;
    a time for looking forward and anticipating his coming again,
    as he returns to establish your kingdom and rule in your name;
    but above all a time for the present moment,
    for examining our lives, searching our hearts,
    exploring your word, and renewing our faith;
    a time for recognising more fully
    that Jesus is with us each moment of every day, now and always.
For your coming and coming again in Christ,
    **we thank you.**

Loving God,
    you came to our world in humility,
        born of Mary in a stable.
You will come once more in glory,
        through the risen and ascended Christ.
You are with us now even as we speak,
        here through your Holy Spirit making Jesus real!
We praise you, the great truth of Advent.
For your coming and coming again in Christ,
    **we thank you,**
    **in his name.**
    **Amen.**

NICK FAWCETT

## Advent expectation

Loving God,
    you have told us to look forward to a time
        when your kingdom will come and your will be done –
        a time when there will be an end to sin and evil,
        suffering and sorrow;
        when all your people will live together in peace and harmony;
        when Christ will come again in glory.
**Come to us now, we pray.**

Loving God,
    forgive us that so often we have lost our sense of expectation,
        content simply to get by,
        settling for the way things are,
        failing to believe you can change our lives or transform the world.
    **Come to us now, we pray.**

    Forgive us that we have been too full of our own expectations,
        believing we know all there is to know,
        pushing you into little boxes we have made for you,
        presuming your thoughts and your ways are the same as ours.
    **Come to us now, we pray.**

    Forgive us that our expectations have been small and limited,
        tied down by our own limited vision,
        restricted to our own narrow horizons,
        shaped by looking at life from an immediate
        rather than an eternal perspective.
    **Come to us now, we pray.**

Loving God,
    help us through all this season of Advent has to say to us,
        to gain a new sense of expectation
        and new confidence in the future;
    Help us to be open to all you would do among us,
        and to gladly respond.
    Help us to catch sight of the wonder of your coming in Christ,
        and so may we be ready to greet him when he comes again.
    **Come to us now, we pray,**
        **in his name.**
        **Amen.**

NICK FAWCETT

## Intercession

*Keep alert, because much is demanded of those to whom much is entrusted.*

When the pressures of the day
fragment our peace,
keep us watchful and alert,
both for ourselves and for the world.

*Silence for prayer*

For who is God but the Lord:
**who is our rock but our God?**

When false values are paraded
among the true,
keep us watchful and alert,
both for ourselves and for our young.

*Silence for prayer*

For who is God but the Lord:
**who is our rock but our God?**

When our tight schedules
leave no time for being merely available,
keep us watchful and alert,
both for ourselves and for those who need a listener.

*Silence for prayer*

For who is God but the Lord:
**who is our rock but our God?**

When the injustice of the world laughs
at our insignificance,
keep us watchful and alert,
both for ourselves and for all who rely
on our solidarity with them.

*Silence for prayer*

For who is God but the Lord:
**who is our rock but our God?**

When we begin to take the wonder of
your creation for granted,
keep us watchful and alert,
both for ourselves and for every person
you cherish.

*Silence for prayer*

Merciful Father,
**accept these prayers**
**for the sake of your Son,**
**our Saviour Jesus Christ, Amen.**

SUSAN SAYERS

## Short prayers

Lord Jesus Christ,
    as you came once so you shall come again
    to establish your kingdom
    and to fulfil the purpose of the one who sent you.

Help us to learn from your first coming –
    to remember that, despite the long years
    of expectation
    and the desire of so many to see you,
    there were few who found room for you
    when you finally came.
Save us, then, from complacency,
    and teach us to live each day to your glory,
    happy at each moment to stand in your presence,
    and ready to welcome you
    on the day of your return.
In your name we pray.
Amen.

NICK FAWCETT

Lord,
    you know
    that whatever we think,
    whatever we say,
    and whatever we do
    has a consequence.
We are not alone
    and we don't live in a void.
There is a world around us
    filled with hurting, crying, worried and frightened people
    who feel as if their life
    has been squashed, crushed, contorted,
    twisted and bruised.
They don't know what the future holds
    and many don't care
    as long as it looks nothing like their today.
While for some of us,
    life seems to pass by
    in a sort of monotonous grey colour
    with no bright bits
    and very few dark bits.
But whatever we think,
    whatever we know, or think we know,
    you've said
    that the only thing we can depend upon
    is you,
    and that really is an unexpected bonus
    considering that we have such
    a fragile grasp
    on life, the universe and everything.

PETE TOWNSEND

# All-age-talk material

## Waiting in hope

Beforehand get a kitchen timer, and one of those automatic timers which you fix on a lamp.

Begin by explaining how you are going to set the timer for X minutes, at which time the talk should be finishing. You are also setting the light to come on half-way through the talk. (Do this.)

Talk about the way things seem to take ages coming, because we want them so much – like birthdays, Christmas, holidays, pension day or tea time. Other things seem to come too fast – like telephone bills, exams or dentist appointments – because we aren't looking forward to them at all.

The early Christians were really looking forward to Jesus coming back in glory, and it seemed to be taking for ever. People who expected it to happen before they were sixteen, grew to seventy-five and died, and still Jesus hadn't come. It has been about 2000 years now, and he still hasn't come.

Now as soon as we start measuring the time for something, it seems to make us impatient. 'A watched pot never boils', they say. Because you know this talk will end when the ringer goes, you are probably all waiting for it to ring at any moment, especially as the light will remind you that it's all being timed. Peter told the people not to think God was slow in coming; he was just patiently waiting for the right time, and that might be any time. That's still true – Jesus could come again at any moment, on any day. All we know for certain is that he is definitely going to return in glory, and we can't give an exact time and date to it. Meanwhile, we can live our lives to the full, living the life of love that God shows us, and keeping in close contact with him through prayer and worship, so that we are ready when he does appear.

SUSAN SAYERS

## The Advent Hope (1)

SUSAN SAYERS

## The Advent Hope (2)

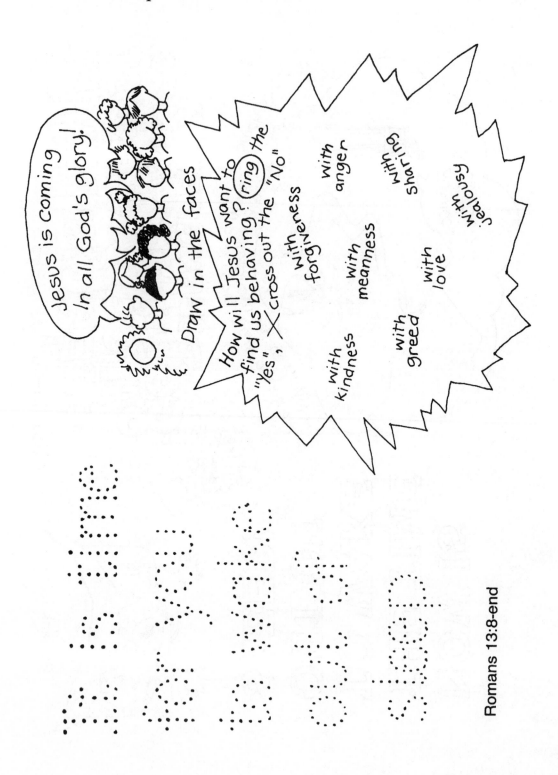

Romans 13:8-end

SUSAN SAYERS

Be ready!

Noah listened to God and was ready when the flood came. What happened to the people who were not ready?

| ▲ | A | T | W | E | Y |
|---|---|---|---|---|---|
| ○ | L | H | M | O | C |
| □ | N | S | D | F | P |
|   | ◆ | ✔ | ✚ | ☆ | ◗ |

**Use the code cracker to find the answer**

▲✔  ○✔  ▲☆

○◗  ▲◆  ○✚  ▲☆

□☆  ○◆  ○☆  ○☆  □✚

▲◆  □◆  □✚

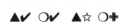
□✔  ▲✚  ▲☆  □◗  ▲✔

▲✔  ○✔  ▲☆  ○✚

▲◆  ○◆  ○◆   ▲◆  ▲✚  ▲◆  ▲◗

Matthew 24:39

KATIE THOMPSON

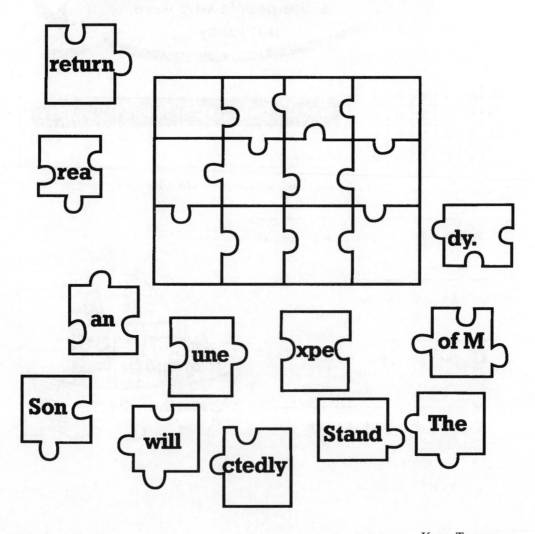

KATIE THOMPSON

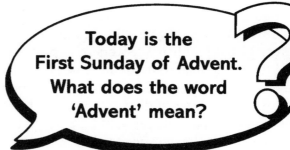

Today is the
First Sunday of Advent.
What does the word
'Advent' mean?

**Write the letter that is missing from
the second word in the box**

In **CARROT**     but not **PARROT**

In **OTHER**      but not **THERE**

In **MAN**        but not **PAN**

In **PIE**        but not **PEN**

In **NICE**       but not **MICE**

In **GOAL**       but not **LOAF**

KATIE THOMPSON

## Read Matthew 24:36-44

If any of us were to say that we weren't just the teeniest bit interested in what the future holds then they've either got life totally sorted and know how to sort out every global problem (answers on a postcard, please) or they're too busy writing their autobiography to care. Life is unreliable. No matter how we look at life or how much we look at the clock and complain about the monotony of our existence, anything, and everything, can change within a split second.

Lots of people spend money and time trying to predict their future and what it holds for them. The question is, does knowing what is going to happen in a few days', months' or even years' time change the way we think and live now?

Just say, for instance, that someone read your palm and said you were going to win a fortune. So, you go and live according to that prediction and use every bit of credit and hire purchase that you can lay your paws on. And . . . the bills arrive quickly followed by a solicitor's letter suggesting that you'd better pay the money back, with mega-large interest, asap. Alternatively, you might decide that if life is so unpredictable and that it could end quite unexpectedly, then you should live life to the full, right now, this instant or even sooner and ignore everyone in the pursuit of pleasure. Pretty soon you've got no friends, no money and no idea how much more of this pleasure trip you can take.

In reality, most of us don't live as if nothing and no one matter. We have people we care for and hope that they care for us. We try and save some money for the future or have an insurance policy as a protection against the unexpected. We are urged to make the most of our future by putting money into a pension scheme just so that we can enjoy our retirement (that is if we aren't too wasted to enjoy it). But the nagging thoughts still continue, 'Is this it?', 'What are we here for?', 'Have I missed the bus?'

As Jesus chats with his disciples, he tells them that at some point he wants to come back. The disciples must have thought he was barking mad but only Jesus knew that his time on earth was limited and the purpose of his human life was soon to be made painfully obvious. Jesus suggests that people will forget or ignore what he's said and done and live as if they weren't accountable to any-one. But, Jesus reminds them, the 'Son of Man' will return when people least expect it. This isn't used as a threat but as a promise that soon evil will become subject to the authority of Heaven, and that Jesus' return will signal the time when the ravages of evil will be put right.

No one knows when all that Jesus said will actually happen. All we do know is to expect the unexpected!                                        PETE TOWNSEND

## Expecting

**Reading** – Matthew 24:36-44.

### Aim

To bring home the fact that Advent is not an excuse for speculating about end times, but rather an opportunity to prepare for the unexpected return of Christ.

**Preparation**

You will need two alarm clocks (one with a loud bell, if possible), a flash gun or camera with built-in flash, two balloons (one inflated), a sharp pin and an empty bucket. Before the service set one of the alarm clocks to go off at the beginning of your talk – this will need some pretty fine judgement on your part!

**Talk**

Tell the congregation that you are going to test their ability to predict the future. Keep talking on this theme – for example, ask them how good they are at predicting the weather or football results – until the alarm you have pre-set goes off. Ask how many expected that! Reset both clocks, one to go off in two minutes and one in three, and then, keeping the clock faces turned away from the congregation, ask them to predict which will go off first. When one eventually goes off, ask who picked the right one. In the meantime pick up the flash-gun/camera, and ask what will happen if you press the 'control button' (demonstrate). Pick up an inflated balloon and a pin, and ask what will happens if the two come into contact (demonstrate!). Blow up the other balloon, then ask what will happen if you let go (demonstrate!). Finally pick up the empty bucket, pretending it is full of water. Ask the congregation how many of them will get a soaking if you throw it over them (demonstrate, and enjoy the consternation giving way to relieved laughter!).

In all of these situations, there was a fair chance of predicting what might happen, and in some it was possible to predict precisely. But there are some things we can't foretell. For example, will there be a white Christmas this year? Who will win the next World Cup? What numbers will come up on the Lottery this week? Such questions are almost impossible to answer with any certainty, despite the attempts of many to try.

And the same thing is true when it comes to Advent – a season for looking forward, anticipating the future, preparing ourselves for the coming again of Jesus Christ. The reason we light our Advent candles is to symbolise our mood of expectation at this time.

But when will he come? The answer is we do not know, we cannot know, and we do not need to know. As Jesus told his disciples:

> About that day and hour, no one knows, neither the angels of heaven, nor the Son, but only the Father. Therefore you also must be ready, for the Son of Man is coming at an unexpected hour.   (*Matthew* 24:36, 44)

It is not *when* Jesus comes that matters, but the fact he will come, in God's own time. There is no point in speculating about times and places; such things are unimportant. What matters is that we live in such a way that, whenever he comes, we are happy to be found by him, and ready to welcome him as our living Lord and Saviour.   NICK FAWCETT

# Reflective material
## (sketches, meditations and poems)

## Morning star of God

*Leader*    Morning star of God,
      rising in beauty from
      the ashes of our night,
      encourage us your servants
      who walk in darkness
      and need the loving
      touch of your light
      to lift us into joy.

*All*    Be gracious to us
      for without your light
      we are left in our
      darkness for ever.

*Leader*    Morning star of God,
      clothed in unattainable glory,
      enfold us in your
      robes of light,
      that we may stand
      in gladness before you
      in the beauty
      of your presence.

*All*    Be gracious to us
      for without your light
      we are left in our
      darkness for ever.

*Leader*    Morning star of God,
      our joy and our desiring,
      come to us we beseech you,
      shine upon us once again
      for life is cold without you.
    Our bodies, minds and spirits
      ache with longing for
      the glory of your light.

*All*    Be gracious to us
      for without your light
      we are left in our
      darkness for ever.

MARY HATHAWAY

## Meditation of Simon the zealot, one of the twelve disciples

We thought the waiting was over.
After all those years looking forward to the dawn of the Messiah,
   we dared to hope the moment had arrived,
     the day when God's kingdom would at last be established
     and his servant would rule over all.
But apparently not,
   for here he was,
     our friend Jesus, whom we had looked to with such confidence,
     such anticipation,
     telling us to be dressed for action,
     prepared once again for his coming.
It left us bemused, bewildered,
   for why did he have to leave us?
Why not simply stay and claim the kingdom now?
Only it wasn't that simple, unfortunately,
   a time apart needed before we could truly be together,
   and it came as a bitter blow.
It had been hard enough for those before us to keep faith,
   to hold on to the belief that the Messiah would come
   despite centuries of disappointment,
   and now here he was talking of another long delay in store,
   no telling how long it might be before his return,
   even, indeed, whether we might see it in our lifetime.
It takes courage to go on trusting then,
   a special kind of faith to keep hope fresh
   and the flame burning as brightly as the day it was lit.
We may think we're ready and waiting,
   but it doesn't take long for carelessness or complacency to set in.
He *will* come, we tell ourselves,
   but not today
   not tomorrow,
   and probably not the next day;
   so relax,
   take it easy,
   plenty of time for more serious discipleship.
He *will* come,
   but there's no sign of it yet,
   not even the slightest indication that the day is near;
   so, for the moment at least,
   let's accommodate the way of the world,
   a little pragmatism to balance faith.
Do you see what I'm getting at?
We say we believe,
   that our faith is as vibrant as the day it was born,

but it no longer makes any difference to our lives,
    its life-giving breath slowly anaesthetised
    by habit and familiarity.
Don't let that happen to you.
Don't be caught short when the day finally dawns.
I know his promise seems a long time ago
    and it's fulfilment equally as far away,
    and I know how easy it is
    to feel like those who waited so long for the Messiah's coming
    yet never saw it.
The difference is that we've seen him for ourselves,
    we've watched as he dwelt among us,
    lived, breathed, suffered and died;
    and we know now, despite everything that may seem to deny it,
    that, as he came, so he shall come again.

NICK FAWCETT

# The Second Sunday of Advent

*John the Baptist – the voice in the wilderness –*
*prepares the way of the Lord*

### Matthew 3:1-12

*(also Isaiah 11:1-10; Psalm 72:1-7, 18-19; Romans 15:4-13)*

## A reading from the Gospel of Matthew (3:1-12)

A man called John appeared in the Judean desert and began to preach to the people. His coming had been foretold by the prophet Isaiah who said:

'A voice calls out in the desert,
prepare a straight path for the Lord.'

John wore a simple camel-hair coat fastened around the middle with a leather belt, and he lived on honey and creatures living in the desert. Soon news of John spread throughout Judea and Jordan, and people made their way to him to confess their sins and to be baptised.

When some of the Pharisees and Sadducees came to John, he gave them this warning: 'Repent and turn back to God, and do not assume that you will be saved because you are descendants of Abraham. Any tree which produces bad fruit will be cut down and burned. I baptise you with water as a sign of your repentance, but someone more powerful is coming after me, and he will baptise with the Holy Spirit. He will sort the good from the bad, and I am not worthy even to carry his sandals.'

This is the Gospel of the Lord
**Praise to you, Lord Jesus Christ**                                    KATIE THOMPSON

## Communal reading of Isaiah 11:1-10

| | |
|---|---|
| **All** | **A shoot will come up from the stump of Jesse:** **from his roots a Branch will bear fruit.** |
| **Children** | The Spirit of the Lord will rest on him – |
| **Women/girls** | the Spirit of wisdom and of understanding, |
| **Men/boys** | the Spirit of counsel and of power, |
| **Women/girls** | the Spirit of knowledge and of the fear of the Lord – |
| **Men/boys** | and he will delight in the fear of the Lord. |
| | |
| **All** | **He will not judge by what he sees with his eyes,** **or decide by what he hears with his ears;** |
| **Men/boys** | but with righteousness he will judge the needy, |
| **Women/girls** | with justice he will give decisions for the poor of the earth. |

| | |
|---|---|
| **Men/boys** | He will strike the earth with the rod of his mouth; |
| **Women/girls** | with the breath of his lips he will slay the wicked. |
| **All** | **Righteousness will be his belt**<br>**and faithfulness the sash round his waist.** |

| | |
|---|---|
| **Men/boys** | The wolf will live with the lamb,<br>the leopard will lie down with the goat, |
| **All** | **the calf and the lion and the yearling together;** |
| **Children** | and a little child will lead them. |
| **Women/girls** | The cow will feed with the bear,<br>their young will lie down together, |
| **Children** | and the lion will eat straw like the ox. |
| **Men/boys** | The infant will play near the hole of the cobra, |
| **Women/girls** | and the young child will put his hand into the viper's nest. |
| **All** | **They will neither harm nor destroy on all my holy mountain,**<br>**for the earth will be full of the knowledge of the Lord**<br>**as the waters cover the sea.** |

SUSAN SAYERS

# Introductory material

We are here to look back. We are here to look forward. We are here to remember Jesus, born in a stable. We are here to worship Christ who shall come again in glory. We come to listen again to the words of Scripture that speak of God's promise. We come to rejoice in the Word made flesh. We come recalling the voice in the wilderness preparing the way of the Lord. We come to hear God's voice speaking to us. Open your ears, open your eyes, open your hearts, open your minds, and may God fill your souls with the living presence of Jesus Christ.

NICK FAWCETT

# Prayers

## Coming in faith

Living God,
  you have spoken to your people across the centuries,
    you identified yourself with humankind in Jesus Christ,
    you dwell within us through your Holy Spirit,
    making your presence come alive.
  Accept now the worship we offer,
    **and use us for your kingdom.**

Loving God,
　　having come to us, you call us to come to you,
　　　　promising that *in* Christ we shall find rest for our souls,
　　　　that *through* Christ our spiritual hunger shall be satisfied,
　　　　and that *from* Christ we shall receive life in all its fullness.
　　Accept now the worship we offer,
　　**and use us for your kingdom.**

Gracious God,
　　we come in response to your call,
　　　　to offer our worship,
　　　　our thanks,
　　　　our confession,
　　　　our lives.
　　Accept now the worship we offer,
　　**and use us for your kingdom.**

Sovereign God,
　　we come,
　　　　seeking your guidance,
　　　　your strength,
　　　　your renewal
　　　　and your will.
　　Accept now the worship we offer,
　　**and use us for your kingdom.**

Lord of all,
　　help us to come to you not just as an outward gesture,
　　　　a matter of routine or duty,
　　　　but in heart and mind and soul.
　　Help us to make space in our hectic lives
　　　　to be still in your presence,
　　　　and so may *we* live in you and *you* in us.
　　Accept now the worship we offer,
　　**and use us for your kingdom.**

We ask it through Jesus Christ our Lord.
**Amen.**                                          NICK FAWCETT

## Confession – rediscovering the word

Sovereign God,
　　we thank you for your word –
　　　　recorded in Scripture
　　　　and handed down over countless generations;
　　　　heard through reading, preaching, fellowship and worship;
　　　　glimpsed in the beauty of our world and the mysteries of life;

brought to life through prayer and meditation,
embodied through Jesus Christ, the Word made flesh.
Speak again now,
**and give us ears to hear.**

Forgive us that we are sometimes slow to listen.
We do not make time to read the Scriptures as we should,
allowing instead the pressures and responsibilities of life,
our many interests, pleasures and concerns,
to crowd out the time we spend with you.
Speak again now,
**and give us ears to hear.**

We become casual or complacent in our worship,
no longer expecting you to challenge us,
no longer moved to a sense of awe,
no longer hungry for spiritual food.
Speak again now,
**and give us ears to hear.**

We neglect the opportunity for fellowship,
turning in on ourselves,
imagining we know all there is to know of you,
more concerned with our own insights
than those we can gain from others.
Speak again now,
**and give us ears to hear.**

We grow deaf to your voice in creation,
our senses dulled by over-familiarity;
no time to pause and ponder,
to reflect on deeper, eternal realities.
Speak again now,
**and give us ears to hear.**

We believe we have listened and responded,
but our focus is on the written word
rather than the Word made flesh,
the letter rather than the spirit of your revelation in Christ.
Speak again now,
**and give us ears to hear.**

Sovereign God,
speak afresh through the pages of Scripture,
through the worship that we share,
the experience and insight of other Christians,
and, above all, through the inner presence
of the living Christ in our hearts.

Teach us, when your voice seems silent,
    to listen again more carefully,
    and to rediscover your word.
Speak again now,
    **and give us ears to hear.**

Through Jesus Christ our Lord.
**Amen.**

                                          NICK FAWCETT

## Intercession – proclaiming God's word

Loving God,
    we thank you today for the Scriptures,
        and the opportunity we have each day
        of reading and studying them for ourselves.
Hear now our prayer for all those denied that privilege.

We pray for those who have not heard the challenge of the Bible,
    who do not possess a copy of it in their own language,
    or who are denied the right to own a Bible or study it freely.
Lord, in your mercy,
    **hear our prayer.**

We pray for those who have heard but closed their minds,
    for those who read but do not understand,
    and for those who have read the Bible so often
    that it fails to challenge as it used to.
Lord, in your mercy,
    **hear our prayer.**

We pray for those who work to make the Scriptures known
    and available to all –
    those who translate the Bible
    into modern language and other tongues,
    who print and distribute it across the world,
    who strive to open its message afresh
    to each and every generation;
    and who preach from it, witnessing to Christ from its pages.
Lord, in your mercy,
    **hear our prayer.**

Loving God,
    may your word be made known
        with clarity, wisdom, faithfulness and power,
        so that many hear its challenge
        and respond in faith to your loving purpose.

Lord, in your mercy,
   **hear our prayer.**

Through Jesus Christ our Lord,
   the Word made flesh.
**Amen.**                                                     NICK FAWCETT


## A short prayer

Living God,
   you spoke, and the world was brought
   into being –
   the heavens and the earth,
   the sea and dry land,
   night and day,
   life in all its variety and abundance.
You spoke again in the book of the law,
   the poetry of the psalms,
   the wisdom of the teacher,
   the chronicling of history
   and the message of the prophets,
   revealing your will,
   proclaiming your purpose.
You spoke through Jesus Christ,
   the Word made flesh,
   through those who witnessed
   to his life and ministry
   and those who shared in the building
   of his Church.
You have spoken throughout history,
   through preaching and teaching,
   through study and quiet devotion,
   through prayer and fellowship,
   through the wonder of this world,
   and still you speak today,
   your word ever old but always new,
   able to redeem, renew and restore.
Speak to us now, we pray.
Help us to use this season of Advent
   to listen more carefully to your voice,
   and so to walk with you more closely,
   this and every day,
   through Jesus Christ our Lord.
Amen.                                                         NICK FAWCETT

# All-age-talk material

If you prefer to emphasise God's word there are several ways in which you can illustrate its impact. You'll need to prepare an appropriate warning sign and a familiar advertising slogan to a scale that can be seen by the whole congregation.

1) *Words convey information*, which is easily demonstrated by holding up an encyclopaedia. We find this everywhere – in books, magazines and in the broadcast media. The Bible also gives us knowledge about certain people and situations, but it goes much further than useful historical facts. It also tells us how to apply that knowledge in our daily lives so that we can live as God means us to.

2) *Words sometimes carry a warning*. At this point display a triangular road sign with an exclamation mark in the middle. It's fairly obvious that there's some danger or hazard ahead, but we need some words to indicate what it is – a flood, an accident or long traffic queues. God's word also contains warnings about the consequences of wrong behaviour or attitudes, and of going our own way instead of following him.

3) *Words also encourage us*. Here you could hold up a familiar advertising slogan which encourages us to buy a particular product. However, you should go on to stress that God's word isn't a sales pitch. God uses his word to encourage us to keep going with the Christian faith when we feel like giving up, to take risks for the sake of his kingdom, to open our lives to his guidance. Through it the Holy Spirit persuades us of the truth, and enables us to act on it.

STUART THOMAS

## Repentance

**Thought for the day**

Let's make a clear road to get
ourselves ready for welcoming Jesus.

**Reflection on the readings**

Isaiah 11:1-10
Psalm 72:1-7, 18-19
Romans 15:4-13 Matthew 3:1-12

Today Paul reminds us of the teaching and encouragement we are given through the Scriptures, so that we maintain our hope. By the end of the passage he's talking about us overflowing with hope, once we've got into the habit of being constantly topped up by God, who is, after all, the ground of all hope. And with the hope come all kinds of other good things, like joy and peace and a life of faith in the Spirit's power.

Hope is linked with longing: longing for all the good things we sense life was meant to be like, but which it so often falls short of. 'One day . . .,' the prophet dreams in our first reading from Isaiah; one day it will be as we all long for it to be, with righteousness and real justice, and no conflict or cruelty.

Is it just a dream? Almost like an alarm clock, John the Baptist bursts into our longings and starts shaking us into action. It is the action of thorough, deep-seated repentance, so that we may be prepared and ready for Jesus to save us and make the dream kingdom a practical reality. So that we are ready to come when he says follow; so that we actually notice him calling us.

Every time we come to the Eucharist we need to prepare ourselves to meet with Jesus, which is why we start off the service with a time of confession. How can we best use this provision? Clearly real repentance is far less likely to happen if we just read through the words on a Sunday without thinking much about them. The truth is that every time we realise we are thinking, acting or speaking unlovingly, bitterly, destructively, dishonestly or unfairly, we need to repent immediately and make ourselves right with God, whose love and truth our living has insulted. Then, when we gather as the community of faith at the Eucharist . . . we shall be making a communal act of real repentance.

### Discussion starters

1. Why do we need to repent and confess our sins when we gather to worship God and receive Communion?
2. Read through the words of the General Confession below, looking at what it suggests we should be sorting out in our lives. Have we become calloused to any of these, so we no longer count them as needing repentance?
3. As the church community here, what things do we perhaps need to repent of together? Are there any long-standing blocks (such as wrong attitudes, mis-placed priorities) on the road which we've stopped noticing because we are so accustomed to them? Get rid of them now by repenting together of them . . .

Almighty and most merciful Father,
    we have wandered and strayed from your ways like lost sheep.
We have followed too much the devices and desires of our own hearts.
We have offended against your holy laws.
We have left undone those things that we ought to have done;
    and we have done those things that we ought not to have done;
    and there is no health in us.
But you, O Lord, have mercy upon us sinners.
Spare those who confess their faults.
Restore those who are penitent, according to your promises
    declared to mankind in Jesus Christ our Lord.
And grant, O merciful Father, for his sake,
    that we may live a disciplined, righteous and godly life,
    to the glory of your holy name. Amen.                    SUSAN SAYERS

TODAY WE ARE LEARNING ABOUT REPENTANCE AND GOD'S FORGIVENESS, WHICH SETS US FREE!

**QUIZZ**

ROUND 1 — FOR THIS YOU'LL NEED ISAIAH 1: 15-16

**TURN YOUR LIFE AROUND**

WHY IS THERE A PRAYER OF CONFESSION AT THE BEGINNING OF WORSHIP?

Well, we're all gathering together to meet with God and worship him, but we all know we haven't been the loving church of people we're called to be.

SO YOU MEAN WE'RE PUTTING OURSELVES RIGHT WITH GOD BEFORE WE HAVE THE NERVE TO WORSHIP HIM?

Exactly. How can we realistically offer worship to the loving God when we haven't apologised for all the unloving stuff we've done, and the loving we haven't bothered to do?

WHAT'S IT CALLED AGAIN — THIS TURNING AWAY FROM SIN TOWARDS GOD?

Repentance. We repent of our sin, and God forgives us, which sets us free of it for ever.

1. **Why is God refusing to listen to the people's prayers?**
   (a) Their lives show they don't mean what they're saying
   (b) They aren't dressed properly
   (c) They aren't speaking loud enough

2. **What does God tell the people to do?**
   (a) Pray with more words
   (b) Stop doing evil and learn to do good
   (c) Stop coming to worship

ROUND 2 — YOU'LL NEED MATTHEW 3: 1-12

1. **When John urged people to repent, what did they do?**
   (a) They decided he couldn't mean them as they hadn't sinned
   (b) They kept quiet about their sins as they were embarrassed
   (c) They publicly confessed their sins and John washed them clean in baptism

2. **How were people told their repentance would be proved true?**
   (a) By going through the water
   (b) By the good fruit their lives would produce
   (c) By pretending they were sorry

ROUND 3 — YOU'LL NEED ROMANS 15: 13

1. **What will God do, as we lead the life of faith?**
   (a) Send us on a guilt trip
   (b) Make us into sad freaks
   (c) Fill us all with joy and peace, until, by the power of the Holy Spirit, we overflow with hope

SUSAN SAYERS

## Read Matthew 3:1-12

Can you imagine what image John the Baptist would have made? Just think, here's a bloke dressed in a camel-hair suit, a leather strap wrapped around his waist and dipping grasshoppers into a pot of honey and popping them into his mouth! In between mouthfuls he gives the crowd a load of verbal about their antics and suggests they have a lot in common with snakes. He then goes on to give them some tips on gardening and hints that they all could do with a dunk in the river. You can just hear the mutterings of 'Been in the sun too long' or 'What can you expect from someone who wanders around the desert all day?' Quite a few folk would have been making gestures indicating that John was a few grains short of a sand-castle.

John the Baptist was a man who had turned his back on the comforts that most people enjoyed and had given himself to reading and meditating about God. Despite his odd appearance and behaviour, John was recognised as a messenger. His message was that all the people should '. . . Get the road ready for the Lord . . .' (Matthew 3:3). This wasn't such a strange thing to say as you might imagine. During, and before, biblical times the roads were almost non-existent. Those tracks that did exist were in a terrible condition and most people who travelled were warned to sort out all their legal affairs and say goodbye to their family because there was no guarantee that you would get to your intended destination safely.

The few good roads that did exist were built for a special purpose. King Solomon built a road of black basalt (a volcanic rock which often contained crystals). These special roads were constructed to reflect the wealth of the king. These roads were built by the king and mainly for the benefit of the king. They were often referred to as 'The king's highway'. Before the king began his travels a message was sent out telling the people to get the roads repaired and looking good in preparation for the king's arrival.

John's message was just the same, the only difference being that the road to be prepared wasn't made of basalt but of flesh and blood, the human heart and mind. John was preparing the people to hear the words of Jesus and the words wouldn't reach their destination if the 'road' wasn't ready to receive a message from the King.

John was concerned that the people were too occupied with their own comforts and had forgotten who God was! The rulers, politicians and religious leaders were too busy building their own little kingdoms to listen to the message of the 'King'. John was determined that when Jesus began his journey the people had at least been warned of his coming.

PETE TOWNSEND

**John said about Jesus . . .**

KATIE THOMPSON

**Some people believed that he was the Messiah. What did John tell them?**

**Match the shapes and copy the letters**

JOHN 1:20

KATIE THOMPSON

# LOOKING AT THE BIBLE

The Bible has lots of books in it. Here are some of them~ cross out every second letter to find them:

AMCSTUSY

LJUBKMEX

JHOMHANS

GBEJNOERSTILSN PRSBALLOMTSJ

ITSWAYIMANHT

One of the ways we can find out what God is like is to read the Bible. The ▢ Testament looks forward to the coming of Jesus. The ▢ Testament is about Jesus and his followers.

Find Psalm 119 verse 105 and write the words here:

Your ___ is a ___ to ___ and a ___ to ~

WORD    IN    GOD    THE    HEAR    AND    THE    OF    WE    READ    BIBLE    CAN

The BIBLE

Design a cover for this bible

SUSAN SAYERS

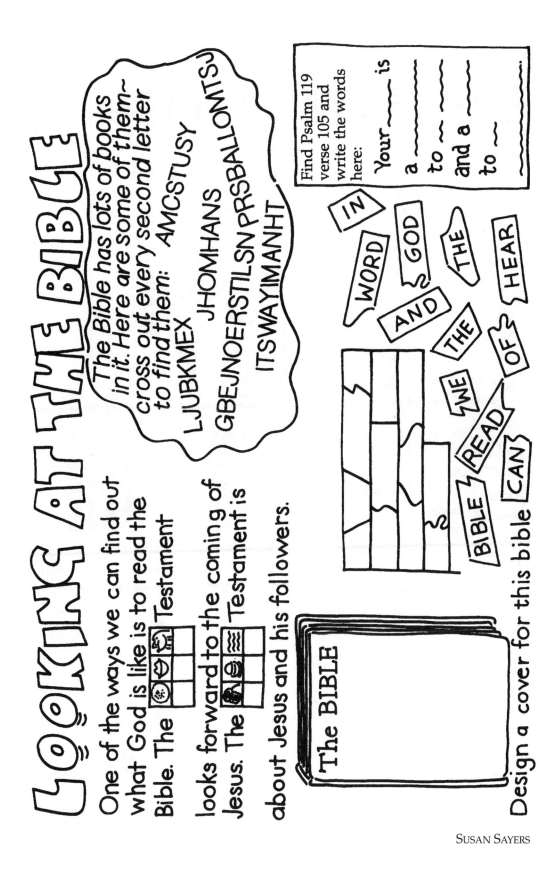

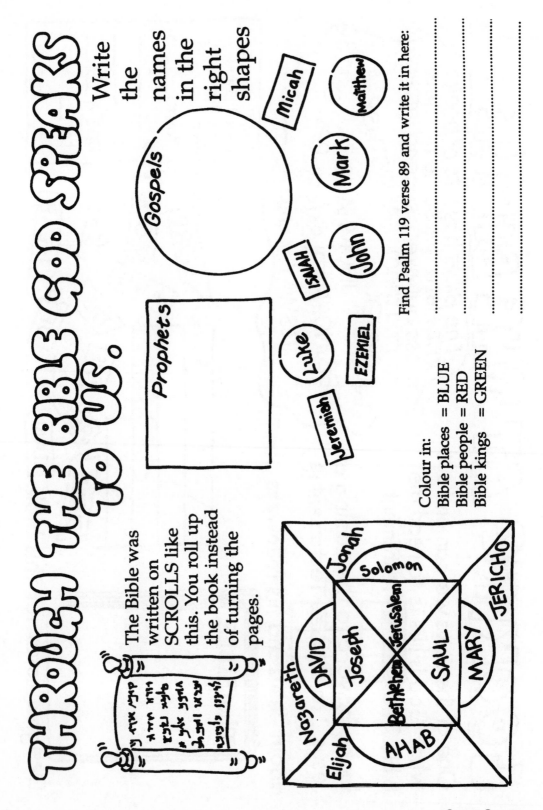

# THROUGH THE BIBLE GOD SPEAKS TO US.

Write the names in the right shapes

Gospels

Prophets

Micah

Matthew

Mark

John

ISAIAH

Luke

EZEKIEL

Jeremiah

Find Psalm 119 verse 89 and write it in here:

...................................................

...................................................

...................................................

Colour in:
Bible places = BLUE
Bible people = RED
Bible kings = GREEN

The Bible was written on SCROLLS like this. You roll up the book instead of turning the pages.

Jonah

Solomon

Nazareth

DAVID

Joseph

Bethlehem

Jerusalem

SAUL

MARY

JERICHO

Elijah

AHAB

SUSAN SAYERS

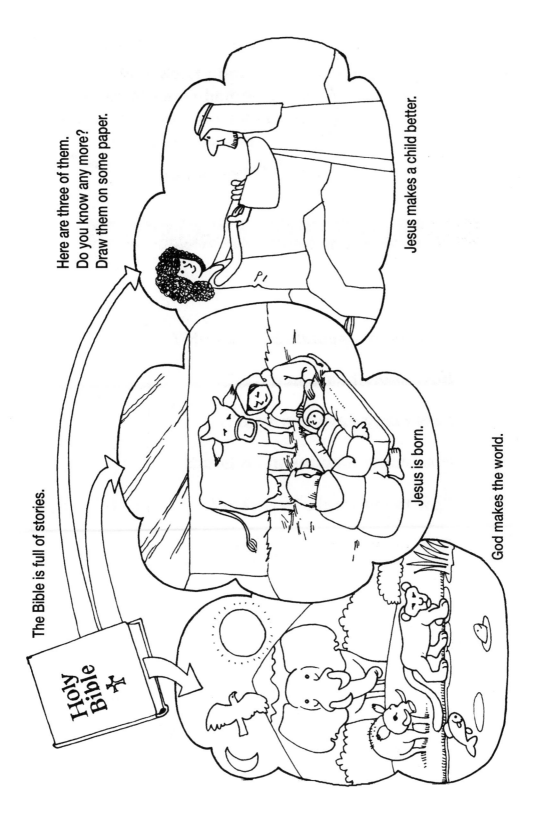

The Bible is full of stories.

Here are three of them.
Do you know any more?
Draw them on some paper.

Jesus makes a child better.

Jesus is born.

God makes the world.

SUSAN SAYERS

John knew that the time had come to 'prepare a way for the Lord'. We must be prepared too!

**How much do you know about time? Try this quiz!**

**How many seconds in a minute?**

**How many hours in a day?**

**How many days in a year?**

**How many minutes in an hour?**

**How many weeks in a year?**

**How many minutes in a day?**

KATIE THOMPSON

John called
the people to say sorry for
turning away from God and to
change their hearts

**Use the code to read the warning he gave them!**

CODE

ABCDEFGHIJKLMNOPQRSTUVWXYZ
zyxwvutsrqponmlkjihgfedcba

'
‾  ‾  ‾     ‾  ‾  ‾  ‾     ‾  ‾  ‾  ‾
z  m  b     g  i  v  v     g  s  z  g

‾  ‾  ‾  ‾     ‾  ‾  ‾     ‾  ‾  ‾  ‾
w  l  v  h     m  l  g     y  v  z  i

‾  ‾  ‾  ‾     ‾  ‾  ‾  ‾'
t  l  l  w     u  i  f  r  g

‾  ‾  ‾  ‾     ‾  ‾     ‾  ‾  ‾
d  r  o  o     y  v     x  f  g

‾  ‾  ‾  ‾,
w  l  d  m

Matt    3:10

**John the Baptist**

**John appeared in the wilderness and preached to the people**

**Follow the arrows to find his words**

Matthew
3:2

| S | P | A | I | M | L | H | E |
|---|---|---|---|---|---|---|---|
| R→ | P | K | N | O | F | A | V |
| E | E | G | D | S | R | E | A |
| F | N | H | B | I | N | E | N |
| O | T | T | S | C | S | M | B |
| D | R | E | G | L | O | F | L |

KATIE THOMPSON

# Reflective material
## (sketches, meditations and poems)

### The Bible

*(The reader should hold a large black Bible)*

I do not love this book because it is
   black enough to please Puritans,
   holy enough to scare demons,
   thick enough to stop bullets,
   heavy enough to squash flies;
   but because sometimes when I read it
   I am moved
   deeper than tears.

I do not love this book because
   they say it is the very words of God,
   and polish every dot and comma,
   like golden ornaments
   in an idolatrous temple;
   but because sometimes when I read it
   God speaks in a strange tongue
   deeper than words.

I do not love this book because
   the passionate preacher
   beats the truth out of it
   with his blunt fist
   and sharp ideas,
   (for some use the book
   to support their opinions,
   as others might use it
   to support their tables).

But I do love this book
   because sometimes when I read it
   I am disturbed by a truth
   deeper than thought.

And when I read of Jesus,
   then I know,
   that *he* is the Truth
   that moves my soul –
   the living Word of God.

PETER DAINTY

## A Plug for the Book

**Logian**   Good evening and welcome again to *On the Spot* in this very special series of interviews. We often have guests appearing on this show with the intention of getting a plug for some book they've written in the hope that it might thereby become a best seller. Tonight it's different. The book is *already* a best seller, and has been since any of us can remember. Some describe it as the greatest literature in the world; others claim that it's riddled with inconsistencies; secular feminists denounce it as patriarchalist propaganda, and more blood has been shed over it than any other document. The book is the Bible, and here to talk about it is its author. Welcome, Big G.

**Big G**   Thank you. Good evening.

**Logian**   Let's get the basic argument cleared up straightaway. Did you write this book, and is it true?

**Big G**   Well, I really would like to help, but I think you'll find that it's not *quite* as simple as that, Theo.

**Logian**   I'd have thought it was *absolutely* that simple. Either you wrote it or you didn't; either it's true or it's not. What could be simpler?

**Big G**   It's a bit like the proverbial 'Have you stopped beating your wife?' question. A straight yes or no doesn't really do it justice.

**Logian**   But surely, that's a deliberate catch question. I asked you a totally straightforward one. Did you write the Bible?

**Big G**   Do you mean, did I actually hold a pen in my hand and create the text letter by letter?

**Logian**   Well, no. Of course I didn't mean it *that* literally. OK, you've made your point. I'll accept that that part of the question is open to interpretation. But what about the second half? It's either true or it's not.

**Big G**   Would you mind if we stay with the first half for a little longer, Theo?

**Logian**   You wouldn't be avoiding the issue, by any chance?

**Big G**   Oh, no – not in the least; we seem to have got a bit hung up on the wording. Look, will it help if I say that the Bible was inspired by me?

**Logian**   I thought that was what I asked.

**Big G**   Not quite, you asked whether I *wrote* the Bible.

**Logian**   But it comes to the same thing in this instance.

**Big G**   Let me put it this way. To say that *I wrote the* Bible is a little like saying you wrote that short story for Dan – the one that won him a school prize.

**Logian**  I did *not* write it! It was all his own work. I never thought I'd say this to you, Big G, but you should be careful what you say. People might misunderstand.

**Big G**  Right! Now you see what I'm driving at? You didn't write that story, of course, but you *did* inspire it.

**Logian**  Did I?

**Big G**  It was about a child who longed to be a journalist, and then grew up and found out that it isn't all it's cracked up to be.

**Logian**  You're right. I'd never realised before.

**Big G**  So you're happy to say you inspired it?

**Logian**  Now you point it out, yes.

**Big G**  But not that you wrote it?

**Logian**  No. And not just because of the split infinitive in the final paragraph.

**Big G**  Why, then?

**Logian**  Because I don't want to detract from his achievement. I'm really glad to have had a part in it, though.

**Big G**  So you won't mind, then, if I say that I inspired the Bible, but didn't actually write it?

**Logian**  I can see the distinction you're trying to make, Big G, but it's still rather unclear. I mean, just *how* did you inspire it?

**Big G**  How did you inspire Dan?

**Logian**  I didn't know I was, to be honest.

**Big G**  That's interesting. So you didn't wake up one morning and think, 'I'm going to inspire Dan to write a prize-winning story about a disillusioned journalist'?

**Logian**  Heavens, no! Sorry, Big G.

**Big G**  Don't worry, Theo. My good friend Paul used a similar kind of phrase in his letters to the churches, but pious translators watered it down to 'by no means' – I ask you! So how did Dan's inspiration come about?

**Logian**  I suppose it must have been happening when we were talking together.

**Big G**  Or, perhaps, playing together?

**Logian**  Yes, maybe.

**Big G**  We're really very alike, you and I, which I suppose shouldn't be surprising. So the inspiration happened in your ordinary relationship. You and Dan have talked together, played together, laughed and cried together I always enjoy your games, you know – and then what he actually wrote was *inspired by* you but *written* by him.

**Logian**  I see what you're driving at. But it doesn't quite work. I didn't interfere with Dan's writing, but I would have done if I'd had to.

**Big G**  Go on?

**Logian**  Well, some of the biblical writers have said some things that I'd *definitely*
have censored if I'd been you.

**Big G**  But you're not me.

**Logian**  No, but don't say it too loudly. My secretary might hear you.

**Big G**  Fair enough, Theo. Can you give me some examples?

**Logian**  There's an awful lot of bloodlust in the Bible; and most of the time
people ascribe it to you. Did you really tell your people to do such
horrible things to their enemies?

**Big G**  What do you think, Theo?

**Logian**  If you did, you'll be getting no more 'alleluias' or 'praise his names'
from me, for a start.

**Big G**  Well said. It's bad enough that people do these horrible things to each
other, but when they convince themselves that I approve of it . . . and
then for people to believe them . . .

**Logian**  I don't *want* to, Big G, but if those passages are wrong why are they
there?

**Big G**  Partly for the same reason that the split infinitive's still in Dan's story.
Because it's inspired, not dictated. But tell me what you learn from
those parts of Scripture.

**Logian**  I don't want to upset you, Big G, but to be candid I've never got anything at all from passages like that.

**Big G**  Bless you, Theo, I'm not *that* sensitive! It's how people treat each other,
not the Bible, that gets to me. Let me put it another way. What does all
that violence and ghastliness tell you *about the writer*?

**Logian**  Seems to me he was sanctifying his own desires by attributing them to
you.

**Big G**  It's not at all uncommon, I'm afraid. People do it all the time, and
things were no different in biblical days.

**Logian**  Andnow?

**Big G**  It's not so long since the Dutch Reformed Church in South Africa were
claiming that I approved of Apartheid. Now that *really* got to me, but I
danced in the streets when they corrected it!

**Logian**  So the kind of biblical verses I've been querying should have been a
warning to them. But what have they got to say to ordinary people
like you and – whoops – like me?

**Big G**   You know, Theo, I rather liked that. 'Ordinary'. Most people put me on a pedestal and then complain they can't relate to me! Anyway, to address your question: I do remember an instance of someone who thought I wanted him to have a bigger house. Before I could get through to him to deny it, he'd got it all worked out. He needed a bigger study so that he could work for me better, and a larger lounge and garden so he could hold functions for the church, and so it went on. Before long, he'd convinced himself that he was really doing it for me.

**Logian**   I don't mind people knowing that was me, Big G. And you're right – I really did convince myself I was doing it all for you.

**Big G**   Of course you did, Theo, and you're very far from alone. So perhaps there is something you can learn from those passages, after all.

**Logian**   So you're saying that the biblical writers can speak to us in ways they themselves didn't even realise?

**Big G**   Close. I'm saying that *I* can speak through the things they write. I love working *with* people – not against them. And however wrong they get things, I can always bring something good out of it, even if it's not what ideally I'd have wanted.

**Logian**   Of course! Redemption.

**Big G**   Exactly! The most rewarding part of my work: taking what is apparently lost and turning it to good.

**Logian**   We seem to have moved on to the second part of my question: about whether the Bible's true or not. I realise now that it isn't.

**Big G**   When did I say that?

**Logian**   Earlier on, I asked whether the Bible was true.

**Big G**   And I haven't answered that, yet.

**Logian**   But everything you've just said –

**Big G**   – suggests that there are parts that aren't *factual*.

**Logian**   That's right.

**Big G**   Not that it's not *true*.

**Logian**   But everyone knows that all facts are true. That's the definition.

**Big G**   Absolutely, Theo. No question about it. But is all truth factual?

**Logian**   You sound like a lawyer.

**Big G**   Some people think I am, but I find grace much more exciting.

**Logian**   Grace who?

**Big G**   Now you're trying to wind *me* up, Theo!

**Logian**   What are you, Big G, a gramophone or a public company?

**Big G**   Boy, I walked into that one, didn't I! Now, this thing about truth and fact: I take it you've heard the story of the boy who cried wolf?

**Logian**   Of course. I was telling it to Luke, my youngest, the other day.

**Big G**   I know, I was eavesdropping at the time. But tell me: is it a factual story?

**Logian**   I haven't the faintest idea, but does it matter?

**Big G**   Not in the least – except presumably to the people involved – but it does contain *truth*, doesn't it?

**Logian**   Right. So it doesn't matter whether the Bible is factual or not, so long as we grasp its truths?

**Big G**   I wouldn't go quite so far as that, Theo, but you're on the right lines.

**Logian**   So those people who say the Bible's history are off their –

**Big G**   Off beam is the word you're looking for, I think, Theo. Not as far off as you're suggesting. The Bible is history.

**Logian**   But you just said it wasn't factual.

**Big G**   To be quite precise, I said it wasn't necessary for it to be factual in order for it to be true. That doesn't mean it's complete fiction.

**Logian**   So some parts are history and some aren't?

**Big G**   You're missing the point, Theo.

**Logian**   Well, perhaps it would be more helpful if you were to clarify the point for me, Big G?

**Big G**   Certainly. I imagine that when you were at school you were taught in History that Columbus discovered the New World.

**Logian**   Yes, I was.

**Big G**   Except that it wasn't 'new' at all, was it?

**Logian**   I suppose it *existed* before, but no one knew about it. So it was new in that sense.

**Big G**   *No one* knew about it?

**Logian**   Well, I suppose the natives did.

**Big G**   So someone *did* know about it before Columbus invaded it?

**Logian**   Invaded?

**Big G**   Just another word, Theo, but one which would seem more appropriate if you were a native of the Americas.

**Logian**   I'd never heard it used that way before.

**Big G**   So, then, who is right? Was it discovery or invasion?

**Logian**   I suppose it depends on your point of view. But what's this got to do with the Bible?

**Big G**   Nothing much, except to show that it can be history without being factual. All history is interpretation, as you've just demonstrated. Especially the history of any relationship.

**Logian**   Go on.

**Big G**   If I ask you about your personal history, you could talk in objective, factual statements: when you were bom, what schools you attended, and so on. But if you start talking about your relationship with me – or with anyone else for that matter – then all you can really do is give your side of it. And that's very subjective.

**Logian**   Of course it is, but that doesn't mean it's any less valuable.

**Big G**   Absolutely. So now we're agreed that statements don't need to be factual to be truthful, and history can be of value even when it isn't strictly objective or accurate. If nothing else, it gives insights into human nature.

**Logian**   So it seems that we need to treat the Bible with a good deal of caution.

**Big G**   You need to treat the Bible with a good deal of *respect* and you don't do that by reading it like a kind of users' manual for the world.

**Logian**   So how *should* we read it?

**Big G**   D'you remember how we set up these interviews, Theo?

**Logian**   Do I just! During the negotiations, you accused me of being deferential. I've been called some things in my time but nobody's ever called me *that* before.

**Big G**   So treat the Bible with the same kind of respect you have me – get into a dialogue with it. Challenge it, probe it, get under its skin. And don't let it get away with anything that doesn't ring true.

**Logian**   Because it might not be.

**Big G**   Because it might not be *factual.* You might have to make a little more of an effort before you understand it properly.

**Logian**   Yes, of course. Well, Big G, it's a pity we can't continue this interview for longer, but time, tide and the late-night movie wait for no man.

**Big G**   Or God.

**Logian**   Big G, thank you very much for being my guest again.

**Big G**   Thank *you*, Theo. And if ever I *do* write a book, I promise I'll give you the first interview about it.

**Logian**   We'll look forward to it. Meanwhile, thanks for watching. See you next week, eleven o'clock, on the dot, *On the Spot.* Goodnight.

MICHAEL FORSTER

# The Third Sunday of Advent

*The words of the prophets are fulfilled in Christ*

## Matthew 11:2-11
*(also Isaiah 35:1-10; Psalm 146:5-10; James 5:7-10)*

### A reading from the Gospel of Matthew (11:2-11)

John the Baptist had been arrested and imprisoned by King Herod, when news of Jesus and his wonderful works reached him. So John sent his friends to ask Jesus, 'Are you the promised one or is he still to come?'

Jesus said to them, 'Tell John what you have seen and heard; the blind can see, the lame can walk, the sick are cured, the deaf can hear and the dead are raised to life. The good news of God's kingdom is being proclaimed to the poor, and blessed are those who believe in me.'

As the men left, Jesus asked the crowds gathered around him, 'Did you go to the desert expecting to see a prophet? Yes, but John is more than a prophet; he is the one of whom the Scriptures said: "I will send my messenger before you to prepare the way." No one greater than John has ever been born, and yet the least in God's kingdom is greater than he.'

This is the Gospel of the Lord
**Praise to you, Lord Jesus Christ**                                    KATIE THOMPSON

# Introductory material

We focus today, this third Sunday in Advent, on John the Baptist, the one who came to bear witness to the light. He stands as a bridge between the old and the new, his unforgettable ministry paving the way for the dawn of the kingdom which Christ was shortly to bring. And in that ministry we see exemplified the call of God to each and every member of his Church since, for the task of witnessing to Christ is as vital today as it has ever been. Many have yet to hear, still more have yet to respond – a desert of doubt and disbelief lies waiting. Are we ready to follow in John's footsteps and to be a voice in the wilderness, a witness to the light of the world?

NICK FAWCETT

# Prayers

## Advent petition

Father God,
> we praise you once more for this season of Advent,
>> for its mood of expectation,
>> its message of hope,
>> its call to prepare ourselves,
>> its spirit of confidence and trust.
> God made flesh,
>> **hear our prayer.**

> We praise you for the way you have spoken,
>> in the fulfilment of ancient prophecies,
>> in promises yet to be realised,
>> and in the living presence of Christ
>> made known through his Holy Spirit.
> God made flesh,
>> **hear our prayer.**

> Touch our lives again at this time,
>> as we remember the coming of Jesus,
>> as we anticipate his coming again,
>> and as we strive to serve him better here and now.
> God made flesh,
>> **hear our prayer.**

> Grant that through this season
>> we shall be renewed in hope and strengthened in faith,
>> trusting more completely in the future you hold.
> May our confidence be deepened
>> in your eternal love and purpose,
>> despite all that seems to work against it.
> And may we be ready to welcome Christ,
>> in the assurance that as he came so he shall come again.
> God made flesh,
>> **hear our prayer,**
>> **for we ask it in the name of Christ.**
>> **Amen.**

NICK FAWCETT

## Advent fulfilment

Living God,
> we remember this day how you prepared the way for your coming.
> To your servant Abraham you promised blessing
>> for all the world through his offspring.

To your prophets you spoke your word,
   promising the Messiah would come,
   bringing peace, justice and deliverance for all your people.
To Elizabeth and Zechariah you promised a son
   who would prepare the way of the Lord,
   making his way straight in the wilderness.
To Mary you promised a child
   who would be called Emmanuel, God with us,
   born to save his people from their sins.
And through John the Baptist
   you announced the fulfilment of those prophecies
   in the person of Jesus,
   the light of the world shining in the darkness.
You promise us that Christ will come again:
   **prepare our hearts for his coming.**

Living God,
   you spoke your word to so many,
   yet when the time came and Jesus was born
   so few were ready to receive him.
He was the word made flesh, but was accused of blasphemy,
   he offered life to the world, but was put to death on the cross,
   he came to his own people, and they would not receive him.
You promise us that Christ will come again:
   **prepare our hearts for his coming.**

Living God,
   help us as we remember his birth, life, death and resurrection,
   to be ready to receive him,
   not just when he comes again,
   but each day into every part of our lives.
Help us to read your word with new insight,
   to offer you our living worship,
   and to turn from all that is wrong and faithless in our lives.
Help us to focus on what is central to this season
   and not on the trappings with which we surround it.
Help us to open our hearts and minds
   to the guidance of your Holy Spirit,
   and respond to his prompting.
Help us to follow in the way of Christ,
   loving him as he has loved us.
You promise us that Christ will come again:
   **prepare our hearts for his coming.**
   **In his name we pray.**
   **Amen.**

NICK FAWCETT

## Advent intercession

*Be prepared for the coming of the Lord. John the Baptist was the promised forerunner to Christ, and his teaching inspired many to turn back to God's ways, making them receptive when Jesus began his ministry. We, too, need to renounce sin and prepare for the time when Christ will come again in glory.*

Let us bring to God our loving Father
all the cares that weigh on our hearts,
knowing that he understands us
better than we understand ourselves.

Father, we bring the daily work of those who labour to
spread the good news of Christ amid apathy, ridicule or
prejudice; may they be encouraged and strengthened.

*Silence for prayer*

Father, hear us:
**and prepare us to meet you.**

Father, we bring our daily work, with all the pressures,
monotony, enjoyment and mistakes;
help your world to recognise your presence
and trust in your love.

*Silence for prayer*

Father, hear us:
**and prepare us to meet you.**

Father, we bring all our loved ones
with their hopes and disappointments,
their struggles and their successes;
may they be guided and nurtured by your love.

*Silence for prayer*

Father, hear us:
**and prepare us to meet you.**

Father, we bring all those
whose lives seem to them bleak,
painful or empty of meaning;
please release them, unburden them,
and fill them with your gift of joy.

*Silence for prayer*

Father, hear us:
**and prepare us to meet you.**

Father, we commend to your unfailing love
all who have died,
especially . . .

*Silence for prayer*

Father, hear us:
**and prepare us to meet you.**

Filled with thankfulness for all
your many blessings to us,
we offer you our praise.
May we never forget your generosity.

*Silence for prayer*

Merciful Father,
**accept these prayers**
**for the sake of your Son,**
**our Saviour Jesus Christ, Amen.**                    SUSAN SAYERS

## A short prayer

Gracious God,
    we come to reflect on your age-old promises,
    your sovereign purpose,
    your constant working within human history.
We remember that you brought this world into being,
    guiding your people across the centuries,
    despite repeated rebellion and disobedience;
    and we rejoice that, in love,
    you took on human flesh,
    coming to our world through Jesus Christ.
We remember his birth in Bethlehem,
    his life and ministry,
    his death and resurrection,
    and we celebrate his living presence with us now,
    through his Spirit.
Open our hearts to everything you would say to us
    through this day and season,
    so that we may understand your love
    more completely,
    and serve you more faithfully;
    through Christ our Lord.
Amen.                                      NICK FAWCETT

# All-age-talk material

**Jesus is the promised one**

**John the Baptist sent some of his followers to ask Jesus a question**

**Add or subtract letters to see what they asked**

**A B C D E F G H I J K L M N O P Q R S T U V W X Y Z**

'

$\overline{\text{F–5}}$ $\overline{\text{M+5}}$ $\overline{\text{G?2}}$     $\overline{\text{W+2}}$ $\overline{\text{Z–11}}$ $\overline{\text{P+5}}$     $\overline{\text{S+1}}$ $\overline{\text{Q–9}}$ $\overline{\text{S–14}}$

$\overline{\text{K+4}}$ $\overline{\text{U–7}}$ $\overline{\text{C+2}}$     $\overline{\text{X–1}}$ $\overline{\text{J–2}}$ $\overline{\text{P?1}}$     $\overline{\text{B+7}}$ $\overline{\text{V–3}}$

$\overline{\text{R+2}}$ $\overline{\text{Y–10}}$     $\overline{\text{H–5}}$ $\overline{\text{J+5}}$ $\overline{\text{L+1}}$ $\overline{\text{L–7}}$ ?'

Matthew 11:3

KATIE THOMPSON

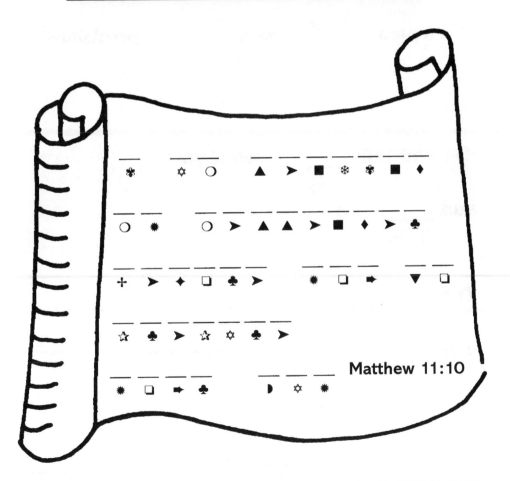

KATIE THOMPSON

Use the picture code to find the
missing words from Matthew 11:4-5

𝔇 = **hear**     ʘ̆ʘ̆ = **see**     ⌠ = **lame**     ✗ = **deaf**

↝ = **blind**     👟 = **walk**     📖 = **Good News**

🖐 = **lepers**     👦 = **John**     🎺 = **proclaimed**

**'Go and tell _____ what you _____**
                    👦                      𝔇

**and _____ !**
         ʘ̆ʘ̆

**The _____ can _____, the _____**
         ↝              ʘ̆ʘ̆                ⌠

**can _____, _____ are cured,**
         👟              🖐

**the _____ can _____, and the**
         ✗              𝔇

**_____ is being _____!'**
         📖                      🎺

KATIE THOMPSON

## Read Matthew 11:2-11

John the Baptist was in prison (he'd got on the wrong side of Herodias, who was the wife of Herod and had previously been the wife of Herod's brother Philip, but that's another story). John had heard a great deal about Jesus and what he was saying. His curiosity aroused, John sent some of his followers to find out who exactly Jesus was. In fact, John told his followers to ask Jesus whether he was the one who they were looking for or were they to expect someone else.

Can you imagine a couple of guys going up to another guy and saying 'Are you the one we're supposed to be looking for or not? 'Cos if not, then we're to look for some other geezer.' This wasn't really meant to sound crazy, it just sounded like it! The problem was that John was expecting the Christ to come and act like a judge, telling people what they'd done wrong and what would happen to them if they continued behaving that way (Jesus did say words to this effect later on). So when John heard what Jesus was saying and doing, it confused him a little bit.

Jesus' reply to the odd question simply reminded John of some predictions from the Old Testament.

### Isaiah 29:18-19

The deaf will be able to hear whatever is read to them; the blind will be freed from a life of darkness. The poor and the needy will celebrate and shout because of the Lord, the Holy God of Israel.

and

### Isaiah 61:1

The Spirit of the Lord God has taken control of me! The Lord has chosen and sent me to tell the oppressed the good news, to heal the brokenhearted, and to announce freedom for prisoners and captives.

Jesus wanted John to know that what God had promised would happen was now happening.

John wasn't accused of doubting or lacking faith in God. All Jesus wanted to do was to open John's eyes to everything that God wanted to do. No one expected John, or anybody else, to immediately recognise who Jesus was and what he had come to say and do. Unfortunately, John had difficulty seeing and hearing much more about Jesus, Herod cut his head off! Fortunately, the disciples and the rest of the population of Israel had a bit more time to get to know Jesus.

For us, getting to know Jesus isn't a snap of the fingers and we know it all and more. Getting to know Jesus is all about a relationship, one which takes time to grow. A lot of the relationship is simply taking the time to chat and experience the day-to-day with Jesus. Another aspect of the relationship is getting to know Jesus through the Bible and accepting that exactly what he said is exactly what he will do. It all takes time but there again, time is all it takes. In other words, enjoy the experience of getting to know Jesus and don't give yourself a headache purely because it doesn't happen overnight.          PETE TOWNSEND

# Reflective material
## (sketches, meditations and poems)

### Meditation of Zachariah, father of John the Baptist

I didn't believe it was possible, not any longer,
   not after all those years of trying.
There had been so many disappointments, so many false alarms,
   and we'd given up, ages ago.
It still hurt occasionally, of course it did.
We love children, both of us;
   and we'd have given anything to see that little crib occupied,
   that lovingly embroidered shawl wrapped around our little baby.
We shouldn't have tempted fate –
   it was stupid, we know that now –
   but at the time we never anticipated any problems,
   and we just couldn't help looking forward,
   planning for the future:
   two bright-eyed young things with so much before us,
   or so we thought.
She used to cry, Elizabeth,
   after her hopes had been raised only to be dashed again.
And although I'd try manfully to comfort her,
   assure her next time it would be different,
   all the while my heart was breaking as much as hers.
But then she started to torture herself,
   feeling she'd failed me somehow,
   that it was all her fault,
   even God's punishment for some unrepented sin.
I don't need to tell you she was wrong,
   but it was hard work making her see that –
   so much extra heartache
   before she finally accepted it was just one of those things.
But then I had this dream –
   at least I think that's what it was.
I was in the temple
   and suddenly a man appeared
   telling me we were to have a child,
   ordained by God and consecrated to his service,
   so he said.
Well, I dismissed it, of course;
   a cruel trick of the mind, that's what I thought.
But the next thing I knew, there was Elizabeth,
   a look of wonder in her eyes,
   blurting out the news that she was expecting!

Well, you could have knocked me down, you really could!
I honestly thought she was having me on,
    that the strain had finally got to her.
But I couldn't tell her –
    I'd been struck dumb since that dream of mine.
So I just stood there, trying to humour her.
I'm glad now I couldn't speak, pour scorn on the idea,
    for she was right.
A child, at our time of life!
I still marvel every day I see him,
    our wonderful little boy.
And I know now never to lose hope
    for with God nothing is impossible.
Yet we were the lucky ones, I realise that,
    and for every one of us
    there's another still enduring the pain,
    still waiting, hoping and praying for a miracle.
I don't know why God lets that happen
    any more than I know why he chose to bless us.
It's a mystery to us both.
But there's an odd twist I have to mention,
    for though our baby brought us joy,
    more than words can ever express,
    somehow Elizabeth seemed even more excited
    by the birth of her cousin's boy –
    Jesus the name was –
    always claimed he was more of a miracle than John,
    though I can't think why.
She's no nearer understanding this crazy world of ours than I,
    but when she looks at Jesus
    sometimes I get this strange feeling it's in him,
    rather than John,
    that she's looking for an answer;
    almost as though she expects him to make sense of it all.          NICK FAWCETT

# The Fourth Sunday of Advent

*God's coming and the dawn of his promised kingdom*
*are revealed to Joseph*

## Matthew 1:18-25

*(also Isaiah 7:10-16; Psalm 80:1-7, 17-19; Romans 1:1-7)*

### A reading from the Gospel of Matthew (1:18-25)

This is how the birth of Jesus took place. Mary, his mother, was engaged to a carpenter called Joseph; before they were married Mary told Joseph that she was expecting a child. Joseph, who was a good and kind man, wanted to protect Mary from gossip and scandal, so he decided to break off the engagement quietly.

Then one night, as he slept, an angel appeared to him and said, 'Joseph, descendant of David, do not be afraid to take Mary to be your wife. This child has been conceived by the Holy Spirit, and Mary will have a son and you must call him Jesus, for he has come to save his people from their sins.' When Joseph awoke, he did as the angel had said and took Mary to be his wife.

When the time came, she gave birth to a son and they called him Jesus. All this happened just as the Lord had promised through the prophet Isaiah when he foretold: 'See! A virgin will conceive and have a son and they will call him Emmanuel' (which means 'God is with us').

This is the Gospel of the Lord
**Praise to you, Lord Jesus Christ**                              KATIE THOMPSON

# Introductory material

'Let us go now to Bethlehem and see this thing that has taken place, which the Lord has made known to us': the response of the shepherds to the good news of Christ's birth, and the beginning of a night which was to see them returning soon after 'glorifying and praising God for all they had heard and seen, as it had been told them'. We cannot, of course, see quite what they saw, even if we were able to go now to the Holy Land and visit the place where these great events unfolded, but we are here now to listen again to words of Scripture which, familiar though they may be, still have the power to speak to us in new and unexpected ways. Let us step back then, and put ourselves in the shoes of those who were part of that extraordinary night of his birth, and let us hear afresh the good news of Jesus Christ, which God continues to make known to us today.

                                                              NICK FAWCETT

## Carrying or lighting a candle

Many churches find that this simple act brings a sense of peace and the presence of Jesus to what can be a very busy time in the church day. As a candle is carried forward, or someone from the congregation is invited up to light it, the symbolism of the light of Christ can be very effective.

*Candle responses*

We welcome Jesus,
the light of the world.

As the candle shines
so your light shines for us.

Jesus is the light of the world.
Let us welcome him now.

Jesus, Light of the world,
shine in our hearts and lives.

Jesus, the light
bring light to our worship.

As we light the candle today,
light a flame in our hearts.

In our dark world
**let Jesus bring light.**
In our dark hearts
**let Jesus bring light.**

## Christingle

### Jesus is part of everything

Christingle services occur in many churches and are part of the annual fund-raising programme for the Childrens' Society.

*Reading*

Christingle services usually take place around Advent or Christmas, and therefore a Christmas reading is appropriate.

*Story and talk*

This story and talk is combined, and is in three parts. Each should be based and told from a different area of the church. You will need the phrase CHRIST IN written up on a large sheet of paper and displayed, and the G, L and E on pieces of paper to put with it.

1. Christ in G. Stand near the crib or tree if you have one in place. Ask a child to hold up the letter G. Explain that G is for gifts. Jesus was a gift which we remember at Christmas, as God sent Jesus as the best present we could ever have. But we all have gifts to use too that come from Jesus. We can share, love, care, etc.

   Key message: Christ is a gift from God, and gives us gifts.

2. Stand near a candle. Ask a child to hold up the letter L. Explain that L is for light. Jesus brought light to the world. When he had grown up he went from town to town and village to village speaking to people, healing and helping them. He also explained who he was, on one occasion saying 'I am the light of the world'. He brings light to the darkness and sad times in our lives.

   Key message: Jesus is the light, and brings light to our dark times.

3. Stand amongst the congregation. Ask a child to hold up the letter E. Explain that E is for Everyone. Because Jesus was the best gift, and because he brings light to all the world, we can all have Jesus with us. Another name for Jesus is Immanuel, which means 'God is with us'. Jesus wants to be with everyone, including all of us here.

   Key message: Jesus wants to be with everyone, but do we want Jesus?

NICK HARDING

# Prayers

## Confession – advent omission

Loving God,
   the great festival of Christmas is drawing nearer
      and we are busy preparing for it –
      choosing presents,
      writing cards,
      planning get-togethers,
      buying food –
      so much that has become an accepted
      and expected part of this season.
   Yet, in all the bustle, we so easily forget
      the most important thing of all:
      responding to the wonderful gift of your Son.
   You have come to us in Christ:
      **forgive us when we fail to receive him.**

We tell ourselves that *we* are different –
   that we will be worshipping you Sunday by Sunday,
   sharing in services of lessons and carols,
   hearing again familiar and well-loved verses of Scripture,

but we know that this isn't enough in itself,
for these too can become just another part
of our traditional celebrations,
washing over us
rather than communicating the great message of the Gospel.
We become so concerned with the wrapping
that we fail to recognise the gift concealed underneath.
You have come to us in Christ:
**forgive us when we fail to receive him.**

Forgive us for relegating Jesus to the periphery of our celebrations,
rather than placing him at the centre where he belongs;
for turning this season into a time for material extravagance,
rather than an opportunity for spiritual fulfilment;
for doing so much to prepare for Christmas on the surface,
yet so little to make ourselves ready within.
You have come to us in Christ:
**forgive us when we fail to receive him.**

Loving God,
open our hearts now to hear again your word,
to welcome the living Christ,
and to reflect on our response to his call.
May this Advent season teach us
to welcome him afresh into our lives
and to rejoice in his love not just at Christmas
but always.
You have come to us in Christ:
**forgive us when we fail to receive him.**

We ask it for his name's sake.
Amen.                                                    NICK FAWCETT

## Year 1

*After years of waiting,*
*the Lord is very near*

Father, we thank you for raising up leaders
and ministers in your church,
and we pray for them now.
*Silence for prayer*
In your way, Lord:
**let your will be done in us**

Father, we thank you for all that is good
in our society and pray now for all in
positions of authority.

*Silence for prayer*

In your way, Lord:
**let your will be done in us**

Father, we thank you for our homes and families,
for our friends and neighbours.

*Silence for prayer*

In your way, Lord:
**let your will be done in us**

Father, we thank you for those who care for the sick,
the distressed and the dying.

*Silence for prayer*

In your way, Lord:
**let your will be done in us**

Father, we thank you for all those who worked with you,
in your plan of salvation for us.
Work also in us for the good of your world.

*Silence for prayer*

Merciful Father,
**accept these prayers**
**for the sake of your Son,**
**our Saviour Jesus Christ, Amen.**                    Susan Sayers

## Closing prayer

Loving God,
   we thank you for the message
      we have been reminded of once more this evening.
   **We praise you for the glad tidings**
      **of your coming to us in Christ.**
   We rejoice in the fulfilment of your word,
      the ancient promises of Scripture.
   **We celebrate with wise men and shepherds long ago**
      **the birth of your Son, our Saviour.**
   Speak to us afresh through all we have heard and shared,
      **so that we, with them,**
      **may go on our way rejoicing,**
      knowing the reality of your love for ourselves,
      **and offering our service to Christ**
      **in grateful praise and heartfelt worship,**
      **for his name's sake.**
   **Amen.**                                      Nick Fawcett

## A short prayer

Lord,
    it's quite a crazy thought
    that somewhere
    in the technicolour maze
    of my dreams, that somehow, somewhere,
    you might want to have a word with me!
I think I'm a bit embarrassed really.
My dreams are what you might call
    a visual dustbin,
    a montage of funny bits, dodgy bits,
    gruesome bits and just plain wacky bits.
I have other dreams of course.
The sort where I want to do
    all kinds of exciting things,
    go to exciting places,
    meet loads of different people
    and immediately forget their names.
There's so much I want to do
    but I'd sort of
    want your opinion on things.
So if you don't mind,
    can we talk about it,
    think about it
    and even dream about it?
'Cos I'm not so sure
    that I can get through this on my own.
Be with me, Lord,
    guide my ways
    and help me through
    whatever comes my way.

PETE TOWNSEND

# All-age-talk material

These pictures tell today's Gospel story but they have been mixed up. Can you put them in the right order?

A

B

C

D

**The order is** ___ ___ ___ ___

KATIE THOMPSON

> **The angel told Joseph to call the baby Jesus (Matthew 1:21)**

**Unscramble the letters to find another name given to Jesus, and then find what it means**

**A M E M L N E U**
**4 3 1 2 8 5 7 6**

—  —  —  —  —  —  —  —
1   2   3   4   5   6   7   8

## WHICH MEANS

—  —  —      —  —      —  —  —  —
9  10  11    12  13    14  15  16  17

—  —
18  19

**S O S W G T U I D H I**
19 10 13 14 9 16 18 12 11 17 15

KATIE THOMPSON

# The angel's visit

God sent an angel to visit Joseph in a dream

## Use the secret code pad to find the angel's message

| SECRET CODE PAD |
| --- |
| A (1)  B (9)  D (14)  E (10)  F (8)  I (11)  K (4)  M (16) |
| N (2)  O (17)  R (22)  S (19)  T (5)  U (12)  W (26)  Y (6) |

'

(14) (17)    (2) (17) (5)    (9) (10)

(1) (8) (22) (1) (11) (14)    (5) (17)    (5) (1) (4) (10)

(16) (1) (22) (6)    (1) (19)    (6) (17) (12) (22)

(26) (11) (8) (10) ,

Matthew 1:20

KATIE THOMPSON

## Read Matthew 1:18-25

Joseph had a dream . . . a great, stonking, technicolour, 3-D, front row sort. Imagine, here's a bloke who's just found out that the woman he was engaged to is pregnant! You know how it is, take it in your stride, no problem, happens every day. Wrong!

The Jewish tradition was for the marriage to be taken in three stages. First was an engagement, often announced while the couple were still children, their engagement having been arranged by the children's parents. Second was the 'betrothal'. This was the official bit which lasted a year and could only be called off if the female was unwilling to go ahead before the formal agreement had been announced. To break off the 'betrothal' was only possible by divorce. The third part was the actual marriage ceremony, which occurred at the end of the year of betrothal.

Tradition had ruled that if a woman was pregnant before marriage then she was considered to be promiscuous and could, after a public trial, be stoned to death. Fortunately, at the time of Mary and Joseph's betrothal, stoning had become history (to a large cheer of relief from a percentage of the female population). It was now custom to conduct a 'secret' divorce and keep the problem as far from wagging tongues as possible. This was the action that Joseph had decided upon before the dream.

So, there he goes, off to bed with a cluttered head full of angry thoughts and feelings of rejection. Then, just as soon as his eyelids hit the cheeks, along comes a gold-framed dream direct from God. Can you imagine, God tells him that it's still OK to marry Mary, she may be pregnant but she hadn't been unfaithful to him and she was still a virgin! Having received all of this, Joseph turned over and carried on snoozing . . . no he didn't! Joseph listened to what he'd heard and did exactly as God had asked him to. He married Mary even though a lot of people would have suggested that he hadn't been able to wait until his marriage before starting a family or that he'd failed to follow customs of the Jewish law and walked in the opposite direction to Mary.

Joseph heard God, did as he was asked and kept faith in God's word. God had used a dream to get through to Joseph and the dream had packed a real punch. Joseph was to remember that dream many times during Mary's pregnancy and afterwards.

Is it possible that we too can hear from God, do exactly as he asks and stick with it even when the gossip suggests that we may be a few biscuits short of a packet? A few years ago, before crossing the road, children were encouraged to 'Stop! Look! And Listen!' Not a bad piece of advice especially when God wants to have a word in our ear.

PETE TOWNSEND

Dreams often feature ours fears, hurts, hopes or a mixture of all three! Ask the group if any of them would be willing to share with everyone an ambition or hope which they have. It may be that someone is hoping to pass their exams and continue their studies but are afraid of failing; it might be that someone feels hurt at being left out of an event that they were looking forward to being a part of. Whatever it may be, you can use this time to encourage that person and maybe offer to help, pray for or just be someone who'll listen to the hassles.

Also, use part of this time to answer one of the questions that one of the group raised last time.

PETE TOWNSEND

# Reflective material
## (sketches, meditations and poems)

### What a way to have a baby!
She travelled on a donkey,
    at night they both slept rough.
In the last stage of pregnancy
    a journey's really tough.
No car ride to the hospital,
    no ante-natal care,
    no hygienic labour ward –
    germs simply everywhere!
Nowhere to go in labour,
    nothing to help the pain,
    not even a bed to lie on –
    just straw where beasts had lain.
No modern central heating,
    just the cold night air,
    no curtains at the windows,
    stone walls, cold and bare.
No white-coated doctors
    with sterile clothes to wear,
    just Joseph and some animals
    and smelly stable air.
What a way to have a baby!
    where are the cards and flowers?
Just shepherds to share their gladness
    in the midnight hours.

> **'Before she married Joseph**
> **she was in the family way.**
> **She said an angel told her . . .**
> **What a thing to say!'**

But Mary had her baby
  before the light of dawn.
This was how it happened,
  how the son of God was born.

*The words in bold could be read by a separate reader*
*to give dramatic effect.*                         MARY HATHAWAY


## Meditation

Why me?
That's what I kept on asking myself.
Why me?
I mean, it was obvious what people were going to say, wasn't it?
The sly looks,
  the knowing grins,
  the wagging tongues.
And Joseph?
Well, he really hit the roof.
Furious he was, and who can blame him?
If we'd been married it would have been different,
  but engaged – it was bound to cause a scandal.
And it hurt, more than anyone will know;
  I never realised people could be so cruel.
I didn't even want a baby, that's what made it worse;
  it was the last thing on my mind.
I was still young,
  not ready for that kind of responsibility,
  wanting to enjoy life a little.
I could have done without those sleepless nights,
  the endless washing,
  the countless extra demands.
And believe me, it didn't get any easier.
Well, it never does, does it?
I'll never forget how he disappeared like that
  on the way back from Jerusalem –
  a right old panic he had us in.
But was he sorry?
Well, if he was he had a funny way of showing it.
'You should have known where to find me,' he said –
  'My Father's house, where else?'
Cheeky monkey!
And then, just when life was plodding along nicely,
  back on an even keel,
  he went swanning off into the wilderness to be baptised.

Oh, I know he had to make his own way, don't get me wrong,
    but I couldn't help feeling
    he was getting mixed up in something dangerous.
And so it proved.
We could all see it coming,
    all except him apparently.
He said the wrong things
    to the wrong people
    in the wrong places,
    and there could only be one result.
It nearly broke my heart to watch it –
    my beautiful boy, broken and bleeding,
    struggling with that cross,
    hanging in agony.
But then he looked down,
    not at the rest of them
    but at me.
And in his eyes was such love,
    such care,
    such tenderness!
I saw suddenly the eyes of God looking at me
    through the eyes of my child,
    and I asked myself then,
    as I'd asked so many times before,
    yet differently this time,
    so very differently:
        Why me?
        Why me?

NICK FAWCETT

# Christmas

# Christmas Day

*The Word is made flesh; God comes to us as a baby*

## John 1:1-14

*(also Isaiah 52:7-10; Psalm 98; Hebrews 1:1-4 [5-12])*

### A reading from the Gospel of John (1:1-14)

At the beginning of time, the Word already existed. The Word was with God; and the Word was God. From the very beginning, all things were created through him. All life came from the Word, and this life was the light for all people. The light shines out from the darkness, and the darkness could never overcome it.

God sent a man called John, to be a witness for the light, so that others would believe because of him, even though he was not the light. The real light was the Word who was coming into the world to give light to everyone.

He was in the world created through him, and yet the world did not know him. He came to his own people and they did not accept him. To those who did receive him he gave the right to become children of God, the offspring of God himself.

The Word became flesh and he lived as a man among us. We saw his glory given by the Father to his only Son, who is full of grace and truth.

This is the Gospel of the Lord
**Praise to you, Lord Jesus Christ**                          KATIE THOMPSON

# Introductory material

We have come today to celebrate an event at the very heart of our faith – the coming of Christ into our world as the Word made flesh, God identifying himself irrevocably with humankind through the birth of Jesus in Bethlehem. A story we have heard retold countless times in countless ways, and yet, however often we hear it, we cannot begin to exhaust the riches of this wonderful season. There is always more to discover, more to understand, more to give thanks for. So we come today to hear words and music familiar and not so familiar, and to consider some of those who shared in the events of that first Christmas and some whose lives were later touched by Christ. We come so that the Christmas story may speak afresh to us, and our lives may be touched by Jesus in turn.

NICK FAWCETT

# Prayers

## A time for worship

Loving God,
  at this time of giving and receiving,
    of showing our love and gratitude to others
    through the exchanging of cards and presents,
    we are reminded of the great gift you have given us in Christ
    and of how little we have to offer in return.
  You have blessed us in so much:
    **receive our worship.**

Whatever we might bring, it can never repay you.
Whatever we might sacrifice,
    it can scarcely begin to express our thanks,
    but what we can offer and gladly bring
    is our praise,
    our homage,
    our adoration,
    offered in the name of Jesus.
  You have blessed us in so much:
    **receive our worship.**

Like the choir of angels on the night of his birth
    we sing your praise and tell out the good news.
Like the shepherds, returning from the manger,
    we give you the glory for all that we have heard and seen.
Like the magi, kneeling in wonder,
    we offer our gifts as a token of our love
    and sign of our commitment.
  You have blessed us in so much:
    **receive our worship.**

Loving God,
  at this time of giving and receiving
    we do not have much to bring to you,
    but we offer this time together –
    our songs,
    our reading,
    our thinking, speaking and listening –
    and we offer ourselves, such as we are,
    in reverent praise and joyful celebration.
  You have blessed us in so much:
    **receive our worship.**

In the name of Christ.
**Amen.**

NICK FAWCETT

## The true meaning of Christmas

Loving God,
    we thank you for this season of Christmas –
        for all it has meant to so many over the years,
        all it continues to mean to us,
        and all it will mean in generations to come.
    You have given us so much:
        **receive our praise.**

We thank you for carols old and new,
    for familiar and much-loved words of Scripture,
    for all that speaks of your coming among us in Christ.
You have given us so much:
    **receive our praise.**

We thank you for reunions with family and friends,
    for the spirit of giving and receiving,
    for the mood of goodwill and celebration.
You have given us so much:
    **receive our praise.**

We thank you for all the good things we will enjoy –
    good food,
    good company,
    good fun.
You have given us so much,
    **receive our praise.**

Loving God,
    help us in all of this to keep sight of the heart of Christmas,
        what it all really means –
        to celebrate the birth of the infant Christ,
        to worship him as joyfully and reverently
        as shepherds and wise men long ago,
        to welcome and follow him as faithfully
        as those who left everything to be his disciples.
    You have given us so much:
        **receive our praise.**

Loving God,
    forgive us if we have lost sight of what this season truly means.
    Forgive us if we have become over-familiar
        with its simple yet wonderful message.
    Forgive us if we have failed to make room for Christ
        in our Christmas celebrations.
    You have given us so much:
        **receive our praise.**

Speak to us now
   through all that we shall do and share,
   all we shall sing and hear,
   so that our lives may be touched by the wonder of his presence.
You have given us so much,
   **receive our praise**
   **through Jesus Christ.**
   **Amen.**

NICK FAWCETT

## Confession – a time for receiving

Lord Jesus Christ,
   we recall today how you entered your world
      and the world did not know you;
      how you came to your own people,
      and they would not receive you;
      how you were born in Bethlehem,
      and there was no room for you in the inn.
From the beginning it was the same old story –
      your love rejected,
      your grace ignored.
**Lord have mercy,**
   **and teach us to receive you with gladness.**

We remember that you came to set people free
      and to offer a new relationship with God –
      breaking down the barriers which keep us apart,
      bearing the price of our disobedience,
      opening up the way to life.
Yet we remember, too, that though some listened for a moment,
      few followed you to the end.
Time and again it was the same old story –
      your love rejected,
      your grace ignored.
**Lord have mercy,**
   **and teach us to receive you with gladness.**

We know we are no better,
      each of us guilty, day after day, of spurning your guidance,
      forgetting your goodness and abandoning your way.
We talk of commitment, but our faith is weak;
      we speak of following you, but follow only our own inclinations;
      we claim to be a new creation,
      but it is the old self that still holds sway.

Time and again it is the same old story –
   your love rejected,
   your grace ignored.
**Lord have mercy,**
   **and teach us to receive you with gladness.**

Lord Jesus Christ,
   we marvel that, despite it all –
      the world's hostility and our own faithlessness –
   still you reach out in love,
      never giving up,
      refusing to write us off.
   We thank you that you are always ready to offer a fresh start,
      a new beginning,
      to anyone willing to receive it.
   Come what may, it is the same old story –
      you continue seeking us out,
      however often we thrust you aside,
      your love rejected,
      your grace ignored.
**Lord have mercy,**
   **and teach us to receive you with gladness.**

In your name we ask it.
**Amen.**                                         NICK FAWCETT

## Intercession

*Christ, our Saviour, is born. Eternal God breaks into human existence to transform and redeem it. In the darkness of night, God's majestic glory becomes a vulnerable newborn baby. Creator of all is entirely dependent on those he has created. Such is the measure of his infinite love.*

As we gather to worship the Christchild,
born today,
let us pray trustfully
to our heavenly Father.

Father, we pray for all Christians
celebrating with us all over the world,
in all climates, times and seasons
as our planet turns.
*Silence for prayer*
Light of ages:
**be born in our hearts.**

Father, we pray for all areas of darkness
where your light is desperately needed to bring peace,
understanding, sensitivity and compassion.

*Silence for prayer*

Light of ages:
**be born in our hearts.**

Father, we commend to you our homes,
families, neighbours and friends;
all children and young babies, all being born today.

*Silence for prayer*

Light of ages:
**be born in our hearts.**

We pray for those who are hungry, cold or homeless;
for all who are separated from their loved ones;
all who find the festivities of Christmas
emphasising their isolation and misery.

*Silence for prayer*

Light of ages:
**be born in our hearts.**

We thank you for all who have
worshipped you throughout the ages;
for the lives and examples of all
who shone with your light
and now rest in your peace.

*Silence for prayer*

Light of ages:
**be born in our hearts.**

Father in thankfulness we praise and worship you.

*Silence for prayer*

Merciful Father,
**accept these prayers**
**for the sake of your Son,**
**our Saviour Jesus Christ, Amen.**                    Susan Sayers

## Short prayers

Lord Jesus Christ,
    you came to our world
    and it did not know you,
    you came to your own people

and they would not accept you;
    you came to the inn
    and there was no room for you there
    as there has been no room so often
    among so many people.
Help us to make room for you this Christmas-time,
    to welcome you gladly
    at the heart of our celebrations,
    and to receive you as our Lord and Saviour
    with body, soul and mind.
Lord Jesus Christ,
    come now, and make your home within us.
Amen.                                                        NICK FAWCETT

Loving God,
    you have given us and all the world
    good news in Christ.
Help us to hear that news afresh each day,
    recognising it as good news for us.
Help us to receive it with both our minds and our hearts,
    always looking to understand more of what it continues to say.
And help us to share what Christ has done for us
    so that others in turn may celebrate
    what he has done for them.                    NICK FAWCETT

Gracious God,
    at this time of giving and receiving
    we remember the greatest gift of all –
    your coming to our world in Christ
    to live and die among us,
    your identifying with humankind
    so that we might become your children
    and know life in all its fullness.
Help us, as we hear again the Christmas message,
    to understand more fully
    the sheer magnitude of all you have given,
    and as we celebrate this glad season
    help us to receive Christ into our hearts,
    and offer to you, through him,
    our heartfelt praise and joyful service.
Amen.                                                        NICK FAWCETT

# All-age-talk material

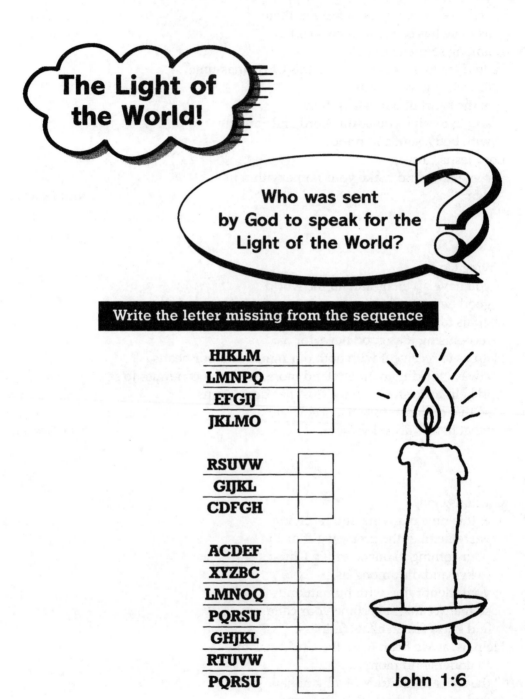

The Light of
the World!

Who was sent
by God to speak for the
Light of the World?

**Write the letter missing from the sequence**

HIKLM
LMNPQ
EFGIJ
JKLMO

RSUVW
GIJKL
CDFGH

ACDEF
XYZBC
LMNOQ
PQRSU
GHJKL
RTUVW
PQRSU

John 1:6

KATIE THOMPSON

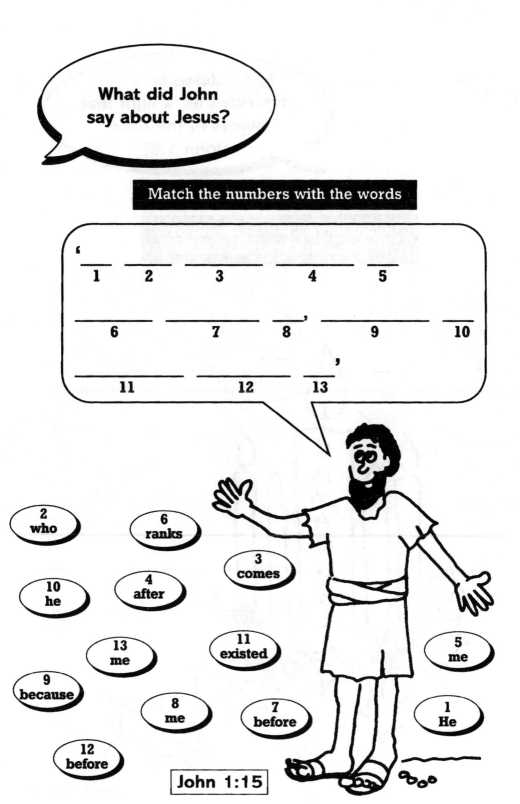

KATIE THOMPSON

Jesus is
described as 'a light that
shines in the dark'
(John 1:5)

Colour this picture of the Advent
wreath and Christmas candle

John 1:4-5

KATIE THOMPSON

# Reflective material
## (sketches, meditations and poems)

Christmas is an ideal time for a sketch to be used in worship. During the Christmas period, the demand for services from church groups, secular groups, schools, etc., is often overwhelming. These are in addition to the many extra services we arrange as part of our own Christmas celebrations. Any additional material we can find is always welcome. Unfortunately, much of the dramatic material available is either a nativity play or a derivative of a nativity play.

This sketch seeks to take a different look at Christmas, rather than simply retelling the story.

We are well used to believing, with some justification, that for most people Christmas is simply a commercial festival with little or no religious content. Like the lady behind me in the supermarket queue (and I swear this is true) who turned to her friend and said, 'It's disgusting, even the churches are trying to take over Christmas now!'

But we are less good at looking inwards at our own preoccupations and examining their relevance and meaning for today. Just as the world can so easily be too worldly, so can the Church be too churchy.

This sketch seeks to question both aspects, and to bring us back to the biblical reality of a God who is magisterial and omnipotent, as well as being present and incarnate. Flowing through all these many perceptions of God is his all-loving nature. For at its heart, this is the true message of Christmas.

> *Knowledge stands on stage, holding a large book, or next to a lectern with a book on it. Two adults stand stage left holding a processional cross. Skint stands centre stage.*
>
> *Enter Pilgrim.*

**Pilgrim**   I'm Pilgrim. *(To Knowledge)* Who are you?

**Knowledge**   I'm Knowledge. I know everything . . . well . . . nearly everything.

**Pilgrim**   What is the good of that?

**Knowledge**   Knowing things gives you power over other people. I'm going to hold up this card to them *(Points to audience)* to prove I know exactly what you will say next. *(Holds up card with WHAT written on it)*

**Pilgrim**   What?

**Knowledge**   *(Shows Pilgrim card)* See?

**Pilgrim**   That is amazing! Perhaps you can help me; I'm looking for God.

**Knowledge**   What do you want to find God for?

**Pilgrim**   Because I'm told he has even more answers than you do.

**Knowledge**  I doubt it. But if you want to find God, you must climb up to him, because he lives far above the sky in his beautiful heaven. *(Points)* Up that way.

**Pilgrim**  How do I get up there?

**Knowledge**  You make your way very slowly, by being good, reading a lot, praying a lot, and generally looking holy.

**Pilgrim**  How do I look holy?

**Knowledge**  Like this. *(He puts his hands together and looks up in a pious way. Pilgrim copies him)*

*Enter Seeker.*

**Seeker**  Hello, I'm Seeker. What are you two doing?

**Pilgrim**  We're looking holy.

**Seeker**  More like senile, if you ask me.

**Knowledge**  What would you know? I'm Knowledge, I know everything.

**Seeker**  If you're so smart, perhaps you can help me. I'm Seeker and I'm looking for the Way.

**Knowledge**  What way?

**Seeker**  I don't know! If I knew that I wouldn't have to find it, would I?

**Pilgrim**  I must be off. Lots of spiritual climbing to do. *(He moves slowly, looking holy, towards something he can climb up, e.g. pulpit or stepladder)*

**Seeker**  So, what about this 'Way', then?

**Knowledge**  Do I have to do everything round here? Find a lively church and join it.

**Seeker**  OK. *(He moves to stage left where the two adults are standing with the cross)*

*Pilgrim climbs part way up pulpit or ladder.*

**Knowledge**  *(Shouts to Pilgrim)* How are you doing?

**Pilgrim**  *(Looking pious)* Very well! I've read two books, said lots of prayers and been on a course about healing. I'm getting much closer now.

**Knowledge**  *(Shouts to Seeker)* How about you?

**Seeker**  *(With arms up in the air)* Wonderful! We sing lots of happy songs, hold prayer meetings and have a really super time. I think I'm finding it.

*Enter Pauper (dressed as a tramp).*

**Pauper**  *(Goes to Seeker)* Spare a coin or two for a poor pauper at Christmas.

| | |
|---|---|
| **Seeker** | Come in! Come in! Join our Group! We'll pray for you. |
| **Pauper** | But I only want a few quid to see me over Christmas. |
| **Seeker** | You will be much better off in here with us. We will help you find the 'Way', once we have cleaned you up a bit. |
| **Pauper** | *(Goes to Pilgrim)* Spare a coin or two for a poor fellow at Christmas. |
| **Pilgrim** | Sorry, but I'm on my way to God. I haven't got time for anything else. Stop distracting me, I'm looking holy. |
| **Pauper** | More like senile . . . *(Goes to Knowledge)* Spare a coin or two for a poor fellow at Christmas. |
| **Knowledge** | I'm Knowledge, I know everything. |
| **Pauper** | If you know everything, how do I get some money? |
| **Knowledge** | Easy, get a job. |
| **Pauper** | But there are no jobs. What do I do now? |
| **Knowledge** | There are some very good government schemes. Try one of those. |
| **Pauper** | Will that get me a job? |
| **Knowledge** | Probably not, but it will give you something to do for a few weeks. There is another fellow over there waiting for the same thing. |

*Pauper goes to join Skint.*

| | |
|---|---|
| **Pauper** | Hello there. Who are you? |
| **Skint** | I'm Skint, and before you ask, that is my name. Skint by name and skint by nature. |

*They shake hands.*

| | |
|---|---|
| **Knowledge** | *(Shouts to Pilgrim who has climbed higher)* How are you doing? |
| **Pilgrim** | Not bad, but I still haven't found him. I thought I was getting nearer, but he seems to have disappeared again. |
| **Skint** | Open those hands if you want to see God. |
| **Pilgrim** | What? |
| **Skint** | Open your hands. What do you see? |
| **Pilgrim** | *(Opens hands and looks at them)* I see the marks of the nails. |
| **Skint** | Then that is where you will find God. Come down. You will never reach him up there. |

*Pilgrim comes down and joins Skint.*

| | |
|---|---|
| **Knowledge** | *(Shouts to Seeker)* Have you found the 'Way' yet? |

| | |
|---|---|
| **Seeker** | No, we still have a lovely time, but we seem to be stuck where we are. |
| **Skint** | Open your doors if you want to see God. |
| **Seeker** | *(Opens pretend doors)* I can't see him. |
| **Skint** | Look closely. You will see him in all those people passing by. |
| | *Seeker and few members of audience join Skint.* |
| **Knowledge** | *(To audience)* That's all the thanks I get! *(To characters on stage)* Don't ask me for help again, if you're going to ignore my advice. I don't know why I bother. |
| **Skint** | Get your eyes out of that book and look around you. Knowledge isn't only in words. It's in all you see, the people you meet, the kindness and the love you give and receive. |
| | *Knowledge looks up and looks around and then joins Skint.* |
| **Pauper** | Who are you really? |
| **Skint** | Who, me? No one important, only God. |
| | *Exit All.* |

DAVID WALKER

## Meditation of the shepherd

It was just an ordinary day, that's what I can't get over;
  nothing special about it,
  nothing different,
  just another ordinary day.
And we were all just ordinary people,
  that's what made it even more puzzling;
  not important,
  not influential,
  just plain ordinary shepherds out working in the fields.
Yet we apparently were the first,
  singled out for special favour!
The first to know,
  the first to see,
  the first to celebrate,
  the first to tell!
I'm still not sure what happened –
  one moment night drawing in,
  and the next bright as day;
  one moment laughing and joking together,
  and the next rooted to the spot in amazement;
  one moment looking forward to getting home,
  and the next hurrying down to Bethlehem.

There just aren't words to express what we felt,
    but we knew we had to respond,
    had to go and see for ourselves.
Not that we expected to find anything mind you,
    not if we were honest.
Well, you don't, do you?
I mean, it's not every day the Messiah arrives, is it?
And we'd always imagined when he finally did
    it would be in a blaze of glory,
    to a fanfare of trumpets,
    with the maximum of publicity.
Yet do you know what?
When we got there
    it was to find everything just as we had been told,
    wonderfully special,
    yet surprisingly ordinary.
Not Jerusalem but Bethlehem,
    not a palace but a stable,
    not a prince enthroned in splendour
    but a baby lying in a manger.
We still find it hard to believe even now,
    to think God chose to come
    through that tiny vulnerable child.
But as the years have passed –
    and we've seen not just his birth but his life,
    and not just his life but his death,
    and not just his death but his empty tomb,
    his graveclothes, his joyful followers –
    we've slowly came to realise it really was true.

NICK FAWCETT

## Meditation of Mary

What a day it's been!
I'm shattered, exhausted,
    and yet I'm over the moon!
Does that sound strange?
Well, let me tell you what happened, then you'll understand.
It could hardly have started worse,
    arriving in Bethlehem like that to find the place packed.
My heart sank.
I knew we wouldn't find anywhere, not a chance,
    but Joseph wouldn't have it.
'Next time,' he kept saying, 'you'll see.'
Next time indeed!

A stable, that's what we ended up with –
   hardly the accommodation I had in mind!
It wouldn't have mattered, mind you,
   not in the usual run of things,
   but I was nine months pregnant
   and my pains had started that morning,
   getting stronger by the minute.
I was in agony by the end, you can imagine,
   just about desperate by then,
   not bothered where we stopped
   just so long as I could rest.
That's why we accepted the innkeeper's offer,
   makeshift though it was.
I lay there with cattle breathing down my neck,
   straw prickling my back,
   and what felt like a gale whistling beneath the door –
   but I didn't care;
   I didn't care about anything by then,
   just wanted the baby to be born.
Poor Joseph, he was beside himself.
No idea how to cope or what to do next,
   but thankfully one of the women from the inn took pity on us.
You'll never know how good it was
   to see her kindly reassuring face,
   her confident smile beaming down at me
   through the haze of pain.
It seemed like an eternity for all that,
   but it wasn't long really.
And then that sound,
   that wonderful exhilarating sound,
   my son, Jesus, crying!
I didn't want to let go of him,
   but I had to, of course, eventually.
I was exhausted, just about all in.
So I wrapped him in strips of cloth and laid him in a manger.
Sleep came easy after that,
   blissful peace at last,
   but a moment ago I woke with a start,
   remembering those words in that vision I had –
   'And they shall name him Emmanuel,
   God with us'.
My child, Emmanuel?
Can it really be true?
God come to his people?
He's everything to me, I admit that.

I could gladly worship him.
But others? I wonder.
Time alone will tell, I suppose.
Anyway, no more time for talking, I need my sleep.
But wait, who's this knocking on the door?
Shepherds!
What on earth can they want at this time of night?
I don't know.
What a day it's been!
What a day!                                          NICK FAWCETT

# Order of service

## The Christmas service

In many Churches the Christmas services are a major highlight of the calendar, with Christingles, carols by candlelight, and cribs dominating the scene. However, strong publicity, hopefully increased attendances, and not least the weight of received tradition mean that Christmas is just about the most difficult time of year to engage in ecumenical worship. The exception to this is found mostly in well-established LEPs*, where the people no longer dream of a united Christmas because it has been made to happen. (Our own LEP has reached this stage, though it has taken a couple of years to merge the two traditions into a coherent programme – and we're not sure it's quite right even now!). Ironically, the mainstream Churches have more in common at Christmas than at almost any other time of year, as the carols, readings and symbolism are recognised by everyone.

Christingle and crib services come in more or less the same form in every tradition and are ideally suited to ecumenical worship, even if there are guaranteed to be a few minor differences in execution. The carol service (often entitled a 'Festival of Carols' or 'Carols by Candlelight') is also familiar to all denominations, though it may vary in style from the formal and tightly structured 'Nine Lessons and Carols' (Anglican in origin and style) through to a more lively and exuberant 'Carol Praise' (in the charismatic tradition). An ecumenical version will probably try to combine the best of both worlds.

From traditional carols to the folk ballads of the Iona Community, from Plainsong to John Rutter or John Taverner, there is a wealth of Christmas music available. What you choose will be determined as much as anything by the available resources. The following outline suggests one way that well-known items can be integrated together by a common thread. Readings 1 and 7 frame the narrative, describing God's eternal purposes, and the rest of the readings and the carols

*LEPs – Local Ecumenical Projects

reflect our response to God's love in Christ. A final reading and song express our commitment to what we have heard and understood. Each reading is concluded with a brief prayer, and an opening bidding in modern style is also included, together with a closing response.

## Bidding

In the name of our Lord Jesus Christ we welcome you all, as we gather together once more to hear the story of his coming among us as a helpless baby, yet Lord of all. With the shepherds we run joyfully to the manger, to see for ourselves the Word made flesh. With the angels we sing 'Glory to God in the Highest', and join with the praises of all heaven as we celebrate the coming of our Saviour. With the wise men we bring to the infant Christ our own gifts and offerings, to acknowledge him as King of kings. With Mary and Joseph we ponder these things in our hearts, as we seek to understand more of God's loving purposes.

We offer to God our prayers for the world into which he sent his Son, with its conflict and chaos, its greed and selfishness, its sadness and pain, especially . . .

We offer to God our prayers for the Church throughout the world, divided and confused, yet united in our one Lord and in seeking to bring the good news of his love to all people . . .

We offer to God our prayers for those whose rejoicing at this Christmas season will be overshadowed by grief, illness, anxiety or loneliness, especially . . .

We pray finally for ourselves, that we may not only hear the familiar story of Christ's birth, but may open our minds to reflect on it, our hearts to respond to it, and our lives to proclaim it, day by day. And so we worship the newborn King, together with the angels and all God's people throughout the world, rejoicing at his coming among us and praying as he taught: **Our Father** . . .

## Carol

O come, all ye faithful (HON 357)*

## First reading

John 1:1-14

## Prayer

Living Word,
who came to be the light for all people;
shine in our darkness
and help us to recognise you living among us,
that believing in your name,
we may become children of God. Amen.

*HON – *Hymns Old and New*, Kevin Mayhew Publishers

**Carol**

Of the Father's love begotten (HON 395)

**Second reading**

Isaiah 11:1-9

**Prayer**

Lord God,
may your Spirit of wisdom and understanding
rest upon us,
that we may deal fairly with the needy
and act justly for the world's poor. Amen.

**Carol**

Who would think *(God's surprise)* (HON 558)

**Third reading**

Zechariah 2:10-13

**Prayer**

Lord Jesus,
as you once came to live among your people,
come now and dwell in our hearts,
that we may rejoice and be glad
as your presence breaks into our lives
with power. Amen.

**Carol**

Lord Jesus Christ (HON 311)

**Fourth reading**

Luke 1:26-38

**Prayer**

Lord God,
as we hear your gracious call,
make our ears open to the message you give,
and our hearts willing to obey you
as faithful servants. Amen.

**Carol**

For Mary, mother of our Lord (HON 136)

**Fifth reading**

Luke 2:8-14

**Prayer**

Lord Jesus,
we hear again the angels' song of praise
at your coming to earth as our Saviour;
rejoicing with them,
may we treasure what we see
and hear in our hearts,
that our lives may reflect
the presence of Emmanuel, God with us. Amen.

**Carol**

Angels from the realms of glory (HON 34)

**Sixth reading**

Matthew 2:1-12

**Prayer**

Lord Jesus,
recognising you as King of kings
and Lord of all,
we offer you our gifts
and ask you to use them
for the glory of your kingdom. Amen.

**Carol**

In the bleak mid-winter (HON 248)

**Seventh reading**

Hebrews 1:1-4 (or 9)

**Prayer**

Lord Jesus,
you are the radiance of your Father's glory
and through you the universe was made;
as you descended from your heavenly home
to share our life and bear our sins,
may we make room for you in our hearts
and be filled with your eternal life. Amen.

**Carol**

Meekness and majesty (HON 335) or
Thou didst leave thy throne (HON 513)

**Final reading**

Philippians 2:5-11

**Carol**

From heaven you came, helpless babe (HON 148)

**Final prayer**

Lord Jesus,
encouraged by our union with you
and comforted by your love,
**make us one in heart and mind.**

Lord Jesus,
may we do nothing out of selfish pride
or ambition,
but regard others as more important
than ourselves;
**make us one in heart and mind.**

Lord Jesus,
may we be filled with your Spirit of humility,
and give priority to the interests of others;
**make us one in heart and mind.**

Lord Jesus,
may we acknowledge you to be Lord of all,
both with lips which sing your praise,
and in lives dedicated to humbly serving you;
**make us one in heart and mind
that together we may confess
that Jesus Christ is Lord,
to the glory of God our Father. Amen.**

**Carol**

Hark, the herald angels sing (HON 199)

**Blessing**

May God, who in his Son
left heaven's glory to take the form of a servant,
make us faithful in his service.
**Amen.**

May God, who in his Son
was obedient even to death on a cross,
make us obedient to his perfect will.
**Amen.**

May God, who has exalted his Son
to the highest place in heaven,
give us grace to acknowledge Christ as Lord
both in word and deed.
**Amen.**

And the blessing . . .

## Choral music

*A number of choir anthems could be prepared to fit in with this pattern, either in addition to the carols, or as an alternative. Many of the carols have themselves been set for performance by a choir – the settings found in* Carols Old *and* New *are well worth exploring, and lie easily within the compass of an occasional 'united choir'. Some splendid new settings for choir can be found in* Songs for the Manger *– the 'Charleston carol', 'See, the Lord of all creation', and 'Peace be yours' are most rewarding to sing.*

*The Christmas music of John Rutter is now becoming familiar to a very wide audience, and some of it is available in relatively simple settings – 'Jesus Child', 'Nativity carol', 'Angels' carol' and 'Shepherd's pipe carol' are all suitable to this outline (though beware the possible 'typo' which led one church to advertise their choir singing the 'Shepherd's pie carol'!). Other well-known possibilities include Peter Warlock's 'Bethlehem down', John Ireland's 'Holy Boy', Herbert Howells' 'A spotless Rose' and Byrd's 'Hodie Christus natus est'.*

STUART THOMAS

# Additional Christmas Material
## (First and second weeks after Christmas or Candlemas)

## A reading from the Gospel of Matthew (2:13-15, 19-23)

After the wise men had left, an angel sent by God appeared to Joseph in a dream with this warning: 'Get up, Joseph! You and your family are in great danger! You must flee to Egypt this very night, and stay there until I tell you that it is safe to return. King Herod means to find Jesus and kill him!'

So Joseph got up and set off for Egypt while it was still dark. Some time later, after Herod's death, the angel returned to Joseph just as he had promised and told him that it was safe for the family to leave Egypt. So they returned once more to Galilee and made their home in a town called Nazareth.

This is the Gospel of the Lord
**Praise to you, Lord Jesus Christ**                                  KATIE THOMPSON

## A reading from the Gospel of John (1:1-18) – Second Sunday

At the beginning of time, the Word already existed. The Word was with God; and the Word was God. From the very beginning, all things were created through him. All life came from the Word, and this life was the light for all people. The light shines out from the darkness, and the darkness could never overcome it.

God sent a man called John, to be a witness for the light, so that others would believe because of him, even though he was not the light. The real light was the Word who was coming into the world to give light to everyone.

He was in the world created through him, and yet the world did not know him. He came to his own people and they did not accept him. To those who did receive him he gave the right to become children of God, the offspring of God himself.

The Word became flesh and he lived as a man among us. We saw his glory given by the Father to his only Son, who is full of grace and truth.

John came to be his witness and he said: 'This is the one whom I spoke of when I said, "He who succeeds me, has passed before me, because he already existed." We received God's law through Moses, but it is through Jesus Christ that we receive many gifts and his grace and truth. God has never been seen, but Jesus, his only beloved Son, has made God known to us as never before, because he is very close to his Father's heart.'

This is the Gospel of the Lord
**Praise to you, Lord Jesus Christ**                                  KATIE THOMPSON

# Prayers

## Approach – a time for us

Gracious God,
> we come to hear the glorious message of this season,
>> the glad tidings of great joy,
>> ever old,
>> ever new.
> We come to recall the faith of Mary,
>> the commitment of Joseph,
>> the response of shepherds,
>> the pilgrimage of wise men,
>> their experience of that life-changing day in Bethlehem.
> But it is not just their story this season speaks of;
>> it is ours too!
> A Saviour has been born to us which is Christ the Lord:
>> **thanks be to God!**

> You told Joseph that the words of the prophet would be fulfilled:
>> that a virgin would conceive and bear a son,
>> and that he would be called Emmanuel,
>> meaning 'God is with us'.
> It was good news not for one but for all,
>> and not simply for then but for now.
> A Saviour has been born to us which is Christ the Lord:
>> **thanks be to God!**

> You proclaimed news of great joy to shepherds out in the fields,
>> the glad tidings that in the city of David a Saviour had been born
>> who was Christ the Lord,
>> the promised Messiah,
>> the one so long awaited.
> It was good news not only for them but for all the people,
>> not just for *that* day but *every* day.
> A Saviour has been born to us which is Christ the Lord:
>> **thanks be to God!**

> You revealed to John the Apostle the meaning of these great events,
>> the astonishing truth that you had taken on flesh and blood,
>> your light, your Word, coming into the world,
>> so that all those who receive him,
>> who believe in his name,
>> can be called your children,
>> children born not of blood,
>> nor of the will of the flesh,
>> but of God.

It was a promise not confined to the past but for the present also,
    not merely for the chosen few but the whole world.
A Saviour has been born to us which is Christ the Lord:
    **thanks be to God!**

Gracious God,
    we thank you for this time,
        this season which speaks so powerfully of your love,
        which reveals so wonderfully your purpose,
        and which demonstrates so clearly your grace.
    A time for praise,
        a time for joy,
        a time for thanksgiving . . .
        a time for us!
A Saviour has been born to us which is Christ the Lord:
    **thanks be to God!**

**Amen.**                                                        NICK FAWCETT

## Christmas petition

Lord of all,
    we pray for all who worship you today,
        all across the world who rejoice
        in the good news of the birth of Jesus Christ.
    Speak your word of life,
        **and be born in our hearts today.**

May the reading of Scripture,
    the singing of carols,
    the offering of prayers,
    and the sharing of fellowship,
    convey something of the wonder of your love.
Speak your word of life,
    **and be born in our hearts today.**

May the faith of all your people be enriched,
    and the life of the Church renewed
    by the presence of the living Christ,
    so that the Gospel may be proclaimed
    through its joyful witness,
    and the glad tidings of your coming in Christ
    bring new hope, joy, meaning and purpose
    to the lives of all.
Speak your word of life,
    **and be born in our hearts today.**

Lord of all,
    reach out to your Church and to people everywhere
        at this glad time of year,
        touching our lives with the living presence of Christ.
    Speak your word of life,
        **and be born in our hearts today,**
        **to the glory of Jesus Christ our Lord.**
        **Amen.**                                                    NICK FAWCETT

## Intercession – a time for change

Lord of all,
    we have heard again the good news of Jesus Christ,
        the glad tidings of his coming,
        and we have rejoiced in the wonder of this season.
    But we pray now for those for whom it brings no joy,
        serving only to remind them of their pain.
    Come again to your world,
        **and turn tears into laughter,**
        **sorrow into gladness.**

We pray for the poor, the hungry, the homeless –
        those for whom this Christmas
        will simply be another day in the struggle for survival;
        for those caught up in war, violence and persecution –
        those for whom this Christmas might be their last;
        for the unloved, the lonely, the homeless –
        those for whom Christmas merely heightens their sense of isolation.
    Come again to your world,
        **and turn tears into laughter,**
        **sorrow into gladness.**

We pray for the anxious, the troubled and the fearful –
        those for whom Christmas will be swamped by worries;
        for the sick, the suffering, the broken in body and mind –
        those for whom this Christmas means only another day of pain;
        and we pray for the bereaved, the divorced, the estranged –
        those for whom Christmas brings home
        the memory of happier times.
    Come again to your world,
        **and turn tears into laughter,**
        **sorrow into gladness.**

Lord of all,
    you give us a vision through the song of Mary
        of the way the world ought to be
        and one day shall be:

a world in which you show the strength of your arm
and scatter the proud,
in which you bring down the powerful
and lift up the lowly,
fill the hungry with good things
and send the rich away empty;
a world of justice,
in which good will triumph,
evil be ended
and the meek inherit the earth.
Give us confidence to believe that day can come
and the resolve to make it happen.
Stir the hearts of your people everywhere
to work in whatever way possible for change –
to bring the dawn of your kingdom closer
and so translate that vision into reality.
Come again to your world,
**and turn tears into laughter,**
**sorrow into gladness.**

In the name of Christ we ask it.
**Amen.**                                                    NICK FAWCETT

## Intercession – a time for giving

Gracious God,
we say that it is more blessed to give than to receive
but in practice we rarely give any indication of believing that.
We claim that Christmas is a time for giving as well as receiving,
but our gifts are usually reserved for family and friends,
the chosen few.
Gratefully, we remember today
that your gift of Christ is so very different –
good news *for* all,
the Saviour *of* all,
given *to* all.
God of grace, you have given us so much:
**teach us to give in return.**

We thank you that you offered yourself freely,
not for any reward, save that of sharing your love,
and you gave everything,
even life itself,
so that anyone and everyone might come to know your goodness,
irrespective of creed, colour or culture.
God of grace, you have given us so much:
**teach us to give in return.**

We pray now for your world in all its need –
  those in lands racked by poverty,
  crushed by debt,
  overwhelmed by famine or natural disaster.
God of grace, you have given us so much:
  **teach us to give in return.**

We remember those who are persecuted,
  denied justice,
  or falsely imprisoned.
God of grace, you have given us so much:
  **teach us to give in return.**

We remember those whose land is torn by hatred,
  scarred by violence,
  broken by war.
God of grace, you have given us so much:
  **teach us to give in return.**

We remember those afflicted by sickness,
  struggling with disability,
  or crushed by suffering.
God of grace, you have given us so much:
  **teach us to give in return.**

We remember those overcome by depression,
  bereavement or broken relationships,
  all for whom the present brings trouble
  and the future seems uncertain.
God of grace, you have given us so much:
  **teach us to give in return.**

Gracious God,
  at this time of giving and receiving
  reach out in love to your aching world.
Bring comfort in distress,
  courage in adversity,
  confidence in uncertainty
  and compassion in suffering.
Strengthen all those who work to build a fairer society
  and a more just world,
  and challenge each of us, who have so much
  to share from our plenty with those who have so little.
May we not just talk in this season about goodwill to all,
  but do something to show what it means.
God of grace, you have given us so much:
  **teach us to give in return.**
Through Jesus Christ our Lord.
**Amen.**                                                NICK FAWCETT

## Something to celebrate

Loving God,
  we praise you for all we have to rejoice in at Christmas,
    this special reminder year by year of your coming to us
    in Christ.
  Come to us now,
    and help us to keep you at the centre of our celebrations.
  Lord, in your mercy,
    **hear our prayer.**

Come to our loved ones,
  our families,
  our friends,
  all those we hold dear
  and whom we shall share with or think of
  over these coming days.
Help us as we celebrate and make merry
  to think also of Christ,
  and through drawing closer to him
  to grow closer together.
Lord, in your mercy,
  **hear our prayer.**

Come to those in special need –
  the poor, the sick, the lonely and sad,
  the homeless, the helpless,
  the oppressed and persecuted;
  all those for whom life is hard and the future seems bleak.
Reach out to them in love,
  and give them something to celebrate.
Lord, in your mercy,
  **hear our prayer.**

Loving God,
  may the light of Christ break into the lives of people everywhere,
    bringing your joy,
    your peace,
    your hope,
    and your love,
    a song of praise on their lips,
    and celebration in their hearts.
  Lord, in your mercy,
    **hear our prayer.**

Come to them,
  come to us,
  come to all,

and send us on our way,
    rejoicing in the Gospel,
    and praising you for the wonder of your grace.
Lord, in your mercy,
    **hear our prayer,**
    **through Jesus Christ our Lord.**
    **Amen.**

NICK FAWCETT

## A short prayer

Lord,
    although I want to understand so much,
    and be able to explain everything that I learn,
    I can't help feeling that it's just not possible
    to put everything into words,
    or reduce what we see and experience
    into a formula or rule.
Some things are just awesome,
    without boundaries,
    without limits
    and are best left
    for the eye and heart to soak in their beauty.
Just as the sun shines on everyone
    without us waking up each day
    and reading a scientific textbook
    or listening to some long-winded debate
    about why and how,
    we accept the fact that it's there.
Surely that's a bit like your love for us?
We really don't need to understand
    every little detail to appreciate it;
    it's simply there,
    for me,
    for them,
    for everyone.
And I think that's totally awesome.

PETE TOWNSEND

# All-age-talk material

## Read Matthew 2:13-23

No sooner had Joseph started to get his head around the idea of a pregnant girl-friend than three wise men turn up with gifts that weren't cuddly, couldn't feed the baby, and certainly wouldn't treat nappy rash!

At some stage Joseph must have dreamt of a normal, traditional betrothal, a nice wedding where aunties cried while uncles drank the wine, and the beginning of a marriage where lots of people gave them gifts and threw confetti . . . or rice, or dates, or orange pips or something. But God had other ideas for Joseph and his bride.

God had already spoken to Joseph in a dream to assure him that Mary was faithful and that the child she would eventually give birth to was special. Now, after using a dream to warn the wise men to make a detour on the way home, God speaks to Joseph again through a dream. So, Joseph and his new family take a long holiday in Egypt, where Joseph has another dream (quite a while later) telling him to go home to Israel then another dream telling them to go and live in Nazareth!

The Bible doesn't tell us whether Joseph had a habit of eating vast quantities of cheese before he went to bed but he certainly had some vivid dreams! But, the most important point is that Joseph was obedient to what he felt God was telling him to do. Even though Joseph would almost certainly have felt fazed, anxious, frightened and a few fries short of a happy meal, he still placed his trust in God. Each time he listened and obeyed God Joseph was building his confidence in what God said and did. Often Joseph wouldn't have a clue what God was up to; he still went ahead and built his faith in God each step of the way. There would have been a lot of criticism and pointing fingers but Joseph was learning to trust in a God who kept his promises.

PETE TOWNSEND

**Escape from danger!**

An angel appeared to Joseph and warned him to take his family and escape from Bethlehem. Where did they go?

**Write the letter that is missing from the second word in the box**

In **PEN** but not **PAN**

In **GAME** but not **MANE**

In **PONY** but not **PONG**

In **PIECE** but not **NIECE**

In **TOAD** but not **ROAD**

Matthew 2:13-23

KATIE THOMPSON

## What warning did the angel give to Joseph?

**Use the numbers written under the lines to find the missing letters and spell out the angel's words**

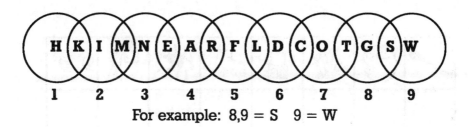

H K I M N E A R F L D C O T G S W

1   2   3   4   5   6   7   8   9

For example: 8,9 = S   9 = W

'

| 1,2 | 2 | 3 | 8 | | 1 | 3,4 | 4,5 | 7 | 6 | | 9 | 4 | 3 | 7,8 | 8,9 |

| 7,8 | 7 | | 5 | 2 | 3 | 6 | | 7,8 | 1 | 3,4 |

| 6,7 | 1 | 2 | 5,6 | 6 | | 4 | 3 | 6 |

| 1,2 | 2 | 5,6 | 5,6 | | 1 | 2 | 2,3 |!'

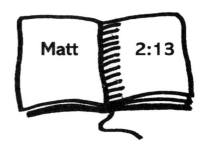

Matt   2:13

KATIE THOMPSON

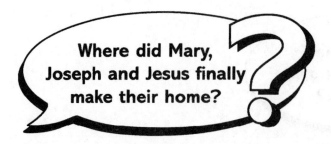

Where did Mary, Joseph and Jesus finally make their home?

**Write the first letter of each picture to spell out the answer**

## IN

| | | | | | | | |
|---|---|---|---|---|---|---|---|
| | | | | | | | |

## in

| | | | | | | |
|---|---|---|---|---|---|---|
| | | | | | | |

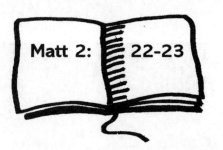

Matt 2: 22-23

KATIE THOMPSON

When Herod died,
Joseph and his family returned to
Israel, but they were still afraid
of the new ruler

Write the word that fits the clue. The missing letters of the
words will spell out the name of the new ruler of Judea

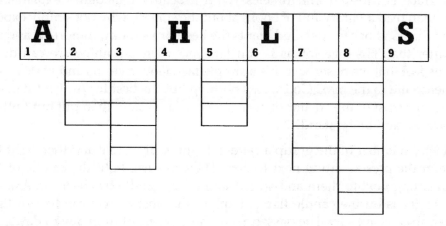

| A | | | H | | L | | | S |
|---|---|---|---|---|---|---|---|---|
| 1 | 2 | 3 | 4 | 5 | 6 | 7 | 8 | 9 |

**CLUES**

2. Water that falls from clouds

3. An orange-coloured vegetable

5. Hens lay these

7. The opposite of never

8. Something used on a rainy day

He was Herod's son!
Matthew 2:22

KATIE THOMPSON

## Read John 1:1-9, 10-18

The whole solar system is so vast that even if we could map every single part of it, the sheer complexity and variety would be virtually impossible to comprehend. It is all so awesome that rather than try and understand every minute detail it's easier just to simply stare at its beauty.

If you look at the night sky, the planets and stars, your senses are overwhelmed. Words fail to describe fully the vision before you. That's something like John the Baptist would have felt when he saw Jesus. Here was God's promise to humankind, in the flesh and offering one blessing after another (see verse 16). Just as the sun provides light and life for the earth, it shines on every one of us and even lights up the other planets without losing any of its brightness. Again, here was Jesus offering God's love and blessing to everyone irrespective of who or where they were. This 'grace', or undeserved kindness from God, is endless. It knows no limits or boundaries. It has no preferences or priorities. God's grace is constant and timeless with a beauty that defies explanation. Rather than read a library full of books about the subject, why not simply experience all that God has for us? God wants the best for us today, tomorrow and the days after that. His love for us is constant and there's nothing we can do to make us feel that we deserve it. It's a simple fact, God loves us and wants us to experience life to the max. God wants nothing but the best for us. Isn't it easier to place our trust in the creator of such a vast solar system than put our faith in what we see and understand?

Give every member of the group a candle. Light your candle and then light the candle of the person sitting next to you. They, in turn, light the candle of the person sitting next to them and so on until every candle has been lit. Ask the group to focus on the candle flame. Explain that just as one candle can light another, so can God's love be passed on to those we meet from day to day.

**(Allow 5 minutes for this)**                                      PETE TOWNSEND

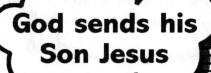

**God sends his Son Jesus**

In today's Gospel, Jesus is called by many different names

Find the different titles used for Jesus

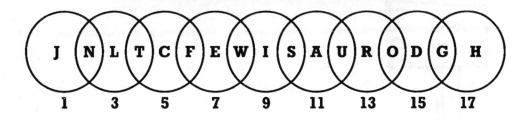

| J | N | L | T | C | F | E | W | I | S | A | U | R | O | D | G | H |
|---|---|---|---|---|---|---|---|---|---|---|---|---|---|---|---|---|
| 1 | | 3 | | 5 | | 7 | | 9 | | 11 | | 13 | | 15 | | 17 |

___ ___ ___   ___ ___ ___ ___        John 1:1
3,5 17 7   7,9 13,15 13 15

___ ___ ___   ___ ___   ___ ___ ___
9,11 13,15 1,3   13,15 5,7   3,5 17 7

___ ___ ___ ___ ___ ___        John 1:14
5,7 11 3,5 17 7 13

___ ___ ___   ___ ___ ___ ___ ___        John 1:9
3,5 17 7   3 9 15,17 17 3,5

___ ___ ___ ___ ___   ___ ___ ___ ___ ___ ___        John 1:17
1 7 9,11 11,13 9,11   5 17 13 9 9,11 3,5

KATIE THOMPSON

Who shows us what God wants us to do?

**Use the code to spell out the answer**

ABCDEFGHIJKLMNOPQRSTUVWXYZ
z y x w v u t s r q p o n m l k j i h g f e d c b a

John 1:18

'
r g    r h    g s v    l m o b

h l m    q v h f h

d s l    n z p v h    g s v

,

u z g s v i    p m l d m

KATIE THOMPSON

God made our
world and sent Jesus to
show us how to take care of
it and each other

**Find eight differences between the two pictures**

KATIE THOMPSON

God sent
Jesus to rescue us from
our wrongdoings and to
be our Saviour

**Use the clues to find the missing letters and decode another word which means Saviour**

**Something you wear on your head in cold weather**

**You use your eyes to . . .**

**Opposite of woman**

**They swim around in ponds**

**The Jews were waiting for the**

__ __ __ __ __ __ __ **to come!**

KATIE THOMPSON

# Reflective material
## (sketches, meditations and poems)

### Meditation of a mother in Bethlehem

It was as though all hell was let loose,
    the most terrible day in my life,
    as suddenly the soldiers burst in upon us –
    cold,
    cruel,
    clinical –
    wresting our little ones from us,
    ignoring *our* screams for mercy,
    *their* screams of terror,
    and hacking them down in cold blood before our very eyes.
There are simply no words to describe how we felt –
    the fear,
    the horror,
    the emptiness,
    the rage,
    and above all, the helplessness –
    unable to do anything but watch grief-stricken
    as our world fell to pieces.
One moment life was full of promise,
    the next, utterly bereft.
One moment we were laughing with our children,
    and the next sobbing our hearts out as we laid them to rest.
Why did it have to happen?
What could have possessed even Herod to do such a thing?
And, most of all, how could God ever have allowed it?
I'll never understand that, as long as I live – never!
It's thrown a cloud over everything, even faith itself,
    for I can't help thinking of an event not so very different,
    that moment of our nation's deliverance,
    centuries back, from Egypt,
    when, after the death of their firstborn,
    Pharaoh at last let our people go.
A glorious chapter in our history, so they tell us,
    and maybe it was,
    but I can't help thinking of all *those* mums
    and the agony *they* must have gone through,
    while we skipped away to freedom.
*We* were spared *then* of course –
    the blood of a lamb setting us apart –
    but not *this* time –

this time we were left to face the full force of unbridled evil,
    hatred incarnate,
    humanity at its most vile –
    and all, apparently, because Herod heard some rumour
    that the Messiah had been born
    somewhere here in Bethlehem.
How much longer must it go on?
How much more suffering must there be,
    before God decides to do something about it?
I'm sorry, but it seems to me
    if he really loves this world as he says he does,
    then it's about time he provided another lamb,
    another sacrifice,
    just like he provided before,
    only this time one to save not just a few of us,
    those specially chosen, set apart,
    but everyone.

NICK FAWCETT

## Meditation of John the Apostle

There's only one word for it,
    one word that gets anywhere near the truth,
    that sums up the wonder of it all,
    and that's 'Jesus'.
Trust me, I know,
    for I've spent a lifetime trying to find the right words.
Since I followed Jesus all those years ago,
    since I sat with the apostles in that upper room,
    since we went out teaching and preaching in the Master's name,
    I've been looking for ways in which to describe my experience,
    and I've used words,
    masses of them,
    more than I can begin to count . . .
When I stood and preached to the multitudes,
    when I nurtured believers in their new-found faith,
    when I prayed for the sick,
    when I led times of worship,
    when I reminisced with friends,
    when I witnessed to strangers,
    words, words, words.
But they've never been sufficient,
    never begun to express what I really want to say.
And now more than ever I find that's true,
    sitting here trying to record the good news
    as revealed to me.

I've written so much,
   page after page,
   my own words and his,
   woven together as best I can
   into a tapestry of his life.
I've told of the beginnings and the ends,
   of his signs,
   of his teaching,
   of his actions.
I've spoken of those lesser-known characters,
   the ones Matthew, Mark and Luke missed out,
   and I've given details of those private moments,
   when it was just us and Jesus together
   as the end drew near.
I've tried,
   I've really tried to get it across,
   to tell you what Jesus meant to me and to so many others.
But there's so much more I could still write,
   so much I've had to leave out.
I could go on to the end of time
   and still not do justice to all I want to tell you.
That's why I say there's only one word,
   one word that says it all,
   because Jesus was the fulfilment,
   the embodiment,
   the personification of God's word.
The Law and the Prophets spoke of him.
The wisdom of the teachers spoke of him.
The universe in all its glory speaks of him.
And if you want to listen,
   if you want to hear,
   if you want to understand what life is all about,
   then take my word for it,
   the only way is to know him for yourself,
   the Word made flesh!                    NICK FAWCETT

## Reflection

People should never apologise for being refugees, nor should they ever despair or allow bitterness to hinder them. Refugees are often, through their pain, very strong people, and all have something to offer. The great need for refugees is that they should organise themselves, so that they have a framework to their lives and a goal. People who are not refugees may help them to do this.

*Bassi Mirzania, who is herself a refugee from Iran*

For many people, differences of background and experience suggest problems. Some people would go so far as to think that those who are different are dangerous, including those who are refugees.

People may especially fear those who have been tortured in their own countries. An asylum-seeker from Zaire was typical of many in that he had been seized and tortured in his own country because he was a member of the opposition to the government and had taken part in a demonstration. He managed to escape from prison and arrived in the UK where he spent six months in prison because he was travelling on false documents. He said, 'I thought I had reached safety . . . My situation was made worse because I could not speak English very well.' Eventually a refugee community organisation arranged legal help and found him accommodation when he was released from prison.

Problems for refugees include the stress they face in being so far away from their homes and often from their families. Like the man from Zaire, they often can't speak the language of the country they are in, they have no money and no way of earning through work. Most of all, they lack people to listen to their stories.

From *Sharing Ways and Wisdom*
Barbara Butler

## Meditation of one of the shepherds

Don't talk to strange men.
Have you ever heard that expression?
I have,
    dozens of times,
    far more than I care to remember.
Why do I say that?
Because all too often it's me they mean by it,
    me the one people look at
    as, arm wrapped protectively round their child's shoulder,
    they usher them away –
    the look on their faces saying it all:
    'Keep away, he spells trouble!'
Yes, that's how they see us –
    not as shepherds,
    but as vermin,
    the lowest of the low.
And the worst thing is
    after a while it's hard not to believe it,
    all one's feelings of dignity and self-respect
    eaten away by the continual suspicion,
    the poisonous asides,
    the sly innuendoes.

I think that's what made the other night so special –
   the night we saw the angels,
   heard the good news,
   went to Bethlehem to see for ourselves.
It wasn't simply that the Messiah was born,
   amazing though that was,
   but the fact we were chosen to hear the news,
   given pride of place before all others!
Don't misunderstand me, we'd have rejoiced whoever was the first,
   for, despite what folk may say,
   we're as God-fearing as the next person,
   and we'd been looking forward to the day of the Messiah
   just like them,
   hoping and praying it might be in our lifetime.
But to hear the news firsthand,
   to be given a personal invitation
   to see the newborn Saviour for ourselves,
   that was beyond all our dreams,
   and it meant more to us than I can ever tell you.
Suddenly we were worth something again,
   recognised and valued as individuals.
Suddenly we could hold our heads up high
   and look the world full in the face,
   confident we had as much right to walk this earth as anyone.
Suddenly it didn't bother us any more what others thought,
   whether they loved us or loathed us,
   for we were important to God,
   and what else could matter?
I've no doubt some will judge even now,
   just as they always have,
   still pass us by with the same dismissive gesture,
   the same self-righteous glance of disdain.
But I don't care any more,
   for there's another saying you may have heard
   which to me says it all:
   'Beauty is only skin-deep'.
I know what that means now,
   for God has demonstrated to me
   that he looks beneath the surface,
   behind the outer show,
   and sees the person hidden there,
   deep within –
   a person more precious to him
   than you would ever dare imagine.

NICK FAWCETT

It takes daily courage to expose oneself to God's word and to allow oneself to be judged by it; it takes daily energy to delight in God's love . . . What shall we do, in order to penetrate into this silence before God? . . . Not one of us lives such a hectic life that he cannot spare the time . . . to be still and let the silence gather round him, to stand in the presence of eternity and to let it speak, to enquire from it about our condition, and to gaze deep into himself and far out . . . beyond and above . . . his soul begins to be replenished and revitalised and to receive strength, then he begins to know the eternal quiet which rests in God's love; stress and anxiety, hurry and restlessness, noise and clamour are stilled within him, he has become silent before God who is his help.

Dietrich Bonhoeffer
From *Beyond Words*, PATRICK WOODHOUSE

## Meditation of Mary, mother of Jesus

I had mixed feelings, to tell the truth,
   not just before the birth but afterwards too.
Does that surprise you?
It did me.
I thought I'd be ecstatic once the child was born,
   over the moon –
isn't that how we mums are meant to feel?
He was my firstborn after all,
   a beautiful bouncing boy,
   so why wasn't I bursting with happiness?
Well, I was, of course,
   part of me anyway,
   yet there was so much I didn't understand,
   and so many things to take the edge off the moment.
There was Joseph for a start.
Oh, he was supportive – don't think I'm complaining –
   once he got over the shock of the pregnancy anyway,
   and you can hardly blame him if that took a while, can you?
But, imagined or not, I always felt there was a shadow in his eyes
   when he looked at Jesus,
   as if to say, 'What *really* happened?'
And then there were those visits after the birth –
   first the shepherds,
   then those strangers from the East with their lavish gifts.
It was gratifying, obviously,
   not every child gets that sort of attention, after all.
But what made them come? – that's what I keep asking.
What did their homage signify?

Don't think I'm ungrateful,
  but I really wish sometimes Jesus could have been an ordinary child,
  and the three of us left to enjoy our happiness –
  no fuss,
  no angels,
  no promises,
  simply the joy of being together.
But any last chance of that disappeared after those words of Simeon,
  that curious warning of his about the future.
I've tried not to let it get to me,
  but it's preyed on my mind ever since,
  always that fear within me of tragedy round the corner.
So, you see, I had mixed feelings,
  very mixed,
  and I still do have, as much now as ever.
I want to rejoice,
  to enjoy my boy while I still have him.
I want to count my blessings and thank God for all he's given.
But there's been a price to pay already,
  and deep within I've a horrible feeling
  that this business of being God's servant,
  of accepting his will and serving his kingdom,
  involves a far greater cost than I'd ever begun to imagine,
  and a price I'd rather not pay.                NICK FAWCETT

# Epiphany

# The Epiphany

*The visit of the magi reveals Jesus as the hope for all nations*

## Matthew 2:1-12

*(also Isaiah 60:1-6; Psalm 72:1-7, 10-14; Ephesians 3:1-12)*

### A reading from the Gospel of Matthew (2:1-12)

Jesus was born in Bethlehem, a small town in Judea when King Herod ruled the land. Some wise men from the east travelled to Jerusalem and asked King Herod where they could find the newborn King of the Jews whom they had come to worship.

Herod was greatly troubled because he didn't want anyone else to be king, so he sent for his advisers. 'Tell me where this child, the so-called King, will be born,' he said.

'It has been foretold by the prophets that he will be born in Bethlehem,' they answered.

For the prophets had written:

> And you, Bethlehem in Judea,
> are not the least important among Judean cities,
> for from you a leader will come,
> a shepherd for my people Israel!

King Herod sent for the wise men privately, and asked them to tell him exactly when the star had first appeared. Then he said to them, 'I will allow you to search for this child, but you must come back and tell me where to find him. Then I too can go and honour him.'

The wise men set off again on their journey. They followed the bright star until it appeared to stop over a house, where they found Mary with the baby Jesus. They were filled with wonder and joy, and, falling to their knees to worship him, they gave him gifts of gold, frankincense and myrrh.

An angel warned them in a dream not to return to Herod's palace, so they went back to their own country a different way.

This is the Gospel of the Lord
**Praise to you, Lord Jesus Christ**                                    KATIE THOMPSON

# Introductory material

What must it have felt like to be one of the wise men at last reaching the end of your journey and finding yourself in the presence of Jesus? How must it have felt for John the Baptist suddenly to see Jesus coming down into the Jordan asking for baptism? Of course, we can never fully answer such questions, but that

shouldn't stop us from asking them, because through reflecting on such experiences – experiences Epiphany Sunday traditionally reminds us of – we may better
understand our own encounter with Jesus Christ. So today try to step back in
time and hear voices from the Scriptures speaking to you.

NICK FAWCETT

# Prayers

## Epiphany praise

Loving God,
we remember today that from the beginning
the good news of Jesus Christ was not just for a few,
but for all.
**Receive our praise.**

You made it known to shepherds
tending their flocks by night,
ordinary, everyday people
pursuing their daily life and work,
unlikely yet special representatives
of your chosen nation.
**Receive our praise.**

But you made it known also to wise men from the East,
strangers living far away,
with no knowledge of you,
and regarded by many at the time
as having no part in your promises.
**Receive our praise.**

Loving God,
for the truth this symbolises –
that there is no one outside your love,
that the message of the Gospel transcends all barriers,
that you want to bring light to all corners of the world –
**Receive our praise.**

For the fact that we are part of your great purpose –
heirs of the promise made to Abraham,
members of the great company of your people,
called to proclaim the gospel to those around us –
**Receive our praise.**

For the knowledge that your light continues to shine –
  despite opposition,
  persecution,
  and rejection by so many –
**Receive our praise.**

For the way so many have followed the example of Jesus
  and responded to your call –
  through the waters of baptism,
  through commitment to your Church,
  through a life of faith and witness –
**Receive our praise.**

Loving God,
  you have made your light shine in our hearts.
  Help us to show our gratitude
    by walking in the path it illuminates,
    and shedding that light on those around us,
    to the glory of your name.
  **Receive our praise,**
    **through Jesus Christ our Lord.**
    **Amen.**                                   NICK FAWCETT

## Epiphany petition

God of love,
  we remember today, on this Epiphany Sunday,
    how wise men from the east came seeking the newborn king,
    how finally they reached the end of their journey,
    and how they knelt in worship before the infant Jesus.
  Help us to learn from their example.
  Guide our footsteps,
    **and lead us closer to Christ.**

Teach us to continue faithfully on the path you set before us,
    remembering that true faith involves a journey of discovery
    as well as arrival at a destination.
  Guide our footsteps,
    **and lead us closer to Christ.**

Teach us to seek your will resolutely,
    even when the way ahead is not clear.
  Guide our footsteps,
    **and lead us closer to Christ.**

Teach us to look at the world around us,
   and to recognise the signs
   through which you might be speaking to us.
Guide our footsteps,
   **and lead us closer to Christ.**

Teach us to keep on trusting in your purpose,
   even when the response of others
   may give us cause for doubt.
Guide our footsteps,
   **and lead us closer to Christ.**

Teach us to offer to Jesus our wholehearted devotion –
   not simply our gifts but our whole lives,
   given to him in joyful worship and grateful praise.
Guide our footsteps,
   **and lead us closer to Christ,**
   **for in his name we ask it.**
   **Amen.**                                           NICK FAWCETT

## Epiphany intercession

Lord of Light,
   we have remembered today the journey of the wise men –
      how, inspired by what they took to be a sign,
      they set off in search of a newborn king,
      a king who would change not simply their lives,
      nor merely the life of his people,
      but the life of the world.
Come again now,
   **and may light shine in the darkness.**

We remember how they persevered in their quest,
   travelling in faith
   even though they had no clear idea of where they were heading,
   or any certainty of what they would find
   when they reached their destination.
Come again now,
   **and may light shine in the darkness.**

We remember how they refused to be discouraged,
   despite their reception in Jerusalem,
   despite the fact that no one seemed to have any idea
   that a new king had been born.
Come again now,
   **and may light shine in the darkness.**

We remember how they kept going,
    single-minded in pursuit of their goal,
    until at last their determination was rewarded
    and they came face to face with the infant Jesus.
Come again now,
    **and may light shine in the darkness.**

Living God,
    we pray for all who seek today,
    all those who are looking for a sense of purpose in their lives,
    all who are searching for spiritual fulfilment,
    all who long to find you for themselves.
Come again now,
    **and may light shine in the darkness.**

Help them to keep looking,
    even when the journey is demanding
    and no end seems in sight;
    to keep believing,
    even when others seem oblivious to their quest
    or scornful of it;
    to keep on trusting,
    even when those they look to for guidance
    seem as confused and as lost as they are.
Come again now,
    **and may light shine in the darkness.**

Living God,
    you have promised through Jesus Christ
    that those who seek shall find.
May the experience of the wise men
    inspire all who seek for truth to keep on searching,
    in the assurance that they too, come what may,
    will one day complete their quest,
    and discover you for themselves.
Come again now,
    **and may light shine in the darkness,**
    **in Jesus' name.**
    **Amen.**

NICK FAWCETT

## A short prayer

Lord of all,
    we are reminded today on this Epiphany Sunday
    of the epic journey of the magi –
    that great pilgrimage of faith

as they stepped out into the unknown,
persevering despite adversity,
searching diligently
until their quest was rewarded.
Lord of all,
we come today, seeking in our turn –
seeking to learn from their experience,
to worship the one before whom they knelt
in homage,
to understand what his birth, his life,
his death and his resurrection mean for us.
Lord of all,
help us through this service
to discover a little more
of what this day has to say,
and a little more of what you would say to us
each day
through Jesus Christ our Lord.                    NICK FAWCETT

# All-age-talk material

*Thought for the day: In Jesus we see God's secret plan revealed.*

## Readings
Psalms 2, 8
Isaiah 42:1-9
John 1:29-34

## Aim
For the children to look at different ways God leads us in our spiritual journey.

Beforehand set up the secret worship place, which is where the trail will end. It might be a large cupboard or under-stair area, a small vestry or even a tent. Whatever you decide, it needs to be out of sight when the children start their trail. Set the children off in groups on a trail, either inside or out, depending on the weather. Each group follows their own colour of stars, which are placed far enough apart for there to be times when the direction is uncertain until they look more carefully (rather like cairns on mountains).

Every group's journey eventually leads to the same finishing point. This worship area is beautiful. It may have flowers placed on a mirror, lights or candles (great care!) an open Bible and a cross. Have a rug or blanket down on the floor and quiet music playing, and make the entrance low, so that they have to stoop to go in. The idea is to make it a secret place of wonder which they are led to find. Have a SILENCE notice outside, and make sure the children come in quietly. When everyone is crowded in, tell them quietly and simply how God led the wise men to find him; how he led John the Baptist to recognise him, and he leads us to find him as well. But we don't all come by the same route. God uses all the different events of our lives, and the different people we meet; he can use sad times as well as happy times.

Sing a worship song together that the children know well, and then pray for people who are going through different bits of their journey at the moment. Have music playing again as the children file out and colour this star prayer to hang up at home.

SUSAN SAYERS

## Visitors for Jesus

Matthew 2:1-12

Three wise men came from the east to find a newborn King

Use the numbers written under the lines to find the missing letters and spell out their names
For example, 1 = M and 3, 4 = P

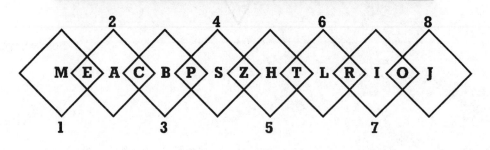

$$\overline{\phantom{x}}\ \overline{\phantom{x}}\ \overline{\phantom{x}}\ \overline{\phantom{x}}\ \overline{\phantom{x}}\ \overline{\phantom{x}}\ \overline{\phantom{x}}\ \overline{\phantom{x}}$$
1   1,2   6   2,3   5   7   7,8   6,7

$$\overline{\phantom{x}}\ \overline{\phantom{x}}\ \overline{\phantom{x}}\ \overline{\phantom{x}}\ \overline{\phantom{x}}\ \overline{\phantom{x}}$$
2,3   2   4   3,4   2   6,7

$$\overline{\phantom{x}}\ \overline{\phantom{x}}\ \overline{\phantom{x}}\ \overline{\phantom{x}}\ \overline{\phantom{x}}\ \overline{\phantom{x}}\ \overline{\phantom{x}}\ \overline{\phantom{x}}\ \overline{\phantom{x}}$$
3   2   6   5,6   5   2   4,5   2   6,7

KATIE THOMPSON

Someone
was not pleased to
see them!

Use the clues to complete the crossword and find out his name

The wise
men had followed a star
to Bethlehem

Use the words to fill in the blanks and find
out what the prophet Micah had foretold

Read
Matthew 2:6

And you, __ __ __ __ __ __ __ __ __ ,

in the land of __ __ __ __ __ ,

you are not least __ __ __ __ __ __ __ __ __

among the __ __ __ __ __ __ __ of Judah.

Because from you will come a __ __ __ __ __ __ ,

who will __ __ __ __ __ __ __ __

my people __ __ __ __ __ __ .

**IMPORTANT   ISRAEL   JUDAH   BETHLEHEM**
**LEADER   PEOPLES   SHEPHERD**

KATIE THOMPSON

**Find out which wise man brought which gift**

KATIE THOMPSON

## Ideas for activities

Take the children on a long journey to different parts of the room, with the star always leading them. Different children can take it in turns to carry the star. As you all trail along you can chant:

Leader:   We're going on a journey,
    All:   we're going on a journey,
Leader:   We're following a star.
    All:   We're following a star.
Leader:   We're going to find Jesus,
    All:   we're going to find Jesus,
Leader:   Hope it's not far.
    All:   Hope it's not far.

SUSAN SAYERS

## The three kings

Here are pictures of the three kings on different stages of their journey. In the space provided write what you think their thoughts or feelings might be.

JILL FULLER

## Read Matthew 2:1-12

When people buy presents for us they usually have a good idea of our likes and dislikes, favourite music, clothes and current rave chocolate bar. The choice of present isn't just a random 'pick anything off the shelf and hope it's OK' type of thing. Presents are given with the hope that the recipient will appreciate (and possibly really like) the choice of gift which will earn the buyer a heartfelt 'thank you'. More often than not, we can even guess what certain people will buy or give us as a present. You know, Gran always buys you a book token equivalent to the price of a book in 1920 while Uncle Arthur never fails to give you a crumpled paper bag containing a selection of boiled sweets. And, on a good year, Great Aunt Dot will give you a box of patterned handkerchiefs which she received for Christmas two years ago.

Often the selection of a present has been given lots of thought and chosen to 'fit' the recipient. Usually a present means something, even if it is only a 'Look, I remembered!'

The wise men didn't just happen to be passing the stable where the infant Jesus was. Neither did they hear about his birth and rush down to the nearest shop and pull any old thing off the shelf. Each present was given for a reason, to mean something, to reflect something of the character of the recipient.

Gold has always, and still does, represent royalty. In Old Testament times it was also a sign of holiness.

Frankincense was a very desirable perfume. It was used by the Jewish priests in the Temple who acted as the 'middle-men' between God and the people.

Myrrh was another perfume used to relieve pain and to anoint the dead prior to burial.

Each of the wise men's gifts represented something of the character of Jesus. He was a Holy King who would act as the bridge-builder between God and the people and would eventually suffer and die as a sacrifice.

The wise men had travelled a great distance to bring their gifts. They knew something of the character of the infant and each gift had a particular significance.

For each of us, Jesus himself became a gift. He became the once and for all sacrifice that would enable us to form an eternal relationship with God. Now, that's a gift that really means something!

PETE TOWNSEND

Give each member of the group a piece of paper and a pen. Chat about what everyone thinks would be the ideal, totally most awesome present. After that, ask everyone to imagine that they are a present which is going to be given to someone they respect, love or admire. What kind of present would they be? Ask them to write their idea onto their piece of paper. Secondly, get everyone to think about what gift they would be if they wanted to make a difference in somebody's life. For example, if they wanted to make a difference to the life of someone who was physically unable to leave their home, they might like to be a car so that they could transport the housebound person wherever they wanted to go. Write the second idea down onto the piece of paper. Compare the two ideas. How different are they? When we are buying a present does it make a difference whether we know the people very well or not?

PETE TOWNSEND

# Reflective material
## (sketches, meditations and poems)

## Star in the night

*Leader*    Lord, when you were born
in Bethlehem
there were armed soldiers
patrolling the streets
and distrust, bitterness
and conflict.

But there came
a star in the night
to lighten the darkness
and because the wise men were ready
to receive its message,
it led them to find you,
a baby in a manger.

We want to be ready to receive your message.
*All*    Help us to find you.

*Leader*    Today, Lord,
in Bethlehem
there are still armed soldiers
patrolling the streets
and distrust, bitterness
and conflict.

But each year
Christmas comes to us
like a star in the night
to lighten our darkness
and if we too are ready
to receive its message,
it still leads us to find you,
not just in Bethlehem
but wherever people truly seek you,

for you came to be the light
of the whole world.

We want to receive your message.
*All*    Help us to find you.                                                   MARY HATHAWAY


## Meditation of one of the wise men

Well, we made it at last.
After all the setbacks,
    all the frustration,
    we finally found the one we were looking for –
    our journey over,
    the quest completed.
And I can't tell you how relieved we were.
You see, we'd begun to fear we'd be too late,
    the time for celebration long since past
    by the time we eventually arrived.
It was that business in Jerusalem which caused the delay,
    all the waiting
    while Herod and his entourage rummaged around
    trying to discover what we were on about.
They were unsettled for some reason,
    taken aback, it seemed, by the news we brought,
    apparently unaware a king had been born among them.
A rival claimant, they must have thought,
    and who could tell what trouble that might stir up?
Anyway, they pointed us in the right direction if nothing else,
    but we'd wasted time there we could ill-afford,
    and although the star reappeared to lead us again
    we were almost falling over ourselves with haste
    by the time we reached Bethlehem.
It was all quiet,
    just as we feared –
    no crowds,
    no family bustling around offering their congratulations,
    no throng of excited visitors,
    just an ordinary house –
    so ordinary we thought we'd gone to the wrong place.
But we went in anyway,
    and the moment we saw the child, we knew he was the one –
    not just the King of the Jews,
    but a prince among princes,
    a ruler among rulers,
    a King of kings!

We were late,
   much later than intended,
   the journey far more difficult than we ever expected,
   but it was worth the effort,
   worth struggling on,
   for, like they say, 'Better late than never!'                NICK FAWCETT

## Thinking about it

*What's the point?*

God doesn't want to exercise coercive power, but rather the persuasive power of a good relationship: the power of love which can transform us, guide us and save us while leaving us free to be truly human. So he came as a baby, because only in that form could he truly appeal for our hearts' and minds' allegiance in a completely unthreatening way.

## Doing it

*Prayer*

Lord Jesus,
thank you for loving us and wanting to share our lives.
Please share in all we do together today,
so that we can grow to know and love you
and one another more.
Amen.

*From the known to the unknown*

Have any of the children got a baby/younger sister/brother? Can they remember the difference their arrival made? You can talk about how a baby inspires love, partly by its very helplessness, but how it also changes the lives of everyone involved! That's rather how Jesus' birth was, as well.

*Tell the story: Matthew 2:1-21*

(See page 149 for a dramatised version of this story.)

### The King of Fear and the King of Love

Wicked King Herod was a very frightened man. 'Someone's after my throne,' he said to Ezra, his chief bodyguard. 'I just know it – someone wants to be king in my place. Well he's not going to get it – whoever he is, he's not going to get my throne.'

   Ezra tried to calm him down. 'There, there, Your Majesty,' he soothed, 'no one's out to get you – and even if they are, they'll have to get past me first.'

   Just then, a servant came in. 'Sire,' he said, 'three wise men from the east have come to ask your advice.'

   King Herod was flattered. 'Show them in,' he said quickly. 'And bring some food and wine – we've got to make a good impression.'

The three wise men were obviously intelligent, well-educated people – and *they* were asking *Herod's* advice! 'So, gentlemen,' he said, 'how can I help you?'

One of the men, Caspar, said, 'We wondered whether you could tell us where the new king is?'

Herod nearly fell off his throne. 'N-n-new k-k-king?' he asked. Then, remembering he had to make a good impression, he pulled himself together. 'I think you are mistaken, gentlemen. I'm the only king here.'

'Oh, no, Your Majesty,' said Melchior – another of the wise men. 'We mean a king who's only just been born. But he's definitely around here somewhere – we've seen his star in the sky and followed it here.'

Suddenly, Herod felt very cold, very sweaty and very weak. 'You're, er, quite sure about this?' he squeaked in a very un-majestic voice.

'Quite sure, Your Majesty,' all the men assured him.

Ezra thought he'd better do something before Herod lost it altogether, so he whispered, 'Your Majesty surely can't be worried about a *baby*? If you can find out where it is, we'll deal with it.'

Herod gave a big sigh of relief. Of course! 'Send for the court prophet,' he shouted. 'Now!'

'Oh, yes, sire,' said the court prophet. 'There's a prophecy in the Bible – something about the town of Bethlehem. "Don't worry about being small," it says, "because you're the town where God's great new king is going to be born." That's good,' the prophet added, 'because it's where King David came from.'

Herod was deathly pale now. 'Good?' he shrieked. 'Good? What's good about a new king? I don't want a new king – what's wrong with the old one, eh? Well? What's wrong with the old one?'

No one answered. They could have – but they didn't. Then Herod had an idea. He turned back to the three wise men. 'Well, now,' he beamed. 'Just joking, of course – just joking. Seriously, I'd like to worship this king, as well. So why don't you go to Bethlehem, find out exactly where he is, and then tell me, so that I can take him a little present? Out of the courtyard, left at the market place and just keep going, and you'll come to Bethlehem. Don't forget, now, will you? Let me know where the dear child is.'

The three wise men went to Bethlehem, and there they found the baby Jesus with his mother Mary and her husband Joseph, and they gave him presents of gold, frankincense and myrrh. What was Herod so worried about? Who could possibly be afraid of a little baby?

'I say,' said Caspar, 'he's rather lovely, isn't he?'

'Ace!' Balthazar always used fewer words than Caspar.

'He's wonderful!' said Mary. 'Isn't it amazing how one little baby can fill the whole world with love!'

That night, Caspar had a dream. An angel appeared and said, 'Don't tell Herod where you found Jesus – he's up to no good.' So the wise men went home by a different route to avoid seeing Herod again.

Herod didn't take long to realise he'd been tricked. '*They're* against me, too!' he thought. He got desperate, and hatched a horrible plan to get rid of Jesus, but God was one step ahead of him there, too. The angel went to Joseph in a dream. 'Get packing,' he said. 'You've all got to go to Egypt – Herod's getting frightened, and you know what that means.'

Joseph woke Mary, and by the time Herod's soldiers arrived in Bethlehem, Jesus was safely away in Egypt where they couldn't get to him.

Now, I ask you: what sort of a king is it that sends an army to defend him against a baby? That's probably why Herod's almost been forgotten now – but millions of people still love Jesus.

**Respond to the story**

*Discussion*

Why did Herod react the way he did?

• Just because he didn't like little boys?

• Because he was afraid of losing his throne?

Why was he afraid?

• Because he knew that everyone hated him?

• Because deep down he knew he wasn't as important as he liked to think?

*Song*

One or more of the following songs might be used:

King of kings and Lord of lords

There was one, there were two (*The children's band*)

Who's the King of the jungle?

You are the King of glory

*Art and craft*

Draw or paint pictures of King Herod and the baby Jesus to put on display. Prepare some cards with words such as Power, Force, Weapons, Army, Fear, to describe Herod's resources, and others such as Love, Weakness, Needs, to apply to Jesus.

Draw or paint a picture of Jesus in Mary's arms.

This is the key picture, but you might want to do others in addition to it, such as:

• King Herod talking to the three wise men

• The three wise men following the star

• The three wise men worshipping the baby Jesus

*Drama*

Have the story read in either narrative or dramatised form. Draw attention to the display pictures of Herod and Jesus, and show the congregation the cards in random order. Ask to which character each card applies, and pin or Blu-Tack the cards around the figures. Then ask whether it's as simple as that. Didn't Jesus have a kind of power that Herod couldn't understand? On the face of it, Herod was strong and the baby Jesus was weak. But if that was really the case, why did Herod feel so threatened? Perhaps the 'power' label ought to be over Jesus, and the 'weakness' label over Herod? When it came down to it, the only power Herod had was based on fear. Jesus' power was based on love. Herod had only the power to destroy, but love is the power of life!

### The King of Fear and the King of Love

**Narrator**    King Herod was very frightened. He sent for Ezra, his bodyguard.

**Herod**    *(Ranting)* Someone's after my throne. I just know it – someone wants to be king in my place.

**Ezra**    *(Soothingly)* There, there, Your Majesty, no one's out to get you – and even if they are, they'll have to get past me first.

**Narrator**    Just then, a servant came in.

**Servant**    Sire, three wise men from the east have come to ask your advice.

**Herod**    *(Flattered)* Show them in. And bring some food and wine – we've got to make a good impression.

**Narrator**    The three wise men were obviously intelligent, well-educated people – and they were asking *Herod's* advice!

**Herod**    *(Grandly)* So, gentlemen, how can I help you?

**Caspar**    We wondered whether you could tell us where the new king is?

**Narrator**    Herod nearly fell off his throne.

**Herod**    N-n-new k-k-king?

**Narrator**    Then, remembering he had to make a good impression, he pulled himself together.

**Herod**    I think you are mistaken, gentlemen. I'm the only king here.

**Melchior**    Oh, no, Your Majesty – a king who's only just been born. He's definitely here somewhere – we've seen his star in the sky.

**Narrator**    Suddenly, Herod felt very cold, very sweaty and very weak.

**Herod**    You're, er, quite sure about this?

**Wise men**    *(Together)* Quite sure, Your Majesty.

**Narrator**    Ezra thought he'd better do something before Herod lost it altogether, so he whispered in his ear.

**Ezra**    Your Majesty surely can't be worried about a baby? If you can find out where it is, we'll deal with it.

**Herod**    *(Relieved)* Of course! Send for the court prophet. Now!

**Narrator**    The court prophet came quickly.

**Prophet**    Oh, yes, sire. There's a prophecy in the Bible – something about the town of Bethlehem. 'Don't worry about being small,' it says, 'because you're the town where God's great new king is going to be born.' That's good, because it's where King David came from.

| | |
|---|---|
| **Herod** | Good? Good? What's good about a new king? What's wrong with the old one, eh? Well? What's wrong with the old one? |
| **Narrator** | No one answered. They could have – but they didn't. Then Herod had an idea. He turned back to the three wise men. |
| **Herod** | Just joking, of course. Seriously, I'd like to worship this king. So go to Bethlehem, find out where he is, and then tell me, so that I can take him a little present. |
| **Narrator** | The three wise men went to Bethlehem, and there they found the baby Jesus with his mother Mary and her husband Joseph, and they gave Jesus presents of gold, frankincense and myrrh. |
| **Caspar** | I say, he's rather lovely, isn't he? |
| **Balthazar** | Ace! |
| **Mary** | He's wonderful! Isn't it amazing how one little baby can fill the whole world with love! |
| **Narrator** | That night, an angel appeared to Caspar in a dream. |
| **Angel** | Don't tell Herod where you found Jesus – he's up to no good. Go home by a different route to avoid seeing Herod again. |
| **Narrator** | Herod didn't take long to realise he'd been tricked. He got desperate, and hatched a horrible plan to get rid of Jesus, but God was one step ahead of him there, too. The angel went to Joseph in a dream. |
| **Angel** | Get packing, you've all got to go to Egypt – Herod's getting frightened, and you know what that means. |
| **Narrator** | Joseph woke Mary, and by the time Herod's soldiers arrived in Bethlehem, Jesus was safely away in Egypt where they couldn't get to him. Now, I ask you: what sort of a king is it that sends an army to fight against a baby? That's probably why Herod's almost been forgotten now – but millions of people still love Jesus. |

MICHAEL FORSTER

## The candle and the flower

Lord Jesus,
   you are the light
   of the world.

And without light
   all shape, form and pattern
   are shrouded in darkness.

Without light
   there is no growth,
   no abundance of living.

Without light
    there is no colour
    in endless variation.

For within you burns
    all light and from you
    blossoms all beauty.

So, Lord Jesus,
    you are truly the light
    of the world.

But in your light
    dwells all the beauty
    of the world also.

MARY HATHAWAY

# Lent

# Ash Wednesday

*Choosing the way of God's kingdom*

## Matthew 6:1-6, 16-21

*(also Isaiah 58:1-12; Psalm 51:1-17; 2 Corinthians 5:20–6:10)*

### A reading from the Gospel of Matthew (6:19-21)

Do not store up for yourself treasure on earth,
   where moth and worm eat things up,
   where thieves break into houses and steal.
Store up for yourself treasure in heaven,
   where no moth or worm eats things up,
   where no thieves break into houses and steal.
For heart and treasure
   go together.

ALAN DALE

# Introductory material

## The season of Lent

Lent is the season offered to us by the Church during which we can make a special effort with self-discipline. It is *offered* to us because we can quite easily sail through Lent without using the opportunity. But if we do that we and our family are the losers. We will receive encouragement but no one will check up to see if we respond or not.

Named after the old English word 'lenten', which means 'spring', the season was first intended as a preparation period for the new converts who were getting ready for baptism. In the early years of Christianity this took place at the Easter Vigil. Later the season was applied to all Christians and their need for an annual effort to renew themselves. Christians who had sinned seriously and now wanted to return to the active life of the community were prepared throughout these forty days for reconciliation at Easter. As a sign of their sorrow they wore clothes of sacking and ashes were sprinkled on their heads. By the ninth century this custom had stopped and was replaced by a ceremony involving the whole Church. To remind the whole community that each and every one was a sinner, ashes were placed on their heads on the first day of Lent. Since this took place on a Wednesday, the day naturally became Ash Wednesday.

### To Easter through Lent

Only Easter makes sense of Lent. Only the resurrection makes sense of Christ's birth, life and death. Jesus' death, on its own, was not special. He offered himself to his Father on the Cross, but if the Father had not accepted his offering that would have been the end of it. However, the Father did show his acceptance by raising his Son up to a new life. Easter is, for that reason, the most important festival in the Church's year, the celebration of the main event of God's work in the world.

Given the great fuss that is made of Christmas it is not surprising that most people fail to appreciate the importance of Easter. Children find it particularly difficult to take in. All those lovely presents, decorations and parties around Christmas time stand in strong contrast to what happens at Easter! A few chocolate Easter eggs do not redress the balance! In the family a great effort needs to be made to give the celebration of Easter a proper emphasis and dignity. And this is not possible without taking the forty days of Lent seriously.

What we have got to absorb and gradually impart to our family is the message of Lent. This is, as we have been saying, that we must die to our own selfishness so that we can rise up joyfully with Christ to a new life.

- It is *a time for – a change of heart*. A time for a new and closer look at the way our lives are lived, for repentance and reconciliation.
- It is *a time for – concern for others*. Caring for others is a valuable weapon in our fight against selfishness. Alms giving has always been a part of Lent.
- It is a *time for – prayer which costs*. That means in terms of time and personal effort.

When any 'giving-up' or mortification is spoken of at the outset of Lent these three things must be kept in mind – our need for a change of heart, an outward and genuine concern for others and, underlying everything, a need to pray much more.

Each of these three parts to Lent must be present if the season is to have any real and lasting value. To go into Lent with a resolution to give up sugar in our tea, for example, is only of any value if it is part of our 'change of heart' campaign. The money saved should go to our deprived brothers and sisters and the action supported by an increased effort at prayer.

TONY CASTLE

# Prayers

## Following Jesus

Gracious God,
we come to worship you at the start of Lent.
**We come in the name of Christ,**
**remembering again those lonely and testing days**
**he endured in the wilderness.**

We come recalling how deliberately he spent time there alone,
    reflecting on who he was and what you wanted of him.
**We come reminded of the courage, the faith,**
    **and the commitment he showed during that time –**
    **qualities that were to characterise the rest of his ministry.**

Gracious God,
    help us to use this time given to us.
**May we draw closer to you through it,**
    **understanding more of your nature and our own.**
May it deepen our faith,
    strengthen our commitment,
    and confirm our sense of calling.
**May we learn what it means to follow Christ**
    **and what it means to serve you.**
May we recognise more clearly the true cost of discipleship
    but equally the rewards.
**May we understand more fully**
    **why you have put us here,**
    **what you would have us do,**
    **who you would have us be,**
    **how you would have us live,**
    **and where you would have us go.**

Gracious God,
    prepare us through this time of worship,
        this day, and this season,
        to understand and celebrate more fully
        all you have done for us in Christ.
**And so may we love you more truly**
    **and serve you more faithfully,**
    **to the glory of your name.**
    **Amen.**
                                     NICK FAWCETT

## Failure to honour our calling

Almighty and merciful God,
    we have done that which we should not have done,
        and failed to do what we know we should have done.
    We have thought that which we should not have thought,
        and failed to think of what is good and pleasing in your sight.
    We have spoken that which we should not have said,
        and left unspoken things we ought to have said.
    We have failed you in so much:
        **forgive us.**

We have sinned against you and one another,
    against many, known and unknown,
    in thought, and word, and deed.
We have failed you in so much:
    **forgive us.**

We are ashamed of our weakness and many faults,
    our greed, selfishness, pride and envy;
    the carelessness of our discipleship
    and the shallowness of our faith.
We have failed you in so much:
    **forgive us.**

We long to serve you better,
    to live as your people and bring honour to Christ,
    but though our hearts say one thing, our bodies say another,
    the spirit willing, but the flesh weak.
We have failed you in so much:
    **forgive us.**

Merciful God,
    deal kindly with us through your grace.
Forgive us our failure to serve you,
    and put a clean heart and a right spirit within us.
Assure us of your forgiveness,
    renew us through your love,
    and give us strength to follow you more faithfully
    in the days ahead.
We have failed you in so much:
    **forgive us.**

Through Jesus Christ our Lord.
**Amen.**                                                        NICK FAWCETT

## A short prayer

Loving God,
    we try to look at ourselves openly and honestly,
    but we find it so hard,
    for we are so often blind to our faults,
    closed to anything which disturbs the image
    we have of ourselves.
So we come to you,
    appealing to your grace and mercy.
Search us, we pray –
    forgive us our sins,
    cleanse us of our iniquities,

have mercy on our weakness,
and through your love create a clean heart
and a right spirit within us.
Remake us,
redeem us,
restore us,
and grant that we may live as your people,
a new creation in Christ,
to the glory of your name.
Amen.                                                    NICK FAWCETT

# Reflective material
## (sketches, meditations and poems)

## The Wanderer
*Matthew 8:19-20; Luke 9:57-58*

A fox has a hole
and a bird has a nest
but Jesus has nowhere
to lie down and rest.
He travels the earth
like a clown or a tramp,
and he knows what it's like
in a refugee camp.

*Jesus, wanderer,*
*travelling alone;*
*knocking on doors*
*in search of a home.*

He's one with the outcast
who's branded at birth.
He's one with the stranger
and pilgrim on earth.
He's one with the poor man
of no fixed address.
He sits with the lonely
and shares their distress.

*Jesus, wanderer,*
*travelling alone;*
*knocking on doors*
*in search of a home.*                                    PETER DAINTY

## Easy is the way

Easy is the way that leads to life,
   through the gates of the kingdom,
   where admission is free
   and the Father runs to greet you with a kiss.
Easy is the way that leads to life,
   but few there be that believe it.

For the other way is hard
   and seems more fitting –
   the way of discipline and self-denial,
   the hair shirt and the bed of nails;
   the way of ritual and right religion,
   fine prayers and costly gifts;
   the moral way of strenuous goodness
   and careful respectability;
   the intellectual way of tortuous reason,
   intense debate and learned books
   and the earnest search for truth.

But that way,
   that broad and steep way,
   that proud and noble highway,
   is the way that leads to destruction
   in the depths of despair,
   where all is vanity.

It is the easier way that leads to life:
   the way of acceptance;
   the narrow way
   that allows us to bring no gifts,
   but empty-handed
   to receive from God.

This is the way of the bird with the air;
   the way of the fish with the sea;
   the way of the seed with the soil and the rain.
It is the way of the child
   with the baptismal waters.
For as we came into the world naked,
   so must we enter the kingdom of God,
   to be born again into his family.

Easy is the way that leads to life –
   if it *is* easy to leave behind
   all the clutter of self-justification,
   and enter into the kingdom
   with nothing.

PETER DAINTY

# The First Sunday of Lent

*Jesus is tempted as we are, so offers hope and forgiveness to all*

## Matthew 4:1-11

*(also Genesis 2:15-17, 3:1-7; Psalm 32; Romans 5:12-19)*

### A reading from the Gospel of Matthew (4:1-11)

Jesus was led by the Holy Spirit into the desert where the devil came to tempt him. After fasting for forty days and nights Jesus was very hungry, and the devil said to him, 'If you are indeed the Son of God, turn the stones around you into bread.'

In reply, Jesus repeated the words of Scripture which said, 'Man cannot survive on bread alone, but needs every word spoken by God.'

Then the devil took Jesus to the Temple in Jerusalem and together they stood on its highest point. 'If you are the Son of God,' the devil said, 'then throw yourself down to prove it, because Scripture tells us that God's angels will protect you from harm.'

Again Jesus answered him with words from Scripture: 'It is not right to put God to the test.'

The devil did not give up easily, so he took Jesus to the top of a high mountain where he showed him the kingdoms of the world in all their glory. 'If you worship me,' the devil said, 'I will give all of these to you.'

Finally growing impatient, Jesus said, 'Devil, leave me alone! For Scripture tells us to worship God and serve only him.'

Finally the devil left Jesus, and angels appeared to take care of him.

This is the Gospel of the Lord
**Praise to you, Lord Jesus Christ**                                    KATIE THOMPSON

# Introductory material

For many people Lent is associated with giving something up. It is seen as an opportunity, perhaps, for kicking that unwanted habit, for going at last on that long-intended diet, or for denying oneself those unnecessary extra luxuries. All such acts of discipline may have their place, but they give a very one-sided view of this season, for, if anything, it should be about taking something on; committing oneself, in the words of Jesus, to going the extra mile. That doesn't mean taking work on for work's sake. Rather, it is about resolving to follow Christ more faithfully, a determination to give him our wholehearted discipleship. It might mean more disciplined devotion, perhaps more practical service, maybe more effective witness, or possibly the offering of previously unused gifts. Whatever it is, it is more than giving something *up*; above all, it is giving something *back* to the one who gave us his all. Consider today what Christ has done for you; then ask what you can do for him, and use Lent as an opportunity to respond.

NICK FAWCETT

# Prayers

## Praise

Loving God,
> we praise you for your coming to us in Christ,
>> walking our earth and sharing our humanity.
> For the wonder of your love,
>> **we praise you.**

> We praise you for the inspiration you give us through him –
>> the knowledge that he experienced temptation,
>> just as we do,
>> yet refused to compromise,
>> staying true to his chosen path despite the awful cost.
> For the wonder of your love,
>> **we praise you.**

> We praise you for the revelation of your purpose in Jesus,
>> everything we see of you throughout his earthly ministry.
> We remember how he taught the multitude,
>> instructed his disciples
>> and interpreted the law;
>> how he healed the sick,
>> responded to the needy
>> and cared for the poor;
>> how he confronted injustice,
>> challenged oppression
>> and overcame evil.
> For the wonder of your love,
>> **we praise you.**

> We praise you
>> for the supreme demonstration of your grace at Calvary –
>> the fact that you were willing to identify yourself with us
>> not only in life but in death,
>> enduring the agony of crucifixion,
>> and the awful burden of our sinfulness.
> For the wonder of your love,
>> **we praise you.**

Loving God,
we come, at this season,
to recall your goodness,
to marvel at your grace
and to commit ourselves to your service.
For the wonder of your love,
**we praise you.**

Through Jesus Christ our Lord.
**Amen.**                                               NICK FAWCETT

## Petition

Gracious and merciful God,
on this first Sunday of Lent we come together to worship you,
to praise and thank you,
to seek your forgiveness and to ask for renewal.
Create in us a clean heart, O Lord,
**and put a right spirit within us.**

We come in the name of Christ,
remembering his lonely days in the wilderness,
his time wrestling with temptation,
and the ministry that followed,
restoring and transforming so many lives.
Create in us a clean heart, O Lord,
**and put a right spirit within us.**

Help us to learn from his example –
to search our hearts as he did,
to consider our calling,
to reflect on our faith,
to resist temptation,
and to commit ourselves more wholly to you.
Create in us a clean heart, O Lord,
**and put a right spirit within us.**

Help us to recognise all Jesus has done for us
through his life, death and resurrection;
and so may we come gladly to you,
confessing our sins,
acknowledging our faults,
accepting our weaknesses,
and receiving your forgiveness.
Create in us a clean heart, O Lord,
**and put a right spirit within us.**

Gracious and merciful God,
we come together on this first Sunday of Lent.
Speak to us today and in the days ahead,
so that we may know you and love you better.
Create in us a clean heart, O Lord,
**and put a right spirit within us,**
**through Jesus Christ our Lord.**
**Amen.**                                                        NICK FAWCETT

## Confession

Loving God,
we remember in this season of Lent
the temptation of Jesus in the wilderness,
the pressures he faced,
the choices he had to make,
the evil he had to resist,
the path he chose.

We remember that though he was tempted as we are
he did not give way,
though he could have used his powers for his own ends
he used them instead for us,
though he could have taken the easy way
he took the hard.

Loving God,
forgive us that our testimony is all too often so different.
**We have failed you in so much,**
**refusing to take up our cross**
**and follow in the footsteps of Jesus.**
**We have not obeyed your commandments,**
**or loved as you have loved us,**
**or in any way lived faithfully as your people.**
**We have been narrow in our vision,**
**weak in our commitment,**
**careless in our worship,**
**self-centred in our attitudes,**
**repeatedly preferring our way to yours**
**and wandering far from you.**

Loving God,
have mercy upon us.
**Renew us in heart and mind and spirit,**
**strengthen our wills and deepen our faith,**
**and send us out once more as your people,**

**forgiven and restored,**
**to live and work for you, in the name of Christ.**
**Amen.**                                                    Nick Fawcett

## Intercession

Lord Jesus Christ,
    we are reminded today, in this season of Lent,
        of the time you spent in the wilderness –
        facing choices,
        wrestling with temptation,
        experiencing a period of testing
        that would shape the course of your ministry;
        a time which reminds us of your humanity,
        which tells us you were one with us,
        tempted just as we are.
    In the wilderness of life today
        **be present, O Lord.**

Lord Jesus Christ,
    we thank you that you came through that time the stronger –
        more sure of the path you must take,
        and more confident of your ability to take it.
    So now we pray for those experiencing similar times of testing.
    In the wilderness of life today
        **be present, O Lord.**

We pray for those facing difficult and demanding choices –
    choices which entail pain and self-sacrifice,
    which mean letting go of cherished dreams,
    which involve facing awkward facts about themselves and others.
In the wilderness of life today
    **be present, O Lord.**

We pray for those wrestling with temptation –
    torn between conflicting desires,
    unsure of where they stand,
    uncertain about their ability to stand firm.
In the wilderness of life today
    **be present, O Lord.**

We pray for those experiencing a period of testing in their lives –
    problems they fear they cannot cope with,
    challenges they feel unable to rise to,
    questions they would rather not face.
In the wilderness of life today
    **be present, O Lord.**

Lord Jesus Christ,
  give strength to all facing such times –
    a sureness of purpose and clearness of mind.
  Give the knowledge of your will –
    then courage to make right decisions
    and resolve to see them through.
  May each emerge the stronger for all they experience,
    and better equipped to face the future.
  In the wilderness of life today,
    **be present, O Lord,**
    **for in your name we pray.**
    **Amen.**                                         NICK FAWCETT


## A short prayer

Living God,
  it's easy to fool ourselves
  that we are observing Lent –
  giving up certain vices,
  denying ourselves particular pleasures,
  making bold resolutions.
It's easy to imagine this is what Lent is all about –
  but it's not.
For Lent above all is a time for reflection,
  for self-examination,
  for prayer,
  for renewed commitment.
We come then today to reflect,
  to search ourselves,
  to seek your guidance,
  to offer you our love.
Help us through this service to hear your voice,
  and to be strengthened in the service of Christ.        NICK FAWCETT


# All-age-talk material

## Choosing God

You need to get hold of someone who can juggle (however badly) with two balls today. If the juggler is really bad, rolled up socks will be better than balls as there is less retrieval time!

Explain that this Lent week is about choices, and the way we choose to live our life. We can choose to live life exactly as we want, buying loads of unnecessary clothes, sweets and luxury goods, yet unable to find more than small change for the Christian Aid collection. Or we can choose to live life exactly as God wants, sharing what we have with other people, being happy to help at home, whether we get paid for it or not, and putting all our time and money at God's disposal.

Perhaps we have already definitely chosen one or other of those ways; for many of us, we try to do it this way. (The juggler does his stuff. It's actually better if he keeps dropping the socks.) We try to juggle our choices, so that sometimes we are holding God at the centre of our lives, and sometimes self. As you can see, it doesn't really work. Sometimes we get into a muddle, all tangled up as we try to serve both God and self at the same time. And we never get to hold on to God long enough to get to know him and understand his will for us in our lives. Having self at the centre of your life will make you possessive and bitter, discontented and miserable. Having God at the centre will make you fulfilled, light-hearted and at peace with yourself. Juggling will make you confused. It's time to make the choice.

SUSAN SAYERS

## Consequences

Ask a couple of volunteers to run up and down, or jog on the spot, and as they do so, point out that if we choose to run fast like this there will be consequences. Stop the runners and demonstrate the way their breathing is much deeper and faster, and their pulse rate higher. They are probably warmer, too. All these things are natural consequences of the action they have been involved in.

If we choose to do something wise, like looking and listening carefully as we cross the road, the consequence will be that we have a far better chance of being safe. If you choose something foolish, like standing on your head when you haven't done that for forty years, the likely consequence is that you will probably damage your neck. We make these decisions all the time and how we choose will actually change the shape of our characters.

If we choose the selfish, unkind, greedy, or cruel way we will become selfish, unkind, greedy or cruel people. If, on the other hand, we choose the friendly, encouraging, honest or loving way, we will become friendly, encouraging, honest or loving people. What we become will be a consequence of what we choose.

SUSAN SAYERS

## Read Matthew 4:1-11

Before Jesus gets on with telling people about restoring their relationship with God, he goes on a walkabout in the desert. It's here that the devil decides to have a go at Jesus and put a bit of temptation his way.

Each time that the devil attempts to divert Jesus' attention away from God, it isn't so much the fact that the devil tries to get Jesus to eat bread, tempt him to demonstrate his authority or offer vast wealth, it's the little word 'if' that is used to sow the first seeds of doubt.

Most of the time we can feel confident about who we are, what we are doing or even where we are going, but it's when someone questions our motives with the 'if' word that the whole thing begins to unravel in our heads.

We can be fairly experienced or have a lot of ability but when the 'if' word is introduced it makes us question everything that we thought we knew or believed.

It's easy to feel confident about being a Christian when we are with a group of people who all think the same way, but when we are alone with a group of people who think a 'Christian' is a species of fish, then it's far from easy to feel quite so confident.

The 'if' word needs to be small so that it can squeeze into the briefest of sentences. It doesn't have to be said very loudly for it to have a huge impact. It's so small that it takes just a split second to write but it can take hours or even days for its effect to dissolve.

Before anyone labels the 'if' word as negative, it's important to say that it is, in fact, a very important word that we should all use. Jesus wasn't afraid to use the 'if' word or deal with the devil's use of it. The important thing is how we react to the 'if' word.

Each time that the devil used 'if', Jesus immediately referred to what God had to say on the subject. This wasn't merely reciting the Scriptures like a parrot but showing that he, Jesus, knew and understood what God was saying and what it meant for everyday living.

The same principle applies to us. We also need to be aware of what God has to say (read the Bible) and how it can affect the way we think and behave (pray and chat with God).

Being afraid of the question 'if' is often the result of being in a desert ourselves, a self-inflicted desert which is the result of choosing not to involve God in our day-to-day lives.

So, rather than think negative, act positive, if you can!

PETE TOWNSEND

Write the word 'temptation' along the left-hand side of a flipchart. Ask the group for examples of temptations that begin with the first letter of the word 'temptation', and so on. For instance: T: threats; E: envy; M: money; P: porn; T: taste; A: anger; T: teasing; I: ignorance; O: outburst; N: nagging.

Put all the definitions that the group think of onto the flipchart.

**(Allow 5 minutes for this)**                                                      PETE TOWNSEND

## Confessing

### Reading

Psalm 32:1-11

### Aim

To remind us that Lent is a time of challenge, urging us to confess our faults, but also a time of hope, bringing the promise of forgiveness.

### Preparation

On pieces of card, or paper, print the following words or part-words:

CONFESSING
(print this horizontally and display on the centre of a board)

A          (print these vertically – see **Talk** below)
QUIT
ABS
LVE
PARDO
ORGIVE
M
RCY
HRIVE
ORRY
ADM
T
REPE
TANCE
APOLO
ISE

Fix magnetic tape or Blu-Tack to the back of each.

### Talk

Tell the congregation that you have prepared a short quiz designed to help explain the meaning of Lent. One of the traditions of the Church over the centuries has been to begin Lent by confessing one's faults and seeking forgiveness. The aim of the quiz is to discover what 'confessing' actually means, and each of the answers will have at least one letter of the word 'confessing' in it. As each correct response is given, arrange the appropriate parts of the word as set out below.

1.  What word means to pronounce someone not guilty? *pardon* *Acquit*
2.  What word means to pronounce forgiveness? *Absolve*
3.  What do we beg if we've done something wrong? *pardon*
4.  What do we ask God to do to our trespasses in the Lord's prayer? *forgive*

5.  What do we show to someone if we let them off punishment?   *Mercy*
6.  What word meaning to cleanse is associated with last Tuesday?   *Shrive.*
7.  What do we say if we have done something wrong?   *Apology Sorry.*
8.  What word means own up to?   *Admit*
9.  What did John the Baptist call people to do before being baptised?   *Repentance*
10. What word means to say sorry?   *apologise*

```
                P                                    A
                A                              R     P
        A       R                       A      E     O
        B       D                       D      P     L
A       S       O       M               M      E     O
C       O   N   F   E   S   S   I       N      G
Q       L       O   R   H   O   T       T      I
U       V       R   C   R   R   A       S
I       E       G   Y   I   R   N       E
T               I       V   Y   C
                V       E       E
                E
```

Today is the first day/Sunday of Lent: a time for CONFESSING everything that is wrong in our lives; a time in which we need to ADMIT our mistakes and show true REPENTANCE through saying SORRY and APOLOGISING to God.

But it is also a time for remembering God is ready to FORGIVE us, a time for rejoicing in his MERCY and PARDON. It is a time which reminds us that, through the grace of Christ, he is ready to ACQUIT and ABSOLVE – or, as the old English word puts it, SHRIVE – us of all we have done wrong.

This, then, is what Lent is all about; a time of challenge but also promise, summed up in the words of Psalm 32:

> I acknowledged my sin to you, and I did not hide my iniquity; I said, 'I will confess my transgressions to the Lord,' and you forgave the guilt of my sin (verse 5).

Thanks be to God!

NICK FAWCETT

KATIE THOMPSON

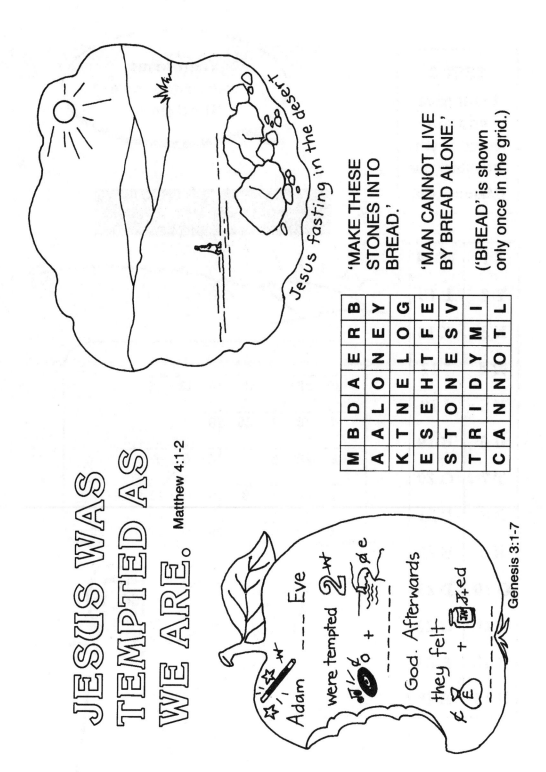

Jesus fasting in the desert

JESUS WAS TEMPTED AS WE ARE. Matthew 4:1-2

'MAKE THESE STONES INTO BREAD.'

'MAN CANNOT LIVE BY BREAD ALONE.'

('BREAD' is shown only once in the grid.)

| M | B | D | A | E | R | B |
|---|---|---|---|---|---|---|
| A | A | L | O | N | E | Y |
| K | T | N | E | L | O | G |
| E | S | E | H | T | F | E |
| S | T | O | N | E | S | V |
| T | R | I | D | Y | M | I |
| C | A | N | N | O | T | L |

Adam ---- Eve were tempted 2

God. Afterwards they felt

Genesis 3:1-7

SUSAN SAYERS

**TEST 3**

**I will give you the world if you worship me**

(Matthew 4:9)

| | |
|---|---|
| Z 1 | M 14 |
| Y 2 | L 15 |
| X 3 | K 16 |
| W 4 | J 17 |
| V 5 | I 18 |
| U 6 | H 19 |
| T 7 | G 20 |
| S 8 | F 21 |
| R 9 | E 22 |
| Q 10 | D 23 |
| P 11 | C 24 |
| O 12 | B 25 |
| N 13 | A 26 |

Then Jesus was tested for a third time!

Use the code cracker to find what Jesus said

```
25 22     20 12 13 22
__ __  __ __ __ __ !
 8 26  7 26 13

__ __ __     __ __ __ __
 2 12  6    14  6  8  7

__ __ __ __ __ __ __
 4 12  9  8 19 18 11

__ __ __     __ __ __ __ __
20 12 23    26 15 12 13 22
```

KATIE THOMPSON

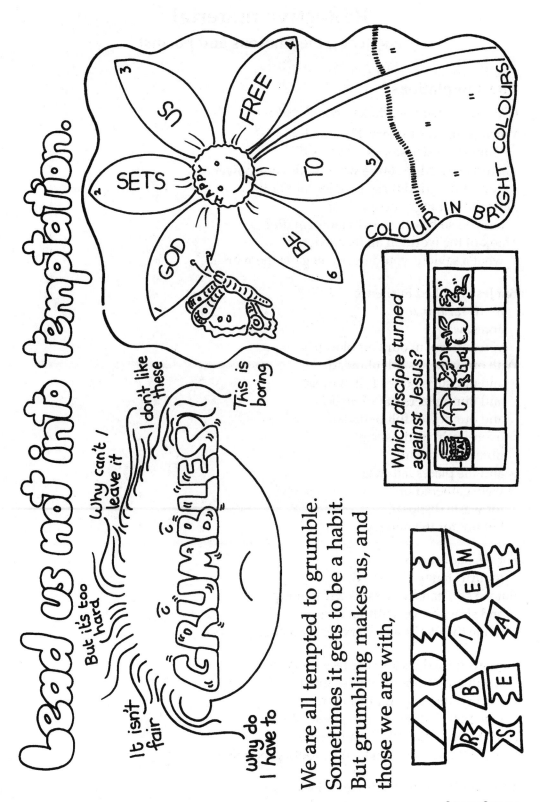

lead us not into temptation.

SETS
US
FREE
TO
BE
GOD
HAPPY

COLOUR IN BRIGHT COLOURS

But it's too hard
Why can't I leave it
I don't like these
This is boring
It isn't fair
why do I have to

GRUMBLES

We are all tempted to grumble.
Sometimes it gets to be a habit.
But grumbling makes us, and
those we are with,

Which disciple turned
against Jesus?

SUSAN SAYERS

# Reflective material
## (sketches, meditations and poems)

## The Temptations

*(This could be shared between several readers)*

When Jesus was hungry, the Devil said,
   'Turn these dry stones into bread.
There's no need to starve when with your power
   you could grind these pebbles into flour.
Hear those hungry people cry;
   are you so heartless as to let them die?
Think of the world in all its need;
   what a saviour you'd be if you gave them bread.'

But Jesus looked in silence
   to the far horizon
   and saw . . .
   you and me, in our complacency.
With our bakeries full of bread,
   and our superstores full of bread,
   and our freezers full of bread,
   and our bellies full of bread;
   oven-fresh, ready-sliced,
   fibre-filled bread;
   and the pieces left over
   were gathered up
   for waste disposal,
   but not for the hungry.

For we had learned
   to turn stones into bread.
But we still had stony faces without joy
   and stony hearts without love;
   while the world was starving for justice.

So Jesus turned back to the Devil and said,
   'I will not turn these stones into bread.
For everyone but you must own
   that man shall not live by bread alone.
And the only thing that really feeds
   is the Word that from God's mouth proceeds.'

Then the Devil tried a different tack
   in order our Lord's will to crack.

He took him to a Temple tower
   and showed him how to get great power:
   by throwing himself from this high steeple
   he would dazzle and amaze the people,
   for angels just in time would fly
   to hold him up lest he should die.

But Jesus looked in silence
   to the far horizon
   and saw . . .
   you and me, in our credulity;
   how we were blinded
   by the glitter of our gods,
   so that open-mouthed
   we could see and believe
   anything but the Truth
   (which is invisible
   and requires inner eyes).

And he saw that
   we had great confidence in tricks,
   and we unwisely followed the stars,
   and we were deafened
   by the purring of public relations
   and swayed
   to the music of mass communications.
And we were the unthinking people,
   spellbound
   by the charisma of false images.

So he turned to the Devil
   and snapped his reply,
   'It shall not be my way to lie,
   and trick and smile and hypnotise
   and wear a conjuror's disguise,
   and use the gift of heavenly power
   to gain men's praise for one brief hour.
What Scripture says is plain and best:
   "You shall not put God to the test."'

But the Devil was not beaten yet;
   he took Jesus from that parapet
   to the top of a mountain where clouds unfurled,
   revealing the kingdoms of the world.
'All that,' said the Devil, 'I'll give to you,
   if you bow to me with worship true.'

But Jesus looked in silence
   to the far horizon
   and saw . . .
   you and me, in our degeneracy,
   bowing beneath the Devil's heavy load,
   having received power to become
   lords of the earth.

He heard the excuses of the exploiters,
   and the explanations of the polluters;
   he saw self-promoting empires,
   and self-infatuated tyrants,
   and self-justifying politicians,
   and self-righteous people
   shrugging technological shoulders
   at the poisoned earth,
   while consumers consumed
   and populations exploded
   the myth of the world's abundance,
   and everybody minded their own business
   greedily.

Then Jesus in anger,
   in red-blooded anger,
   cut the Devil down to size.
He glared at him with blazing eyes
   and asked him who gave him the right
   to dole out this world's wealth and might
   and call on all the human race
   to bow down low before his face.
For only one God reigns above;
   him only should we serve and love.
'So begone Satan!' Jesus cried,
   'with your foul conspiracies I'll not side.'

Then angels came to help our Lord
   with heavenly power to preach the Word,
   and live a life of burning love
   which all this aching world would move.

PETER DAINTY

# The Second Sunday of Lent

*Nicodemus learns that Jesus offers new life
and a new beginning for all who believe*

## John 3:1-17

*(also Genesis 12:1-4; Psalm 121; Romans 4:1-5, 13-17)*

## A reading from the Gospel of John (3:1-6; 19:38-42)

Now there was a Pharisee named Nicodemus, a leader of the Jews. He came to Jesus by night and said to him, 'Rabbi, we know that you are a teacher who has come from God; for no one can do these signs that you do apart from the presence of God.' Jesus answered him, 'Very truly, I tell you, no one can see the kingdom of God without being born from above.' Nicodemus said to him, 'How can anyone be born after having grown old. Can one enter a second time into the mother's womb and be born?' Jesus answered, 'Very truly, I tell you, no one can enter the kingdom of God without being born of water and Spirit. What is born of the flesh is flesh, and what is born of the Spirit is spirit.'

*(Later, following the death of Jesus, we read)*

Joseph of Arimathea, who was a disciple of Jesus, though a secret one because of his fear of the Jews, asked Pilate to let him take away the body of Jesus. Pilate gave him permission; so he came and removed his body. Nicodemus, who had at first come to Jesus by night, also came, bringing a mixture of myrrh and aloes, weighing about a hundred pounds. They took the body of Jesus and wrapped it with the spices in linen cloths, according to the burial custom of the Jews. Now there was a garden in the place where he was crucified, and in the garden there was a new tomb in which no one had ever been laid. And so, because it was the Jewish day of Preparation, and the tomb was nearby, they laid Jesus there.

NRSV

## A reading from the Gospel of Matthew (17:1-9)

One day Jesus asked Peter, James and John to come and pray with him. He led them to the top of a steep mountain, where it was peaceful and quiet, and where they could be alone.

Jesus began to pray to his heavenly Father and suddenly he appeared to change! His face and clothes shone with a brilliant light, as dazzling as the rays of the sun.

Then the disciples saw Moses and Elijah on either side of Jesus, talking to him. Peter jumped up with excitement and said, 'Lord, this is wonderful! I could make three shelters – one for each of you!'

At that moment a cloud streaming with light appeared above them, and a voice said, 'This is my Son, whom I love very much. Listen to what he says.'

The disciples were so terrified that they threw themselves to the ground and hid their faces.

Then Jesus said gently, 'Get up, my friends, do not be afraid.'

When they looked up, Jesus was standing alone. As they came down the mountain together, Jesus told them firmly, 'You must not tell anyone about what you have seen today, until the Son of Man has risen from the dead.'

This is the Gospel of the Lord
**Praise to you, Lord Jesus Christ**                                          KATIE THOMPSON

# Introductory material

Who was Jesus? What lay at the heart of his message? Why had he come? What did it all mean? These and a host of other questions must have teemed in the minds of all those who glimpsed anything of the earthly ministry of Jesus. No one who heard his words or witnessed his actions could have been untouched by the experience, for here was a man who spoke and acted with an authority no one has ever matched. The result may have been more questions than answers, as much rejection as acceptance, but one thing is clear: when people came into contact with Jesus they had to decide for themselves just who it was they were dealing with; there could be no sitting on the fence. And as we listen today to words of Scripture and reflect upon the encounters they record, the same challenge is put to us: what do we make of this man and his message?

NICK FAWCETT

# Prayers

## For the grace of God

Gracious God,
>    we come to declare your goodness –
>        to celebrate again the awesomeness of your love
>        and the wonder of your grace.
>    Though we fail you, you never fail us:
>        **receive our thanks.**

>    Undeserving though we are, you have shown us mercy –
>        accepting our feeble faith and hesitant discipleship,
>        understanding our weakness,
>        putting our faults behind us and helping us to start again.
>    Though we fail you, you never fail us:
>        **receive our thanks.**

However much we fail you,
   however far we wander from your side,
   you continue to seek us out and lead us forward,
   your patience never exhausted,
   your love refusing to be denied.
Though we fail you, you never fail us:
   **receive our thanks.**

We offer so little, yet you give us so much,
   our love is so weak, yet you respond so richly,
   our faith is so small, yet you bless us so constantly –
   your generosity towards us far beyond our deserving.
Though we fail you, you never fail us:
   **receive our thanks.**

Gracious God,
   your grace defies expression,
   too wonderful for us ever to understand,
   and yet it goes on being real, day after day.
Gratefully we praise you
   and joyfully we celebrate your astonishing love.
Though we fail you, you never fail us:
   **receive our thanks.**

In Jesus' name.
**Amen.**                                                NICK FAWCETT

## Resisting Jesus

Loving God,
   you have come to us in Jesus Christ,
   offering us life through his love,
   calling us to live as his disciples,
   speaking to us through his life and ministry,
   his death and resurrection.
**Help us to open our lives to him.**

Forgive us that all too often we do not want to hear.
Forgive us that all too frequently we refuse to listen.
We claim to be followers of Jesus Christ,
   and there is so much that draws us to him,
   but when his message is too demanding –
   when he asks from us what we would rather not face,
   when his words make us feel uncomfortable,
   striking too near the mark –
   we try then to resist him,
   closing our ears and pushing him away.
**Help us to open our lives to him.**

Loving God,
  forgive us for following only when it is convenient,
    only when it fits in with our own assumptions,
    only when little is asked of us.
  Give to us real faith and true commitment,
    so that we will be ready to hear what is painful to hear,
    ready to listen to what is challenging and unwelcome,
    and ready to respond when Jesus calls
    even when our every impulse is to shy away.
  **Help us to open our lives to him.**

Loving God,
  you have come to us in Christ.
  **Help us to open our lives to him.**
    **Amen.**

NICK FAWCETT

## The Transfiguration

*God's glory is shown in Jesus at the transfiguration. The disciples were given a glimpse of Jesus' divinity which strengthened their faith and upheld them. Through their account, we also become witnesses: Jesus is indeed the Son of God.*

In faith, knowing that where two or three are gathered
in your name you have promised to be among them,
let our minds and hearts be filled
with stillness as we pray.

We pray for the Church;
that all your ministers may be given
perception and understanding,
to lead people into the light of your truth.
*Silence for prayer*

Lord of glory:
**make us more like you.**

We pray for all councils, committees and conferences;
that a spirit of integrity may underlie all discussion and
a desire for goodness inspire all decisions.
*Silence for prayer*

Lord of glory:
**make us more like you.**

We pray for all families,
especially those who have troubles;
that they may not be damaged through their suffering,
but rather grow in compassion and understanding.

*Silence for prayer*

Lord of glory:
**make us more like you.**

We pray for those in pain and distress;
for the mentally, physically and emotionally disabled;
that they may be comforted and strengthened
by your presence, trusting in your love
which never fails.

*Silence for prayer*

Lord of glory:
**make us more like you.**

We pray for the dying and those who have
already moved on from this world into eternity;
may they rest for ever in your peace.

*Silence for prayer*

Lord of glory:
**make us more like you.**

In thankfulness and praise we remember
all your many blessings, given to us each day,
and ask you to help us become
more generous-hearted and appreciative.

*Silence for prayer*

Merciful Father,
**accept these prayers**
**for the sake of your Son,**
**our Saviour Jesus Christ, Amen.**

SUSAN SAYERS

# All-age-talk material

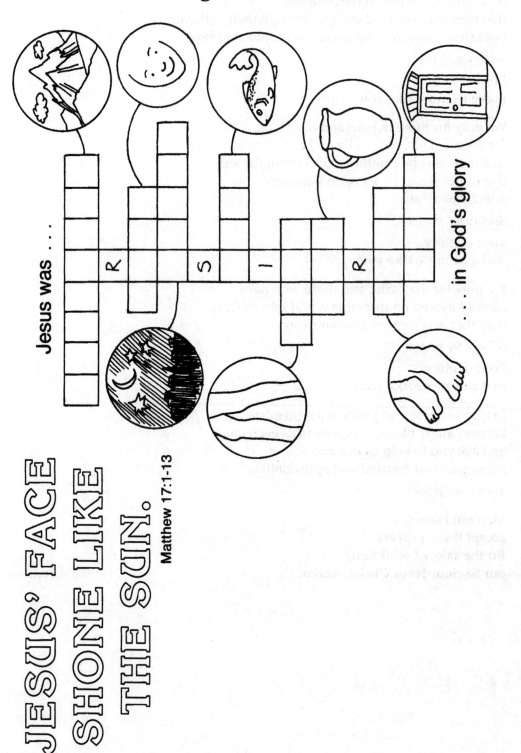

Jesus was . . .

. . . in God's glory

JESUS' FACE SHONE LIKE THE SUN.

Matthew 17:1-13

SUSAN SAYERS

"THIS IS MY SON,
MY CHOSEN;
LISTEN TO HIM."

Luke 9:28-36

Peter, James and John were
allowed to see the

GLORY

of God's son.

CODE KEY

| A | D | E | F | G | H | I | J | L | M | N | O | R | S | T | U |
|---|---|---|---|---|---|---|---|---|---|---|---|---|---|---|---|
| U | T | S | R | O | N | M | L | J | I | H | G | F | E | D | A |

They saw Jesus ...

| D | F | U | H | E | R | M | O | A | F | S | T |
|---|---|---|---|---|---|---|---|---|---|---|---|
|   |   |   |   |   |   |   |   |   |   |   |   |

and talking with .... 

| I | G | E | S | E |
|---|---|---|---|---|
|   |   |   |   |   |

and

| S | J | M | L | U | N |
|---|---|---|---|---|---|
|   |   |   |   |   |   |

Colour the picture

SUSAN SAYERS

John 3:1

KATIE THOMPSON

He belonged to
a religious group called
the Pharisees

**Use the clues to spell out his name**

1. The third letter of
2. The second letter of
3. The first letter of
4. The fifth letter of
5. The first letter of
6. The sixth letter of
7. The second letter of
8. The third letter of
9. The fifth letter of

KATIE THOMPSON

Jesus told him something which puzzled him!

Write the letters in reverse order on the lines below to read what Jesus said

ON   ENO
'N__   ___ __

NAC   EES   EHT
___ ___   ___ __   ___

MODGNIK   FO   DOG
___ ___ ___ ___ ___ ___   __ __   ___ __

SSELNU   YEHT   ERA
___ ___ ___ ___ ___ ___   ___ ___ ___ ___   ___ ___

NROBER,
___ ___ ___ ___ ___ ___,

KATIE THOMPSON

## Read John 3:1-17

When you fill in a form which asks you for your nationality, the majority of people will claim the nationality of the country where they were born, for example, English, Dutch, American, Australian or French. To many people this national identity is a form of pride, a sense of belonging.

In the Bible reading, Nicodemus is described as a Pharisee and a Jewish leader. To be a Pharisee was to be a member of an elite, a special group of people who thought of themselves as very different from the ordinary citizens. As a Jew, Nicodemus would have been extremely proud of his cultural heritage. Fearful of damaging his reputation he went at night to discuss some issues with Jesus. Jesus knew exactly who Nicodemus was and of his reputation. In response to a comment by Nicodemus, Jesus tells him that he must be born again!

Can you imagine the look on Nicodemus' face and the confusion that he must have felt? Because of a simple comment he was being told that his prestige and cultural heritage were meaningless! But, rather than argue and justify himself, Nicodemus asks how it is possible for a grown man to be born again.

To restore the relationship between God and humankind, Jesus came down from heaven to tell everyone of the good news about God's love. Later, when Jesus dies, we are told (Mark 15:38) that the curtain in the temple was torn from top to bottom. In other words God's love was brought down to earth to bring salvation (to be freed from the power of sin).

Before a person agrees that they've been living a life without God's love and living under the shadow of sin, they are outside the kingdom of God. To be a part of the kingdom of God, a person must acknowledge that they've ignored God's love and that Jesus died to become the bridge between humankind and God. At some stage Nicodemus must have asked God for his forgiveness and invited him to become the centre of his life. Nicodemus and everyone who asks for God's forgiveness turn their backs on their old life, in which they were vulnerable to the power of sin, and enter into a new life with God.

Through the Holy Spirit (which took the place of Jesus) we have a relationship with God which is precious. We are no longer subject to the power of sin, although we have a free will to get ourselves into all sorts of mess. As Christians we have placed our trust in God and refuse to ignore his love for each of us. Being born again is exchanging a way of life in which God has no part for one where we have an intimate relationship because of the sacrifice that Jesus made.

PETE TOWNSEND

# Reflective material
## (sketches, meditations and poems)

## Nicodemus

### Scene

*Nicodemus enters. He is looking very nervous, glancing all around as he slowly walks forward.*

| | |
|---|---|
| **Nicodemus** | It's very dark. Very dark. I suppose it is night-time and night-times usually are dark. I don't like the dark. There could be animals out there, there could be ferocious creatures, or, even worse, tax collectors. |
| | *Nicodemus walks slowly forward. Walking towards him is Joseph of Arimathea. They do not see each other in the dark and collide.* |
| **Nicodemus** | Ow! |
| **Joseph** | Ouch! |
| **Nicodemus** | Watch where you are going! |
| **Joseph** | I can't see a thing! |
| **Nicodemus** | You've bruised my ribs. |
| **Joseph** | You nearly blinded me! |
| **Nicodemus** | I thought you couldn't see a thing? |
| **Joseph** | Nicodemus? |
| **Nicodemus** | Joseph? |
| | *They go to hug each other and completely miss.* |
| **Nicodemus** | What are you doing out here tonight? |
| **Joseph** | I'm just on my way home. |
| **Nicodemus** | Oh. |
| **Joseph** | What are you doing out here tonight? |
| **Nicodemus** | Going to meet someone. |
| **Joseph** | Who? |
| **Nicodemus** | You don't know him. |
| **Joseph** | Oh. |
| **Nicodemus** | Better be on my way. Good to see you, Joseph. Well, if I had seen you, that is. |
| **Joseph** | You too, Nicodemus. Goodnight. |

**Nicodemus**    Goodnight.

*Joseph exits.*

**Nicodemus**    My sides are aching. Imagine bumping into Joseph – literally! Still, I couldn't do this in the light, could I? What would people say? What would people think? What would happen to my career? No, it had to be tonight. It had to.

*Nicodemus moves slowly and cautiously.*

**Nicodemus**    I've never met anyone like him. Never heard words like his before. Never felt like this in my whole life.

*He pauses to think and reflect.*

**Nicodemus**    But what did he mean? What was he saying?

*Nicodemus stops, stands still, and shakes his head, trying to understand.*

**Nicodemus**    You must be born again.

*Pause. Nicodemus turns to the audience, almost pleading with them as he raises his set of questions.*

**Nicodemus**    You must be born again. 'How?' I asked him. How can a man be born when he is old? How can he be born from his mother's womb again? My mind was doing cartwheels. How can it be? That's when he said it. He looked into my eyes, but not just into my eyes. It felt like he was seeing straight into my soul, searching the depths of my heart.

    'I tell you the truth,' he said, 'no one can enter the kingdom of God unless he is born of water and the Spirit. Flesh gives birth to flesh, but the Spirit gives birth to spirit.'

    I don't know if I understand, but I know I must. I know I need to understand. Flesh gives birth to flesh. The Spirit gives birth to spirit. You cannot enter the kingdom unless . . . How could he say that to me? I am a religious man. I am a believer of the true faith. I keep the commandments and rules laid down by our ancestor, Moses. How can this not be enough to enter God's kingdom? If a man like me can't enter, then who can?

*Nicodemus pauses, slowly shakes his head, then looks up.*

**Nicodemus**    It will soon be light. Maybe in the morning I will see clearly the mysteries of tonight.

*Nicodemus turns to walk off stage, repeating over and over:*

**Nicodemus**    Unless you are born again, unless you are born again, unless you are born again.

TONY BOWER

## Born again blues *(See also pages 214-217)*

**Narrator**  An official and a soldier discuss a report about the miracles of Jesus, for instance his turning water into wine.

**Official**  You found that amusing?

**Soldier**  Hysterical.

**Official**  One of the Jewish religious leaders absolutely baffled, confused and confounded, and all you can do is break out into a silly, cheesy grin.

**Soldier**  More of a belly-laugh than a cheesy grin, Sir.

**Official**  I know one thing.

**Soldier**  You do, Sir?

**Official**  Yes, I do.

**Soldier**  Sir?

**Official**  I am cheesed off.

**Soldier**  You are, Sir?

**Official**  No, I tell a lie. I am tickled pink. I am in the clover. I am like a lamb in the springtime. I am . . .

**Soldier**  You are cheesed off, aren't you, Sir?

**Official**  One hundred per cent.

**Soldier**  Is there anything I can do to cheer you up, Sir?

**Official**  No!

**Soldier**  A few jokes?

**Official**  No!

**Soldier**  Just asking, Sir.

*The man holds his head and picks up the report. He reads through it.*

**Official**  What are we going to do about this Samaritan woman's report?

**Soldier**  Sir?

**Official**  It's an incredible story.

**Soldier**  No one's going to listen to her, Sir.

**Official**  No one else is going to listen to her. Are you trying to be funny?

**Soldier**  No, Sir.

**Official**  Half the village believed because of her story.

**Soldier**  They did?

**Official**  Have you not read this?

*The man slides the report across the table. The soldier picks it up and begins to read.*

*Freeze.*                                                           TONY BOWER

## Meditation of Nicodemus

It was dark when I went to him that first time,
　　the middle of the night when all was quiet –
　　and can you blame me?
It just wouldn't have done, would it,
　　a man in my position to be seen associating with Jesus?
Even a hint of involvement
　　and my fellow Pharisees would have lynched me on the spot!
He was the enemy,
　　the blasphemer,
　　the one who threatened everything we stood for –
　　not just misguided,
　　but dangerous,
　　evil –
　　a threat to our society,
　　a challenge to the very heart of our religion.
I knew all that,
　　or at least I knew the theory,
　　and, yes, I'd been as shocked as any
　　by some of the things he'd said,
　　not to mention the things he'd done.
Yet I couldn't get him out of my mind, try as I might.
I can't say why exactly,
　　for it wasn't any one word or deed that hooked me –
　　it was all of them together,
　　the way each reinforced the other,
　　combining to make him the person he was.
He spoke of love,
　　and he showed what love was all about.
He talked of forgiveness,
　　and I simply haven't met a more forgiving man.
He talked of life,
　　and there was a quality to his own life that I couldn't help but envy.
He talked of God,
　　and I could see God was more real,
　　more personal,
　　more special to him,
　　than I'd ever have dreamed possible for anyone.
So I went
　　and I talked.

I listened
  and I learned.
Nervous, true,
  hesitant,
  strictly incognito,
  and so very, very slow to understand.
Yet, little by little, the truth broke through my confusion,
  a ray of light in the darkness,
  new birth for my parched and barren soul.
It was dark when I went again,
  a night far blacker than that first night,
  for they'd taken their revenge by then, as I knew they would,
  done him to death on the cross.
And as he hung there in agony,
  his gasps piercing the air,
  suddenly the sun vanished and darkness fell.
That had them worried, you can well imagine,
  more than a few scuttling off in panic.
But not me,
  for I had seen the truth he spoke of
  and found the life he promised.
So, while others stumbled blindly in the darkness,
  for me it was lighter than the lightest day,
  and brighter than the brightest sunshine.

NICK FAWCETT

## Transfiguration

The mountain flames with light
  as Christ, heaven's window,
  opens this dark world
  to divine glory.
He glows with a strange radiance
  normally hidden from earthbound eyes,
  but now revealed
  to dull disciples
  facing the unknown.

And meanwhile,
  down in the valley,
  not lit by other worlds,
  untransfigured suffering
  distorts humanity.
Wretched bearers of pain
  cry out for healing.
Well-meaning helpers
  offer ineffectual suggestions,

while bystanders move in
  with trivial objections.
Unillumined disciples
    fail
    and turn away,
    embarrassed and ashamed.
Is their faith
    not even the size
    of a mustard seed?

Our earthly light is not enough,
    unless transfigured
    by the light from heaven.
Thank God that Christ's true glory
    was not left to be enshrined
    on some irrelevant mountain top;
    but he came down
    into the valley
    to embrace the human beast
    with arms stretched out
    in sacrificial love,
    that we might share
    his royal beauty,
    and dark earth at last
    be radiant with heaven.

PETER DAINTY

## Meditation of John the Apostle

It was fantastic,
    extraordinary,
    mind-blowing;
    a once-in-a-lifetime experience,
    and I was lucky enough to be there –
    me, and Peter and James up on the mountain with Jesus.
We knew something was going to happen;
    we could see it from his manner when he asked us to join him,
    but we never dreamt of anything like that.
He seemed to change before our eyes,
    his clothes to glow,
    his face to shine.
And then – would you believe it –
    who did we see with him but Moses and Elijah!
Clear as day they were,
    chatting together like old friends.
We were struck dumb for a moment,
    lost for words,
    and then dear old Peter got stuck in as usual.

'Can I do something?' he blurted out,
   'You will stay, won't you?'
And why not?
I mean, we were all enjoying ourselves,
   didn't want the moment to end,
   almost too good to be true!
But strangely, as soon as Peter finished speaking,
   the spell seemed to break.
The sky darkened as clouds came over
   and then, as a peal of thunder broke the silence,
   Moses and Elijah disappeared,
   leaving Jesus standing there alone,
   looking just as he always had,
   as ordinary as you or me.
Did we imagine it?
We've often asked ourselves that.
Or was it a vision,
   brought on perhaps by the heat
   or the altitude,
   or simply having one too many before we set off?
It must have been something like that, surely?
There's no other logical explanation.
Yet it's funny how we all saw the same thing,
   all down to the last detail.
I don't know what to make of it,
   but I wouldn't have missed it for the world.
It helped me understand what Peter had already begun to grasp,
   that Jesus was the Messiah,
   the answer to all our prayers,
   the fulfilment of the Law and the Prophets.
It was just a glimpse,
   a moment's wonderful insight
   which I thought at the time could never be repeated.
And that was true in a sense,
   for no one will ever witness quite what we saw in the way we saw it.
But we have all seen his glory now,
   not just the three of us,
   but Thomas, Andrew, Mary, Matthew, and so many others –
   the glory of the Father revealed in him.
We see it day after day after day,
   full of grace and truth,
And, believe me, that too is fantastic,
   extraordinary,
   unforgettable!                                    NICK FAWCETT

# The Third Sunday of Lent

*The woman of Samaria learns that, whoever we may be,*
*God offers us living water in Christ*

## John 4:5-42

*(also Exodus 17:1-7; Psalm 95; Romans 5:1-11)*

### A reading from the Gospel of John (4:5-42)

Jesus came to a Samaritan town called Sychar and stopped to rest about midday at a place known as 'Jacob's Well'. While his disciples went into the town to buy food, Jesus waited beside the well, and before long a woman came there to draw water. When Jesus asked the woman for a drink she was taken by surprise because Jews and Samaritans rarely spoke to each other.

'Surely, sir, you are a Jew,' she said. 'So why do you ask me, a Samaritan, for a drink?'

Jesus said to her, 'If you knew me, it would be you asking me for a drink, because I would give you living water.'

The woman was puzzled and asked him, 'The well is deep and you have no bucket, so how could you reach this 'living' water?'

Jesus said, 'When you drink the water from this well, your thirst always returns. Anyone who drinks the water that I can give will never be thirsty again. This water will become a spring inside them, and fill them with eternal life.'

The woman said to him, 'Sir, share this water with me so that I never feel thirsty again.'

Jesus talked to the woman about her five previous husbands, and the man she now lived with, and he told her many things about herself that no other person knew, and she was amazed.

Then the woman said to Jesus, 'I see you are a prophet from God, whom we Samaritans worship in our own Temple instead of the Temple in Jerusalem.'

Jesus said to her, 'It is not important where you worship, but how you worship God. Through his Spirit people will worship him in the way they should.'

The woman said to Jesus, 'I know that one day everything will be explained by the Messiah who is coming.'

Jesus said to her, 'Even now he is speaking to you. I am he.'

Just then the disciples returned, and although they were surprised to see Jesus talking to a Samaritan woman, they said nothing. Leaving her jar by the well, she ran to tell the people in the town everything the stranger had said to her, and they began to make their way to the well to meet him.

Meanwhile, the disciples encouraged Jesus to eat some of the food they had brought for him, and were puzzled when he said to them, 'I already have food which you do not know about.'

Then he explained to them, 'When I complete the work of the one who sent me, and do his will, then that is my food. You know that the harvest only begins when the crops are ready. Look around you, and see how the harvest is ready to reap. Whoever gathers in this harvest will have eternal life, and the one who sows and the one who reaps will celebrate together.'

When they heard what Jesus had told the woman at the well, many of the Samaritans believed in him. After convincing Jesus to stay in their town for a few days, the Samaritans said to each other, 'Now we have heard him for ourselves, we know that he is indeed the Saviour God promised to send.'

This is the Gospel of the Lord
**Praise to you, Lord Jesus Christ**                          KATIE THOMPSON

## Grace before a meal – alternative translation
### John 4:5-29

*John's Gospel needs to be read slowly and meditatively. This is no mere anecdote about a chance meeting at a well. It is a preview (as all John's stories are) of what is made explicit in his final chapters, where the pierced side of the crucified Christ pours out the lifegiving waters of the Spirit on the world, to wash away the barriers that have for too long separated race from race, and faith from faith.*

On a journey from Jerusalem to Galilee,
Jesus and his disciples had to cross
the hostile territory of Samaria.
About midday they reached Jacob's Well,
just outside the town of Shechem-Nablus.
While the disciples went on into town
to get something for lunch,
Jesus, exhausted by the long walk
slumped down by the side of the well.
It was the hottest part of the day.

A Samaritan woman came to draw water.
'Could you give me a drink?' Jesus asked her.
She laughed. 'You're a fine Jew,' she said,
'asking me, a hated Samaritan, for a drink!
You know we're not supposed even to talk to each other,
let alone drink from the same cup!'

'What *you* don't know,' said Jesus teasingly, 'is who I am!
Perhaps you should be asking *me* for a drink!
I'd have given you fresh, running water,
not the still water from the bottom of a well.'
'A fine lot of water you'll get,' she retorted.
'You haven't even got a bucket!

Old Father Jacob dug down 150 feet to make this well,
and for 1700 years his descendants and their flocks
have had to make do with it.
But you, of course, can do without it!'

'This water won't really quench your thirst,' Jesus replied.
'Before long you'll be back here, thirsty all over again.
The water I'm talking about isn't like that.
When you drink it, you'll never be thirsty.
It will be as if you had a spring of living water inside you,
providing you with life after life after life.'
'Ooh!' said the woman. 'That's useful.
I'll have some of that. Save me a lot of bother
slogging down here and back each day!'

Seeing he was getting nowhere, Jesus said,
'Go fetch your husband, and bring him here.'
'I haven't got a husband,' the woman replied.
'Exactly!' said Jesus. 'You've been married five times,
but you never married the man you're living with now.
You're being very honest!'
'You must be a man of God,' the woman gasped.
Then, after a bit, 'Ah, then perhaps you can tell me
whether we Samaritans were right in building God's Temple
here on Mount Gerizim 500 years ago,
or you Jews in building one on Mount Zion in Jerusalem?'
'Believe me,' said Jesus, 'the time is near
when that miserable dispute between Samaritans and Jews will be over.
Everyone who believes in God will worship him everywhere.
God is not someone you meet on a mountain.
He is Spirit, and what he wants is people who worship him
in the Spirit of love he pours out on them.'

The woman was by now utterly lost.
'Oh well,' she finally said, 'I suppose the Messiah
will make it all clear when he comes.'
'You're speaking to him,' Jesus replied.
The woman dropped her bucket, and chased back into town
to bring everyone out to meet Jesus.
'He read my whole life like a book,' she gasped.
'Do you think maybe this is the Messiah
we've been waiting for?'                                    H. J. RICHARDS

# Prayers

## Facing truth

God of truth,
    you know us better than we know ourselves.
    You search our hearts and minds,
        seeing us as we really are,
        and confronting us with our true selves.
    Teach us to face the truth,
        **for the truth will set us free.**

    Forgive us that all too often
        we shy away from what is hard to accept,
        refusing to countenance anything
        which contradicts the image we have of ourselves.
    We find it so hard to be honest,
        closing our ears to truths we would rather not hear.
    We avoid those who challenge and disturb us,
        preferring instead those who soothe and flatter our egos.
    Teach us to face the truth,
        **for the truth will set us free.**

God of truth,
    we thank you today for all those
        with the rare gift of speaking the truth in love –
        not spitefully, vindictively, or harshly,
        nor from any ulterior motives,
        but because they genuinely care.
    Teach us to face the truth,
        **for the truth will set us free.**

    We thank you for those who are willing
        to risk our resentment,
        our misunderstanding or anger,
        our retaliation or rejection,
        to help us grow as individuals.
    Teach us to face the truth,
        **for the truth will set us free.**

God of all,
    give us true humility and meekness of spirit,
        so that we may be ready to listen and examine ourselves,
        ready to ask searching questions about who we are
        and to change where necessary.
    Teach us to face the truth,
        **for the truth will set us free.**
        **In the name of Christ we pray.**
        **Amen.**

NICK FAWCETT

## Thanksgiving – the mercy of God

Gracious God,
  we thank you that you are a God
    who sees not the outside but the inside,
    a God who is not taken in by external appearances
    but who looks into the inner depths of our heart and soul.

  We thank you for the reassurance which that brings,
    the confidence we can have
    that, though we repeatedly disobey you,
    consistently breaking your commandments
    and failing to live as you have called us to,
    still you know that we earnestly desire to be your people,
    that we long to be better disciples of Christ.
  For your unfailing mercy,
    **receive our thanks.**

  We thank you that you see not merely the end product
    but the initial intention,
    not just the final results but the desire that precedes it.
  But we recognise also the challenge that truth brings,
    for we know that we can never deceive you
    with outward show.
  Though our lives may appear blameless,
    our faith strong,
    our works good
    and our words right,
    you and you alone know the reality in our hearts,
    the truth beneath.
  For your unfailing mercy,
    **receive our thanks.**

Gracious God,
  help us not just to lift up our hands but our hearts,
    not just our voices but our souls.
  Fill us with the power of your Spirit
    and the love of Christ,
    so that we may become more like the people
    you would have us be.
  For your unfailing mercy,
    **receive our thanks.**

In the name of Jesus we pray.
**Amen.**

NICK FAWCETT

## Intercession

Almighty and everlasting God,
   we do not always know what to ask for in our prayers
     for there is so much that we do not know or understand,
     yet we know that you are active in our world,
     moving in human hearts and in the events of history
     to fulfil your purpose.
   So we come now to you,
     and, in quiet faith, we place ourselves and our world
     into your hands,
     asking that your will may be done,
     despite everything that conspires against it.
   All things are yours:
   **we entrust them into your keeping.**

We bring ourselves,
   weak, faithless, hesitant, foolish.
We bring all we are and all we long to be,
   seeking your help and your transforming touch.
All things are yours:
   **we entrust them into your keeping.**

We bring those who are part of our lives –
   family and friends,
   neighbours and colleagues at work,
   all those whom we meet in the daily round of life.
All things are yours:
   **we entrust them into your keeping.**

We bring our world –
   the rich and poor,
   powerful and weak,
   well-fed and hungry,
   healthy and sick;
   those who enjoy peace and those who endure war,
   those who revel in freedom and those who fight for justice.
All things are yours:
   **we entrust them into your keeping.**

Almighty and everlasting God,
   we thank you that you are involved in our lives,
     active in our world,
     concerned about everything you have made.
   We rejoice that you hold all things ultimately in your hands.
   And so we leave them confidently with you,
     asking only this:

'Your will be done,
your kingdom come,
on earth as it is in heaven.'
All things are yours:
**we entrust them into your keeping.**

Through Jesus Christ our Lord.
**Amen.**                                           NICK FAWCETT


## A short prayer

Lord,
I suppose I don't like to think about it too much,
you know,
all those annoying ways that *other* people
behave, act, speak and just, well, you know, live.
Why can't they all be like me?
It would make things so simple.
Just imagine,
no hassles over language,
no arguments over how or what to eat,
no disputes over borders or land,
no complicated debates about nationality,
no violent confrontations about race,
or ethnic origins.
No pointing fingers
about the way people look, their skin tone –
in fact, no problems whatsoever.
But, there again,
I suppose,
knowing the human race to be what it is,
sooner or later
we'd find something to argue about,
and someone, somewhere,
would claim to be superior to other people,
even though
we all bleed when we're cut,
we all cry when we're sad,
we all crumble to dust,
when death stakes its claim.
Lord,
I'm just so thankful
that, despite who we are
or what we may claim to be,
you love us unconditionally,

with no cultural filters
to weed out the undesirable elements
who you'd rather not have anything to do with.
Your love knows no boundaries,
    nor skin tones,
    or anything else for that matter.
You love us, full stop, period, without end,
    for ever and ever.
Amen to that!

PETE TOWNSEND

# All-age-talk material

**The Water of Life**

Jesus stopped to rest at Jacob's Well when a woman came to fill her water jug. Jesus asked her for a drink

Find out why the woman was surprised when Jesus spoke to her. Use the code cracker!

**CODE CRACKER**

|   | | | | |
|---|---|---|---|---|
| 1 | B | A | C | R | E |
| 2 | T | N | S | M | W |
| 3 | E | H | I | U | A |
|   | ☀ | ☽ | ★ | ◯ | ⌒ |

1☀ 3☀ 1★ 1☽ 3◯ 2★ 1⌒  2★ 3☽ 1⌒

2⌒ 1☽ 2★  1☽

John 4:9

2★ 1☽ 2◯ 3⌒ 1◯ 3★ 2☀ 1☽ 2☽

KATIE THOMPSON

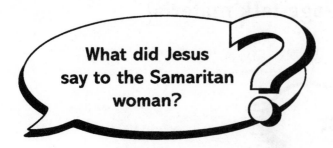

**What did Jesus say to the Samaritan woman?**

**Follow the arrows to find his words**

| B | E | H | E | I | R | L | N |
|---|---|---|---|---|---|---|---|
| M | S | T | A | W | L | I | E |
| K | O | R | E | L | N | K | A |
| P | N | I | G | V | E | A | G |
| M | I | K | E | I | Y | Z | J |
| N | Y | R | H | R | B | T | R |
| A | D | O | W | A | E | I | S |
| J | O | N | E | S | B | T | H |

'A __ __ __ __ __   __ __ __

__ __ __ __ __ __   __ __ __   __ __ __ __ __

__   __ __ __ __   __ __ __ __

__ __ __ __ __   __ __   __ __ __ __ __ __ __ ,

__ __ __ __ __

KATIE THOMPSON

Jesus told the woman many things that no one else knew, and she believed in him

What did the other Samaritans say when they met Jesus? Choose the right words and write them in the spaces

We _____ he ____ the
        1              2

_____ of _____ _____
        3              4        5

1
WONDERED
KNOW
COULD

3
SON
FRIEND
SAVIOUR

2
ON
AT
IS

4
THE
IS
ARE

5
SEA
WORLD
CITY

John 4:42

KATIE THOMPSON

## Read John 4:5-42

The Pharisees had been active in spreading some malicious gossip suggesting that Jesus and John the Baptist were competing with each other to see who could baptise the most people. Although this wasn't true, and even John had acknowledged that he wasn't good enough to tie Jesus' shoelaces, the gossip had annoyed a lot of people who were wondering whether any of the rumours were true.

Rather than ignore the situation, Jesus decided to leave the area and make his way back to Galilee.

At this time, the map of Palestine would have shown Judea at the bottom, Galilee at the top and Samaria sandwiched in between. Looking at the map, the most obvious route for Jesus to take would have been to take the direct road from Judea to Galilee. However, to the majority of Jews this would not have been an acceptable route. Instead they would have travelled east, then north and then west to avoid going anywhere near Samaria.

The relationship between the communities of Samaria and Judea were cool, verging on hostile. No self-respecting Jew would ever be seen near a Samaritan or walk anywhere near Samaria.

Several hundred years before, the area of Samaria had been invaded by the Assyrians who had taken the Jews, who lived in that area, captive. After a while the Jews and Assyrians had intermarried and, when they returned to Samaria, they became known as the Samaritans.

The Jews of Judea themselves had been taken captive by the Babylonians, but the Jews had refused to intermarry and, when they returned home claimed to have retained their pure Jewish blood. From that time, the Jews and the Samaritans had developed a level of hostility rarely seen away from a battlefield.

Jesus chose to ignore the cultural differences and instantly displayed an important aspect of God's love; that his love was for everyone irrespective of race, colour or culture.

Even after leaving the malicious gossip behind, Jesus still chose to be controversial and do the very thing that was unheard of for a Jew to do. Jesus didn't take the shorter route because he couldn't face walking any further than he had to, nor did he take the shorter route because he wanted to get home as quickly as possible. He took the direct route through the heart of Samaria to express God's heart for everyone.

Jesus still takes the direct route, direct to each one of us irrespective of who or what we are. God doesn't let culture, race, colour or tradition alter the fact that he loves each of us passionately. Perhaps we should also apply a little bit of God's perspective to our relationships?

PETE TOWNSEND

# Reflective material
## (sketches, meditations and poems)

## Meditation of the woman at the well

He was full of surprises, that man,
   from the moment I first met him.
I thought he'd just push me aside like all the rest;
   either that or walk away with his head in the air.
He was a Jew, remember, and I a Samaritan;
   and worse than that,
   a woman,
   alone.
Yet he stayed where he was, a smile on his face,
   quite happy, apparently, to be associated with me.
Well, call me suspicious if you like, but I wasn't sure what he was up to,
   so I asked him straight out, 'What's your game?'
He laughed at that, and then offered me a drink of water –
   at least I thought that's what he was doing though I wasn't sure.
You see, he had no bucket,
   and he could hardly shin down the well, could he?
So where was this water he was on about meant to come from?
To be frank I suspected he was pulling my leg,
   but I was beginning to like him despite the nonsense he talked.
He had a nice way with him,
   kind,
   gentle,
   a bit of all right in an unconventional sort of way.
So I played along, wondering where it would all lead.
If only I'd known –
   what an embarrassment I might have saved myself.
I'll never know how he guessed,
   but suddenly he looked straight at me
   and for the first time I noticed his eyes.
They didn't undress you like so many men's seem to do,
   but looked much deeper,
   almost as if into my very soul.
And then he started talking about my lovers,
   my husbands,
   my past,
   every detail correct.
It was uncanny,
   frightening,
   far too near the knuckle,
So I tried to fob him off with some old chestnut about worship.

But even then he threw me;
  none of the usual pat answers
  but a response that reached right to the heart of the matter,
  cutting through all the trivia.
And it was after that he produced the biggest surprise of all –
  told me he was the Messiah!
I didn't know what to say,
  just stood there gawping, flabbergasted.
I mean, I realised he was a prophet,
  but the Messiah?
It couldn't be, I told myself,
  no way.
I went back down to the village, seeking reassurance,
  wanting someone to tell me he was just another religious nutcase.
But they didn't.
They were curious,
  wanted to see for themselves.
And when they heard him,
  listened to his teaching,
  they believed he was the Messiah.
Me? I still don't know, but I wouldn't be surprised,
  not if I'm honest;
  nothing would surprise me about him.                    NICK FAWCETT

## I thirst

### Soak it up

Two old friends meet in the pub and discuss some of the amazing things that
have happened recently. Not least the gossip about a Jew who visited the village's
well recently, asked for a drink and then started saying some strange things. He
may have been out in the sun too long. The one who thirsts is also the one who
offered others the chance to drink from the well that never runs dry.

| | |
|---|---|
| *Characters* | Sop and Binge are two of the village 'soaks'. They like nothing better than a lubricant for the throat to enable them to chat about whatever gossip happens to be worth making a bit of a scandal about. If there is no current gossip, they pass the time by inventing potential gossip which the two old soaks will enjoy telling to anyone willing to listen. They are dressed in baggy sweaters, old trousers and worn-out boots. |
| *Scene* | The inside of the village watering hole is murky, damp and smelly (and that's just the clientele). The two old soaks sit at a small table with litter covering most of the surface. Each of the old soaks has a large glass of liquid sitting amongst the litter on the table. |

| | |
|---|---|
| *Props* | Two old sweaters, trousers and boots. A rough-looking table, assorted litter and two large glasses. |

You can either depict the interior scene as just the old soaks and the table or complete the scene by adding a few extras and a bar. The sketch starts with the two soaks sipping their drinks against a soundtrack of subdued voices and the occasional snippet of music.

| | |
|---|---|
| **Sop** | *(Empties his glass and wipes his mouth across his sleeve)* Ah! I needed that. *(He nods to Binge)* Another one? |
| **Binge** | Yeah. Why not? *(Pushes his glass towards Sop)* |
| **Sop** | Heard any decent gossip lately? |
| **Binge** | I did hear tell that Old Man Armitage found his teeth yesterday. Been missing for three weeks. |
| **Sop** | I bet he was glad to get them back. |
| **Binge** | He'd been living on soup and grape juice all that time. |
| **Sop** | Where'd he find them? |
| **Binge** | Over in Zac's field. |
| **Sop** | What had he been doing there then? Surely not having a kiss and cuddle with Mrs Armitage? *(Pulls disgusted face)* |
| **Binge** | No. He'd been helping Zac spread manure on the field. |
| **Sop** | And he lost them . . . |
| **Binge** | You've guessed it. Somewhere in the middle of three tonnes of the stuff! |
| **Sop** | Hope he washed them well once he got them back. |
| **Binge** | Couldn't tell you. His teeth always look a bit stained. |
| | *Sop goes to the bar and returns with two full glasses.* |
| **Sop** | There you go. *(Places glasses on table)* Get your slurping tackle around that. |
| **Binge** | *(Licks lips)* Better than a plate of cow's innards this be. |
| **Sop** | Oh, I dunno. Nice to have a bit of both, I say. Anyway, enough of this dreaming. Heard any other gossip? |
| **Binge** | You'll never guess what happened to me today. |
| **Sop** | Let me see. *(Places finger on chin)* How about, you changed your socks in time for the summer? |
| **Binge** | No. *(Shakes head)* Too early for that. I'll give 'em another month before I change into my summer pair. |

**Sop**     Well, *(Frowns)* have you had some success with the cream?

**Binge**   Ooh! You wouldn't believe the agony I go through at night. Not something that I would wish on a camel trader.

**Sop**     Go on, you'll have to tell me.

**Binge**   The wife arrived back from shopping.

**Sop**     Typical. *(Tuts and shakes head)* Nowadays, give 'em a shopping bag and a few coins and they don't stop until the well runs dry.

**Binge**   She said she was only going out to get a loaf.

**Sop**     That's what they all say. The time it takes 'em, you could have ploughed the field, sown the wheat, watched it grow and harvested it in by the time it takes them to fetch a loaf.

**Binge**   You're telling me.

*Both take a swig of their drink.*

**Sop**     *(Wipes mouth on sleeve)* How long had she been gone, then?

**Binge**   Two years!

**Sop**     Bet the loaf was stale!

**Binge**   She hadn't got a loaf with her.

**Sop**     Bet she got talking and didn't notice the time, eh?

**Binge**   Something like that. Said she came home 'cos she met this weird guy at the well.

**Sop**     He was brave going to the well. That area is a gossip battle zone. It's a wonder he wasn't tongue lashed to death by the female mafia.

**Binge**   *(Shrugs)* Apparently he went at midday when no one else was about.

**Sop**     Sensible bloke.

*Both nod wisely.*

**Binge**   The wife went up to get some water.

**Sop**     She'd need it to soften the bread.

**Binge**   The bloke asked her for a drink of water.

**Sop**     He's definitely not from around here, then.

**Binge**   He's an out-of-town geezer. Obviously doesn't know the first thing about our customs.

**Sop**     Yeah. *(Puts down empty glass)* Like how long it takes to get served a beer around here!

**Binge**   Anyway, he gets talking to the wife, like. And he starts talking daft to her.

**Sop**   Been out in the sun too long.

**Binge**   Well, listen to this. He reckons that he can give you 'living water' so that you'll never get thirsty again.

**Sop**   He don't work for this brewery then, do he!

**Binge**   You bet he don't. Anyhow, he tells the wife to clear off and come home to me.

**Sop**   Where else would she be going?

**Binge**   Well, I ask you. I knew she'd come home eventually. She'd left her purse under the pillow.

**Sop**   You can always guarantee if they leave their purse under the pillow they'll not be gone long.

**Binge**   S'right. A woman's heart is where her purse is, I always say.

**Sop**   Definitely. So what did she say when she came home?

**Binge**   I'd just got in from feeding the chickens and I heard a voice shout, 'Have you cleaned the goats' pen out?' I knew it was the wife then. Couldn't mistake those honey'd tones of hers.

**Sop**   You get used to their voices like a pair of well-worn socks.

**Binge**   Yeah. All comfortable and warm.

**Sop**   (*Sniffs the air*) Are you sure it's not time to change yours yet?

**Binge**   (*Sniffs and then looks under table*) Don't think so.

**Sop**   I think somebody must be burning cabbage, then.

**Binge**   Disgusting.

**Sop**   Yeah, absolutely disgusting.

*Both pick up their glasses and walk off towards the bar.*

Water is the very element of life. Without it nothing survives. By saying he was 'living water', able to give eternal life, Jesus gave everyone the ability to be reconciled to God.

There is no need for anyone to be thirsty on their journey through life. There is no longer any need for anyone to feel dried-up, parched or suffering as they put one foot in front of the other day by day. Jesus became thirsty, took on the dust of humanity so that our hearts would always have a source of 'living water'. It is no longer 'dust to dust' at the end of our journey but eternal life through God's Son.

PETE TOWNSEND

## The woman at the well

In the fourth chapter of John's gospel we have the beautiful story of Jesus resting beside Jacob's Well at Sychar in Samaria, and his long conversation with the woman there who had come to draw water. Eyebrows were raised by the disciples of Jesus when they returned and found him speaking alone with this woman. It could even be that she had come to the well at an unusual time of day because she was not welcome to rub shoulders with the other women of the town.

To me it is an ever-fresh fact that Jesus was quite happy to talk with her on highly spiritual subjects though he knew she had had five husbands and was with a sixth partner now, outside marriage. He did not say, 'You wicked woman!' He did not say, 'You complete failure!' He did not say, 'Go home and find your first husband (or the first in line out of the five that is still alive). Give up your present man and go back to the first; then come back and we will talk.' He did not say, 'Go and get shut of the present man at all costs, then maybe we'll talk about living water.'

As he would later do with Zacchaeus, he treats this woman as being worthy of respect, and she responds in kind. When she begins to comprehend what Jesus is offering, she is thrilled and delighted, and goes off to bring most of the town to listen to Jesus. To begin with, they came to investigate what she was saying to them; but they stayed, and wanted Jesus to stay, because of what he himself was able to give them. The woman became an ambassador of the good news. And not even at the end of the chapter are we told that Jesus set conditions for her. He does not even say, 'Go, and sin no more.'

GERALD O'MAHONY

## Well, well, would you believe the woman at the well?

### Scene

*Three women walk onto stage. They are carrying baskets full of clothes and are busy talking to each other.*

**Woman 1**   'Come and see a man who told me everything I ever did.' That's what she said!

**Woman 2**   Well, I never.

**Woman 3**   Who wants to hear about her sordid life? How many husbands has she had?

**Woman 2**   I stopped counting after she got to five.

**Woman 1**   And that man she's living with now . . .

*They all look at each other, turn away in disgust and say at the same time:*

**Woman 1**   Ugh!

**Woman 2**    Ugh!

**Woman 3**    Ugh!

*They put their fingers in their mouths to indicate their disgust.*

**Woman 2**    I'm not saying he's ugly, but my donkey closes his eyes every time he goes past.

**Woman 1**    I just hold my nose.

**Woman 3**    She didn't just scrape the bottom of the barrel when she found him . . . He is the barrel! Have you seen the size of him?

*The second woman puffs out her cheeks, holds out her arms to exaggerate how wide, how big and how fat the man is.*

**Woman 3**    Don't do that.

**Woman 2**    Why not?

**Woman 1**    You're doing him far too much justice.

*They all laugh and giggle. After a few seconds, they stop and look up.*

**Woman 1**    Where's that crowd going?

**Woman 2**    No idea.

**Woman 3**    Why are they following her?

*The women look and give disdainful expressions. On one side of the stage the Samaritan woman enters with a small crowd following her. They walk slowly off stage.*

**Woman 2**    Because they're men.

*They look at each other in disgust.*

**Woman 1**    'Could this be the Christ?' she said.

**Woman 2**    Who does she think she's kidding?

**Woman 3**    She chats up a man at the well.

**Woman 2**    A Jewish bloke.

**Woman 1**    And tries to make out he's some holy Joe.

**Woman 3**    Or holy Jew.

*She nudges her friends and they all giggle.*

**Woman 1**    No one in this village is going to fall for that line. That is desperate. Why can't she admit that she was chatting him up, instead of trying to make out that he's the Messiah?

**Woman 2**    Just because he knows everything about her.

**Woman 3**    I bet everyone knows her reputation.

**Woman 2**   What reputation?

*They nudge each other and giggle a high-pitched, hysterical laugh.*

**Woman 1**   When that lot meet this bloke, they'll soon suss him out.

**Woman 2**   Soon sort him out, you mean. He's a Jew!

**Woman 3**   He'll wish he never sat on that well.

**Woman 2**   One push is all it will take!

*They giggle.*

**Woman 1**   They're coming back, look.

**Woman 3**   That didn't take them long.

*The Samaritan woman is walking into town with a crowd of people around her. She is talking excitedly and the crowd are listening to everything she says.*

**Woman 1**   Look at them.

**Woman 2**   What has she got that we haven't?

**Woman 3**   She's not got our good looks.

*The three women start preening themselves.*

**Woman 1**   Who's that man?

*She points into the distance.*

**Woman 2**   Don't know. Never seen him before.

**Woman 3**   You don't think it's . . . him?

**Woman 2**   Well, it's not the Messiah, is it?

*They giggle again.*

*Freeze.*                                                    TONY BOWER

## Well, what do you think?

**Soldier**   You see, Sir, those women didn't believe the woman at the well.

**Official**   They were the only three in the village who didn't!

**Soldier**   But they were the village gossips, Sir. Perhaps they told lots of people not to believe her.

**Official**   It was too late by then. The people had met Jesus.

**Soldier**   Oh.

*There is an awkward silence.*

**Official**   Then there is the Official's report.

| | |
|---|---|
| **Soldier** | What's this then, Sir? |
| **Official** | The official report. |
| **Soldier** | But you said there was the 'Official's report'. |
| **Official** | I meant the Official's report in the official report. |
| **Soldier** | I suppose that makes it very official. Officially official. The Official's officially official report. Have you ever noticed that when you keep on saying the same word over and over again it sounds really weird? Official. Official. Official. Official. Official. |

*The man gives the soldier a withering look.*

| | |
|---|---|
| **Soldier** | He may be an Official, but his report isn't very believable, is it? All coincidence really. |
| **Official** | Coincidence? |
| **Soldier** | Yes, Sir. You know, his son is really ill, he goes to see Jesus, Jesus says his son is healed, he meets his servants on the way home who say his son is better. 'What time did my son get better?' he asks. They tell him the time and it just so happens that it's the exact same time that Jesus says he will be healed. If that's not coincidence, Sir, I don't know what is. |

*The official starts to bang his head on the desk.*

| | |
|---|---|
| **Soldier** | Are you all right, Sir? |
| **Official** | I've felt better. |
| **Soldier** | What about that other guy, the one who really lost it. |
| **Official** | Which man? |
| **Soldier** | You know . . . |

*Freeze.*                                                          TONY BOWER

# The Fourth Sunday of Lent
## (Mothering Sunday)

*Mary learns through Simeon of the cost of motherhood*
*God loves us as a mother loves her children*

### John 9:1-41
*(also 2 Corinthians 1:3-7 or Colossians 3:12-17; Exodus 2:1-10)*

## A reading from the Gospel of John (9:1-41)

One day Jesus saw a blind man begging by the roadside. The man had been blind since birth and the disciples asked Jesus, 'Master, is he blind because of sins committed by himself or his parents?'

Jesus answered, 'Neither is true! This man was born blind so that the power of God could be seen working through him. I am the light of the world, and we must do God's work while we still can.'

Then he bent down and made a paste with some spittle and a little mud. He put this on the man's eyes and said to him, 'Go to the Pool of Siloam, and wash your eyes.'

The man did this, and to his amazement found that he could see! The people of the town could not believe it. 'Is this really the blind beggar?' they asked.

Some said, 'Yes, it is', but others disagreed and said, 'No, but he resembles him.'

The crowd took the beggar to the Pharisees to tell them what had happened. The Pharisees argued amongst themselves. 'No man of God would do such a thing on the Sabbath!' some said, but others answered, 'No sinner could do such an extraordinary thing!'

Many of the people doubted that the man had really been born blind, so they sent for his parents to see what explanation they could give. 'Yes, this is our son,' they said, 'and he was born blind but now he can see. Only he can explain how this has happened, so ask him. He's old enough to answer for himself.'

So they sent for the beggar again and asked him. 'Who is this man you say cured you?'

'I do not know where he came from, or who he is, but I know that he made me see. Unless this man was sent by God he could not have done such a marvellous thing.'

The Pharisees grew angry with the man and shouted, 'Do not try to teach us when you are nothing but a sinner yourself,' and they banned him from the synagogue.

Later Jesus found him sitting alone: 'Do you believe in the Son of Man?' he asked.

'Yes, sir, I believe in him, but I do not know him,' he answered.

Jesus said, 'You can see him for he is speaking to you.'

At once, the man fell to his knees and said, 'Lord, I believe in you!'

And then Jesus said, 'I have come to make the blind see and those who can see, blind!'

'Surely you aren't implying that we are blind?' asked some of the Pharisees who were there.

Jesus said, 'You are guilty because you believe you can see already.'

This is the Gospel of the Lord
**Praise to you, Lord Jesus Christ**                                      KATIE THOMPSON

# Introductory material

## Mother's Day

The Fourth Sunday of Lent, which is also called *Laetare Sunday*, is traditionally known as 'Mothering Sunday' or, in our secular world of today, 'Mother's Day'. In modern times, probably due more to the influence of the large greetings card companies than the Christian Church, it is one of the most popular celebrations of the year. It is of interest to note that it often falls close to 25 March, nine months prior to Christmas Day, when the Virgin Mary was invited to be the mother of the Lord.

For centuries before the Reformation, devout parishioners used to go to the mother church of their diocese, the cathedral, to make special offerings on this Sunday. Exactly when the day also became a festival of human motherhood is uncertain, but 'going a-mothering', that is, visiting your mother with a gift, was well established in Britain by the seventeenth century. Apprentices and servants were given the day off to take a cake or a posy of primroses or violets, gathered in the hedgerows on the way, as a gift to their mothers.

All families develop their own way of celebrating this day; all that needs to be added is to remember a special prayer of thanksgiving, especially as part of the grace that day, for the mothers, including the grandmothers, of the whole extended family.

TONY CASTLE

# Prayers

## Mothering Sunday praise

Gracious God,
    as a mother loves her child so you love us.
    For that great truth
        **we praise and thank you.**

We owe our very lives to you.
You have watched over us from our birth,
    tenderly nurturing us,
    showering us with love.
When we have needed you, you have been there.
For that great truth
    **we praise and thank you**.

You have given us strength in times of need,
    comfort in times of distress,
    encouragement in times of despair,
    guidance in times of uncertainty.
Whatever we have faced, you have been with us.
For that great truth
    **we praise and thank you**.

Gracious God,
    we have not always appreciated your love,
        all too often ignoring what you would teach us,
        disobeying your instructions,
        taking you for granted and wandering far from your side.
    Yet through it all your love has remained constant.
For that great truth
    **we praise and thank you**.

Gracious God,
    caring for us more than you care for yourself,
        sacrificing your all for our sakes,
        loving us with an unquenchable love,
        you have called us all to be your children.
For that great truth
    **we praise and thank you,
    in the name of Christ.
    Amen.**

NICK FAWCETT

## Confession – appreciating mothers

Gracious God,
    we are reminded today
        of how easily we take a mother's love for granted,
        failing to express our thanks for the care we receive,
        slow to demonstrate our appreciation
        for the patient nurture given over so many years.
    For forgetting to show our gratitude,
        **Lord, forgive us.**

We are reminded equally of how easily we take *your* love for granted,
    failing to thank you for the blessings you shower upon us,
    the care with which you daily surround us,
    and the joy with which you fill our lives.
For forgetting to show our gratitude,
    **Lord, forgive us.**

We have assumed that words do not need saying,
    that our thankfulness can be taken as read.
We have believed love comes easily,
    failing to recognise what it can sometimes cost.
We have imagined because no thanks is asked
    that no thanks is necessary.
For forgetting to show our gratitude,
    **Lord, forgive us.**

Gracious God,
    help us to understand the joy we can bring
        through saying thank you,
        not just today but every day,
        not just to our mothers but to everyone,
        and not just to everyone but to you.
    And help us, through the act of thanksgiving,
        to recognise how much we have to be thankful for.
    For forgetting to show our gratitude,
        **Lord, forgive us.**

In the name of Christ we ask it.
**Amen.**                                                 NICK FAWCETT

## Thanksgiving – qualities of mothers

Loving God,
    we thank you for mothers –
        for all they mean or have meant to us,
        for the love they have shown,
        and the care they have given.
    Creator of all,
        **receive our thanks.**

We thank you for the dedication of mothers –
        the sacrifices they make,
        the support they offer,
        the comfort they bring,
        and the guidance they provide.
    Creator of all,
        **receive our thanks.**

We thank you for the qualities of mothers –
  their patience,
  kindness,
  concern
  and understanding.
Creator of all,
  **receive our thanks.**

We thank you for the role of mothers,
  the part they play in our lives,
  our homes,
  our society
  and our world.
Creator of all,
  **receive our thanks.**

We thank you for the joy of mothers –
  the pleasure,
  enrichment,
  laughter and fulfilment,
  which raising children brings.
Creator of all,
  **receive our thanks.**

We thank you for time spent with mothers –
  the learning,
  playing,
  caring and sharing
  which are part of family life.
Creator of all,
  **receive our thanks.**

Loving God,
  we thank you for this day of saying thank you,
    this opportunity to say what we so often mean to say
    but so rarely do.
  For mothers and motherhood,
    for children and families,
    we bring you this day our grateful praise.
  Creator of all,
    **receive our thanks.**

Through Jesus Christ our Lord.
**Amen.**                                        Nick Fawcett

## Intercession – the responsibilities of mothers and those denied the joy of motherhood

Gracious God,
  on this Mothering Sunday we bring your our prayers
    for all entrusted with the responsibility of motherhood.
  Loving Lord,
    **hear our prayer.**

We pray for mothers the world over,
    recognising both the joys and demands they experience –
    the privilege and pressures,
    hopes and fears,
    pleasure and pain that motherhood entails.
  Equip them with the love, wisdom and strength they need.
  Loving Lord,
    **hear our prayer.**

We pray for single mothers,
    bearing the responsibility of parenthood alone,
    struggling sometimes to make ends meet,
    and stigmatised by certain sections of society.
  Grant them the emotional, physical and financial resources they need.
  Loving Lord,
    **hear our prayer.**

We pray for mothers who have experienced heartbreak –
    their children stillborn or seriously disabled,
    injured, maimed or killed through accident or assault,
    struck down by debilitating disease or terminal illness.
  Comfort them in their sorrow.
  Loving Lord,
    **hear our prayer.**

We pray for those denied the joy of motherhood –
    enduring the trauma of infertility,
    prevented on health grounds from risking a pregnancy,
    or unable to establish a relationship
    into which children can be born.
  Help them to come to terms with their pain.
  Loving Lord,
    **hear our prayer.**

We pray for those who foster or adopt children,
    those who long to do so but who are denied the opportunity,
    and those who for various reasons
    have given up their children
    and who are haunted by the image of what might have been.

Grant them your strength and support.
Loving Lord,
**hear our prayer.**

We pray finally for those who long to discover their natural mothers,
those who have become estranged from them,
and those whose mothers have died –
all for whom Mothering Sunday brings pain rather than pleasure,
hurt rather than happiness.
May your love enfold them always.
Loving Lord,
**hear our prayer.**

Gracious God,
we pray for mothers and children everywhere.
May your blessing be upon them,
your hand guide them,
and your love enrich them all.
Loving Lord,
**hear our prayer.**

Through Jesus Christ our Lord.
**Amen.**                                            NICK FAWCETT

# All-age-talk material

## Read John 9:1-41

When we are faced with situations or have behaved in a way which we are not too impressed with ourselves, there is a tendency to see if we can shift the blame or responsibility onto someone or something else.

Often we question why something happens and wonder if there is a God. If he exists why do accidents happen or why do people act so violently towards each other? Do some people deserve what happens to them? These are not new questions. Even the disciples questioned what was going on and whether disease or illness was a result of someone's wrongdoing.

In verse 2 of the reading, the disciples ask Jesus whether it was his parents' sin or the man's sin that led to him being born blind. Jesus answers with an emphatic 'No!'

It is easy to blame God for something which we consider unfair or unjust. We can meet someone or see a situation which makes us feel angry at the injustice of it. The question 'why' echoes around our heads until we can no longer pretend to be satisfied with being told that we should be thankful that we're not like 'that'.

Jesus made it extremely clear that we live in a world which is corrupt and where evil will always attempt to destroy what is good. The very purpose of

God sending Jesus to eventually act as our sacrifice was because sin had invaded every aspect of life. But, because Jesus had power over sin and death he could turn a desperate situation into one of rejoicing.

The presence of Jesus and his actions became a light in a world which was choked by the shadow of sin. Even today, through the Holy Spirit, Jesus acts as a light in situations where it seems impossible to see any light.

We may never know the answers to some of the world's problems but the promise of Jesus to be a light in the darkness is a constant reassurance when the shadows begin to blot out the sun.

PETE TOWNSEND

Give each member of the group a piece of paper and a pen. Ask them to think of a situation, or someone, they feel needs the light of Jesus. The issue can be global, national, local or personal. It doesn't matter if it's only important to the group member or if it concerns a lot of people. Ask the group to write the issue onto the piece of paper and attach it to a noticeboard so that it acts as a reminder for everyone to chat to God about that particular issue.

PETE TOWNSEND

**Help us to see!**

Jesus met a man who had been born blind

## Add or subtract letters to complete the words and find out what Jesus did

A B C D E F G H I J K L M N O P Q R S T U V W X Y Z

_E_ ___ _A_ _E_ _A_   ___ _S T_ ___   ___ _I T_ ___
J-2   H+5 A+3       W-7 D-3 D+1    X-1 L-4

_M_ ___ ___   _A N D_   ___ _P I T_ ___ , ___ _N_ ___
Q+4 H-4           P+3       T+0 I+3 N-9  H-7  C+1

___ _U T_ ___ _T_ ___ _O_ ___ _H E_ _M A_ ___ ___
R-2      F+3   K+3   V-2       G+7 G+12

___ _Y_ ___ _S_ . _T_ ___ _E N_ ___ _E_ ___ _S_ ___ _T_
F-1   A+4    D+4     O-7      I-4 M+1

___ _I_ ___ _T_ ___ ___ _A S_ ___ _I_ ___ ___ _H_ ___
P-8   C+10   J+5 Z-3   X-16   O-1   Q+3 M-8

___ _O O_ ___ ___ ___ ___ _S_ ___ _L_ ___ _M_ .
L+4     Q-5  P-1 J-4   E+4  E+10 J-9

John 9:6-7

KATIE THOMPSON

KATIE THOMPSON

Later, Jesus found the man sitting alone

Figure out the maths problems and use the answers to decode what they said to each other

| 4 | 7 | 8 | 8 | 12 |
|---|---|---|---|---|
| x 5 | + 4 | – 6 | x 2 | + 5 |

**Number**

**Letter**    A      E      I      O      U

D__ Y____ B_L___V__ __N
16   16 17   11 2 11   11   2

TH__ S__N __F G__D?
11    16    16    16

SH__W H__M T__ M__ __ND
16   2   16   11   20

__ W__LL B__L___V__
2    2    11 2 11   11

Y____ __R__ L____K__NG
16 17   20 11   16 16   2

__T H__M!
20   2

L__RD __ B__L___V__
16    2   11 2 11 11

__N Y____!
2    16 17

KATIE THOMPSON

Mothers are kind, loving,
generous, forgiving
and very precious!

Can you find and circle the words in the puzzle below?

**KIND  LOVING  GENEROUS  FORGIVING
PRECIOUS  GENTLE  THOUGHTFUL**

| S | A | H | G | E | O | L | N | L | T |
|---|---|---|---|---|---|---|---|---|---|
| M | G | E | N | E | R | O | U | S | H |
| E | E | F | I | Q | P | V | M | Y | O |
| F | N | I | V | K | Z | I | D | E | U |
| G | T | G | I | S | T | N | F | A | G |
| O | L | V | G | U | I | G | N | I | H |
| P | E | J | R | K | R | C | J | A | T |
| Q | S | U | O | I | C | E | R | P | F |
| S | B | W | F | G | Q | P | M | L | U |
| M | C | B | R | X | H | K | O | D | L |

KATIE THOMPSON

Exodus 2:9

KATIE THOMPSON

# Reflective material
## (sketches, meditations and poems)

## Good parenting

God loves us, not because we are good children, but because we are God's children. Jesus, as God's final messenger, tells us that the best and truest way to think of God is by way of our own experience of good parents. The covenant made with Moses long before Jesus' time was more like the arrangement between an emperor and a subject race. 'Keep the laws of my empire and I will repay you by keeping you safe and prosperous.' When time and again the people broke God's laws, and yet time and again God renewed the covenant, the prophets began to think the covenant was becoming permanent, but they did not know how to express the new covenant. Jesus gave the clue, which no other before or since would have dared to be the first to give: God is first-generation Father to each human person.

In that context, the story of the prodigal son is the story of God's relationship with each sinful human being. All the father wants is to have his son back safe and sound; the adventures the son went through while running away simply do not matter by comparison. Mothers and fathers fret over their children as long as the children are in any kind of trouble. They do not love the children less on that account: if anything, they love them more. And the saying of Isaiah and the saying of the Psalm – that even if a father or a mother did ever forget their child, God would not forget – this is now applied by Jesus in effect not just to the people as a whole but to each poor lost or wayward human being.

I am loved, not because I am good but because I am God's. There is no way I can ever earn a gift like that. God loves me because God wants to, not for anything I have done in the past or will do in the future.

GERALD O'MAHONY

## Meditation of one of the children brought to Jesus

I was scared at first,
    scared of the noise, the crowds, the confusion –
    a sea of faces unlike anything I'd seen before.
It seemed that everyone wanted to see Jesus –
    everyone, that is, except us;
    we just wanted to get back to our friends
    and enjoy ourselves as we'd been doing before.
Who was he anyway?, that's what we wanted to know.
What made him so special, so important?
Yet it was no use arguing,
    one look at my mother's face told me that –
    she was determined I was going to see him, like it or not.

So there we were, pushing through the crowd,
    her hand clasping mine
    in case I should have any ideas about escaping –
    and slowly fear turned to rebellion.
OK, I'd go if I had to,
    but if she imagined I was going to play the sweet innocent child
    she could think again.
I resolved instead to give Jesus an audience he wouldn't forget in a hurry,
    to scowl, sulk, scream the place down if I had to,
    anything to make clear whose idea this daft business was.
Yet that's not the way it worked out.
I had the scowl ready all right,
    a sullen snarl to be proud of,
    but the moment I saw him it just melted away,
    all hostility and resentment forgotten.
I can't tell you why exactly,
    but there was something quite extraordinary about him,
    an interest, warmth and concern which seemed to flow over you,
    impossible to resist.
Instead of treating us like kids he made us feel important,
    as though we were real people,
    worth something to him,
    special –
    and suddenly, instead of sulking,
    we were beaming with sheer delight,
    even, would you believe, when he picked us up
    and started to pray for us.
There's not many I'd have let do that, I can tell you!
He was so different from the rest of those with him –
    you could tell they were itching to get rid of us,
    their annoyance at our intrusion all too clear.
Yet do you know what Jesus said to them?
That the kingdom of God belongs to children like us!
I can't think why, for we were no angels, not by a long way,
    and I can't imagine he was under any illusions –
    presumably he saw something in us we didn't.
I tell you what, though –
    we'd have followed him anywhere after that,
    walked to the ends of the earth and back had he asked us.
No, we didn't understand quite who he was
    or what he'd come to do –
    but that didn't matter –
    we knew instinctively that he was someone special,
    a man we could trust completely,

with our very lives if necessary,
and that was enough.
What more could we have wanted?
What more could anyone ask?                                    NICK FAWCETT


## We recognise truth

We sometimes talk about recognising the truth; yet, when we use the word
'recognise' we usually mean we have seen whatever-it-is before. In the matter
of the good news, to see it is to recognise it for the truth, and how could we
recognise it for the truth unless we had seen it before?

We all come from God, and our human reality comes from the truth. There is
a kinship between the way we are and the way God is. When we die we go
home to God, not to any strange land. Those who are in touch with their own
reality and their own being as creatures (created beings) will have eyes open to
receive further truth as it is revealed.

Jesus used the cure of blind persons as a sign of what he was most concerned
about, namely that people should recognise his teaching for the truth that it
is. His enemies were the really blind, the ones he called blind guides, only
good for leading other poor blind folk into the ditch. They thought they were
independent; they did not see their need. They did not see their need of forgiveness; they were unable to think of all sins being forgiven; they wanted to think
they were sinless, and that the sinful should be condemned.

Jesus cured two kinds of physical blindness. The first was of those who were
blind from birth, like the man who became able to see but not understand (mis-
taking humans for walking trees), then able to understand what was what. The
second kind was that of Bartimaeus, who used to be able to see but had lost his
sight. We all have something of both kinds of blindness. How could we ever
understand God's goodness all at once, even if we have seen it before?

GERALD O'MAHONY


# Order of service

## A reflective service for Lent

Although more substantial services for the start of Lent and Palm Sunday are
described in this book, it may be that church diaries make it impractical to
organise something as elaborate as these. The reflective service described here
is designed for use on the Fifth Sunday in Lent (Passion Sunday), but could be
adapted for any of the others, or even used on a weekday. As with the reflective
service for Advent, it can be led by anyone, ordained or lay, and is ideally suited
to a smaller congregation.

## Introduction

Jesus said: 'Anyone who loves his life will lose it, while anyone who hates his life in this world will keep it for eternal life. Whoever serves me must follow me, and where I am, my servant will also be.'

*Silence*

## Song

Come and see (HON 88)*

## Prayer of approach

Lord Jesus,
Redeemer of the world,
you left your home in glory
to be lifted up on the earth
so that all people might be drawn to you.
As we look on you suffering humiliation,
and dying in agony on the cross,
may we also see you there
in power and majesty.
In recognising you as victor
over sin and death,
may we know our sins forgiven,
and enter into eternal life with you. Amen.

## Responsive words of praise

*Leader:*    Just as you have received Christ Jesus as Lord, continue to live in him; do not let your minds be captured by deceptive philosophies, which depend on human tradition and the principles of this world rather than on Christ.

*Group A:* In Christ the complete being of the Godhead lives in bodily form;
*Group B:* We have been brought to completion in him.

*Group A:* In Christ we have been purified by the removal of our sinful nature;
*Group B:* We have been buried with him in baptism, and raised with him through faith in the power of God.

*Group A:* In Christ God has made us alive by forgiving all our sins.
*Group B:* He took away the written law which condemns us, nailing it to the cross.

*Group A:* In Christ the powers and authorities of this world are disarmed.
*Group B:* He made a public spectacle of them, leading them as captives in his victory procession.

*Leader:*    Since we have died with Christ to this world, let us therefore no longer behave as though we belonged to it, but set our hearts on things above.
*(from Colossians 2)*

*HON – *Hymns Old and New,* Kevin Mayhew Publishers

**First reading**
Romans 8:6-11

**Song**
Lord Jesus Christ (HON 311)

**Second reading**
Mark 10:32-45

**Meditation**
The four evangelists are unanimous in portraying the disciples as decidedly human and fallible. Along with Simon Peter, James and John were the two disciples closest to Jesus, and not long before this disagreement they'd witnessed his transfiguration. Yet they still managed to get into an argument with the others over their future status in God's kingdom. Possibly they thought their closeness to their master entitled them to the place closest to him at the eternal banquet. Or maybe they simply thought their efforts deserved more recognition. It's interesting that Matthew records the involvement of James' and John's mother in the dispute. Whatever the motivation for their request, the effect was to trigger off a squabble with the other ten disciples, whose response was hardly more commendable – no doubt they all felt they should be granted the same special place!

Despite having seen and learned so much over the previous three years, the disciples hadn't yet understood that to share Jesus' status also involves sharing in his suffering, nor that in God's kingdom the values of this world are completely reversed. Following the way of Jesus doesn't mean we're automatically exempt from the temptation to seek status and power, and lord it over others. The divisions this causes have frequently torn the Church apart throughout its history. Too often we ask what we can do to project our image more effectively or gain more influence in the community, rather than asking what God wants us to do to serve those around. The only antidote is to turn the world's standards and values upside down as Jesus did, and choose instead the way of willing service, which will lead us through pain and inconvenience to true greatness.

Four questions to reflect on:

i.   In what situations are we tempted to seek status or greater influence over others, and how can we resist this?

ii.  How do we exercise authority and influence over others, and acknowledge those in authority over us?

iii. How willing are we to accept the role of servant for the sake of God's kingdom, and what might this involve?

iv.  How willing are we to accept suffering or inconvenience as we follow Christ, and what might we find hardest to sacrifice?

**Silent reflection**

### Passiontide response

We approach the throne of the Servant King,
who kneels and washes his disciples' feet,
saying, 'Lord Jesus, wash us clean';
**make us alive in you.**

When we feel tempted
to turn away from suffering
and choose the easy path,
Lord Jesus, wash us clean;
**make us alive in you.**

When we feel tempted
to seek personal recognition
and status above others,
Lord Jesus, wash us clean;
**make us alive in you.**

When we feel tempted
to pursue our own interests
but disregard the needs
of the underprivileged and exploited,
Lord Jesus, wash us clean;
**make us alive in you.**

When we feel tempted to strive for power
and forget our calling to serve others
in your name,
Lord Jesus, wash us clean;
**make us alive in you.**

As you have washed our feet,
setting us an example to follow,
**may we do for others
what you have done for us,
for the sake of your kingdom. Amen.**

### Hymn

Praise to the Holiest in the height (HON 426)

### Intercessions

We bring to God our prayers for all those who are faithfully serving him in hard
or demanding situations, for all those whom we serve in our community, and
for our shared commitment to Christ's way of humble service . . . *(a time of open
intercession may follow, concluding with the Lord's Prayer).*

*After each petition, or group of petitions, may be sung the Taizé chant 'Stay with me'*
(HON 458).

**Song**

From heaven you came (HON 148)

**Final prayer**

We ask God to put within us
the mind of Christ,
and make us willing to serve him
wherever he gives the opening.

In our homes and families
**may we serve you joyfully.**

At work and at leisure
**may we serve you faithfully.**

In times of stress and exertion
**may we serve you loyally.**

In times of quietness and reflection
**may we serve you devotedly.**

In times of sorrow and times of joy
**may we serve you wholeheartedly,
seeking no reward other than knowing
we are doing your will. Amen.**

Following the teaching of Jesus,
we pray as he taught:
**Our Father . . .**

For Jesus, who stoops in humility
to wash our feet,
**let us bless the Lord.**

For Jesus, the Servant King,
who gave his life to be a ransom for many,
**thanks be to God.**                              STUART THOMAS

# The Fifth Sunday of Lent

*Through the raising of Lazarus, Jesus shows himself as
the resurrection and the life, offering life to all*

## John 11:1-45

*(also Ezekiel 37:1-14; Psalm 130; Romans 8:6-11)*

### A reading from the Gospel of John (11:1-45)

Lazarus and his two sisters, Martha and Mary, were very good friends of Jesus.
They lived in a town called Bethany, not far from Jerusalem.

One day, the sisters sent an urgent message to Jesus, because Lazarus was
very ill and close to death. When he heard this message, Jesus said, 'This illness
will not bring death for Lazarus, but glory for God and his Son.' And he did not
set off immediately, even though he was very fond of Lazarus and his sisters.

When Jesus and his disciples arrived in Bethany more than two days later,
they found that Lazarus was dead, and had already been buried for four days.

Martha ran to meet Jesus and said to him, 'Lord, if you had been here, you
could have saved our brother.'

Jesus said, 'Your brother will live again.'

'I know that on the last day he will come back to life,' she answered.

Jesus turned to her and said, 'I am the resurrection and the life. Anyone who
believes in me will have eternal life, and he will never die. Do you believe this?'

Martha answered him, 'Yes, Lord, because I know that you are the Christ, the
Son of God.'

When Jesus saw the great sadness of Martha and Mary and their friends, he
wept with love and sorrow. 'Show me where he is buried,' he said. So they took
him to the tomb, where Jesus said to them, 'Roll away the stone, and you will
see God's glory.'

'Lord,' Martha said, 'Lazarus has been dead for four days and by now he will
smell.'

Jesus said to her, 'You will see God's glory if you believe in me.'

So they did as he said, and, looking up to heaven, Jesus prayed, 'Father, I
thank you, for I know that you always listen to me. Let these people see and
believe.' Then he called out in a loud voice, 'Lazarus, come out!'

To everyone's amazement Lazarus appeared, still wrapped in burial cloths,
and walked from the tomb. Many people saw what happened that day, and
they believed in Jesus.

This is the Gospel of the Lord
**Praise to you, Lord Jesus Christ**                              KATIE THOMPSON

# Prayers

## The God who does more than we can ever ask or think!

Sovereign God,
    we praise you that you are able to do more
        than we can ever ask or imagine –
        where we can do so little, you can do so much,
        **when we can do nothing, you can do everything.**
    Teach us to believe that,
        **not just with our heads but in our hearts.**

When life seems dark,
    the future frightening,
    our problems insurmountable,
    and our resources to meet them all too few,
    **we praise you**
    **that you are able to see us through.**

When life feels good,
    the days ahead full of promise,
    our worries are few,
    and our joys many,
    **we praise you**
    **that you are able to offer more still.**

When loving is hard,
    caring involves pain,
    sharing means sacrifice,
    and believing entails cost,
    **we praise you**
    **that you are able to give us strength.**

When loving is easy,
    our relationships bring joy,
    our friends bring pleasure,
    and our faith brings rewards,
    **we praise you**
    **that you are able to bring yet greater happiness.**

When hopes are dashed,
    dreams lie broken,
    visions have faded,
    and plans are thwarted,
    **we praise you**
    **that you are able to bring new purpose.**

When opportunities excite us,
    prospects beckon,
    possibilities unfold,
    and challenges present themselves,
    **we praise you**
    **that you are able to help us grasp them.**

Sovereign God,
    in these things and so many more,
        you are able not simply to meet our needs
        but to transform our lives –
    **able to bless us beyond words.**

Receive our praise,
    and teach us that whatever we face,
    whether good or bad,
    whether we feel able to meet it or not,
    **you are able to do more**
    **than we can ever ask or think of!**
    **Amen.**                                              NICK FAWCETT

## For those who mourn

Loving God,
    you have promised your special blessing to those who mourn,
        your comfort to those overwhelmed by grief,
        your joy to those enduring sorrow.

So now we pray for those facing sadness,
    those burdened by misery,
    those weighed down by despair,
    those who have lost loved ones
    and who are striving to come to terms
    with the emptiness and heartbreak they feel.
Lord, in your mercy,
    **hear our prayer.**

We pray for those among our families and friends
    who are facing such times,
    all those in this church and in our world.
Lord, in your mercy,
    **hear our prayer.**

Loving God,
   grant to those who grieve your special blessing.
   May they know that your hand is upon them,
      your arms encircling them,
      and your heart reaching out to them.
   Lord, in your mercy,
      **hear our prayer.**

May all who mourn discover the comfort you have promised,
      and find strength to face tomorrow,
      until that time comes when light shall dawn again,
      and hope be born anew.
   Lord, in your mercy,
      **hear our prayer,**
      **through Christ our Lord.**
      **Amen.**                                        NICK FAWCETT

## A short prayer

God of life and love,
we come to worship you
and acclaim you as truly the Lord of life.
We thank you for all that is good
in the lives we live now.
Please forgive us for the times
when our lives don't reflect your love,
and help us to live as true disciples of Jesus
and signs of your love of life.
Through Jesus Christ our Lord.
Amen.                                              MICHAEL FORSTER

# All-age-talk material

'I am the resurrection and the life! Whoever believes in me will never die' (John 11:25-26)

**Jesus called Lazarus from the tomb!**
**Join the dots and read what happened next**

KATIE THOMPSON

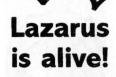

**Lazarus is alive!**

**Martha and Mary's brother, Lazarus, was very ill, so the sisters sent a message to Jesus**

CODE BREAKER

Can you decode their message?

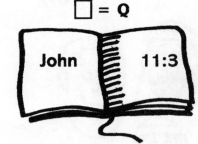

John 11:3

KATIE THOMPSON

When Jesus arrived, Lazarus had already been buried for four days. Martha ran to greet Jesus

Write every second letter on the lines below to find Martha's words

B L L O A R M D E I O K R N S O A W N T E H D A P T
Q G B O L D A W E I O L U L I G N R B A C N F T K W
D H L A P T S E R V N E E R G Y O O N U Y A K S R K

John   11:22

KATIE THOMPSON

| | | | | | | | | | |
|---|---|---|---|---|---|---|---|---|---|
| A | R | C | S | O | N | M | H | D | D |
| S | E | K | I | B | W | O | D | I | W |
| D | H | B | R | E | A | T | H | E | U |
| A | T | P | E | C | A | D | G | D | J |
| I | O | N | R | L | H | O | U | S | E |
| L | M | B | I | A | I | W | D | T | T |
| L | Q | V | J | B | Y | H | Q | H | K |
| Z | E | I | X | O | V | E | R | E | N |
| D | L | I | H | C | F | E | D | A | S |
| E | O | Y | G | R | E | U | M | W | P |

The SON of a WIDOW got ILL and DIED. ELIJAH was staying at the HOUSE at the time. Elijah PRAYED and stretched himself over the child THREE times. The CHILD started to BREATHE again. Elijah brought him to his MOTHER. "Look," he said, "your son is ALIVE!"

JESUS SAID, 'I AM THE RESURRECTION AND THE LIFE!'

John 11:17-27

LAZARUS IS BROUGHT TO LIFE

SUSAN SAYERS

Which route will lead Lazarus to life?

Lazarus and his friends are celebrating – but can you find 6 differences in the pictures?

WORDSEARCH

Find the following words in the grid:

LAZARUS, MARTHA, MARY, BETHANY, JESUS, GOD, GLORY, THOMAS, DEATH, LIFE, FREE, SAVED, GRAVECLOTHES, MESSIAH, STONE

```
F R E M A R T S U S E J
L A Z A R U S A R F A B
S A V R E E A G I G Z E
T P R T N Y M L A Z A T
O B S H R C O H M Y R H
N H T A E D H A O R U A
E A M D V E T I H O S N
T H O M A E S S T L T Y
G R A V E C D S X G O D
S F R E E S D E A T G E
B E T H A N Y M A R T A
G R A V E C L O T H E S
```

MICHAEL FORSTER

## Read John 11:1-45

Lazarus was a really good friend of Jesus. So when Jesus received word that Lazarus was sick you would have thought that the natural reaction would be to get up straightaway and go and see how he was. John tells us that Jesus loved Martha, Mary and their brother Lazarus but instead of rushing to them he stayed where he was for another two days.

The disciples may have thought that Jesus was being cautious and didn't want to go to Judea because he had been threatened with being stoned to death. When Jesus announced that he was now ready to visit Lazarus the disciples were totally surprised and just a little bit concerned for their own safety as well!

When Jesus said that Lazarus was simply asleep the disciples must have thought, 'Great! That means he's getting better and so we don't have to walk into danger.' But then Jesus made it quite plain that he meant Lazarus was actually dead!

Before, and during, the time of Jesus, death was feared by everyone. Death didn't seem to respect anyone and there seemed no way of defeating the finality of it. However, to Jesus, death wasn't to be feared and was subject to his power and authority. Although the disciples were probably not aware of the relevance of the situation, Jesus was making a vital statement concerning his own death and resurrection. Death couldn't hold him and it didn't have any power over him.

When Jesus finally reached Lazarus' home, he spoke to him as if he'd simply been asleep. Jesus didn't speak with sadness in his voice and certainly didn't speak with a questioning voice. It wasn't 'Lazarus, come out . . . if you can', or 'Lazarus, can you hear me?' Jesus spoke with authority because he knew that nothing was more powerful than God. Even before he told Lazarus to come out, Jesus thanked God for answering his prayers! This wasn't because Jesus was unsure what God wanted to do or that he needed to boost his confidence, it was purely because Jesus wanted to encourage those around him to have faith in a God who expressed his love even in the face of death.

If God can express his love in this way, surely we can begin to depend on him for the slightly less difficult situations which we face each day.

PETE TOWNSEND

# Reflective material
### (sketches, meditations and poems)

## Lazarus is called back to life

### What's the point?

We need to be careful not to present the *resuscitation* of Lazarus as comparable with the *resurrection* of Jesus. Lazarus came back *from* death to resume his old life – Jesus went forward *through* death to the new! However, we can see it as showing Jesus as Lord of life, and that he wants us to have real life here and now. We don't have to wait for the next world!

### Prayer
Loving God,
thank you for sharing in our lives,
and wanting them to be as full and satisfying
as they can be.
We thank you for all that we are going to share
this morning,
and ask you to help us know you better, through it all.
Amen.

### From the known to the unknown
Do the children know people whose lives are sad? Perhaps they know someone who's lonely because they can't get out very much, or someone who isn't able to make friends. Sometimes that can feel like no kind of life at all – and Jesus wants them to have a life, just as we do.

### Tell the story: John 11:1-45
*(See page 252 for a dramatised version of this story.)*

#### Get a life, Lazarus
Martha and Mary were friends of Jesus, and they lived with their brother Lazarus at a little town called Bethany, about two miles from Jerusalem.

One day, Lazarus was taken ill. At first his sisters weren't too worried. 'Trust him to catch a cold just as there's housework to be done!' said Martha.

'As far as you're concerned,' Mary answered, 'there's *always* housework to be done.'

'Well, we can't *all* sit around thinking beautiful thoughts all day,' Martha retorted. 'Oh, don't sit on that cushion – I've only just fluffed it up!'

Before long, though, even Martha had to admit that Lazarus had a bit more than a cold. 'We'd better send for Jesus,' she said. 'Now, he'll be hungry when he gets here, so I'll make a few cakes – about five dozen ought to be enough.'

Jesus was with his friends. He was very sad when he heard Lazarus was ill, but he didn't hurry over straightaway. 'We'll go in a couple of days,' he said.

'You'd be mad to go so close to Jerusalem,' Peter objected. 'You know there are people there who are out to kill you – don't you ever learn?'

'What, kill me in broad daylight?' Jesus replied. 'Listen, our friend Lazarus has fallen asleep, and we must wake him up.'

Matthew was amazed. 'You're going to risk your neck to give Lazarus an alarm call?' he said. 'I mean, he's not going to die of too much sleep, now is he?'

'Oh, come on, Matthew,' Jesus answered. 'D'you have to take everything so literally? He *is* dead – *now* d'you get it? It's going to take a little more than an alarm clock to wake him – even if they had been invented, which they haven't. Anyway, it's all working out well – stick with me and you'll see something special.'

The disciples still weren't happy – they thought it was far too dangerous – but Thomas said, 'Have a bit of faith! If he's going to die, let's go and die with him – he'd do that much for us.'

So it was that Jesus and his friends arrived in Bethany, four days after Lazarus died. Martha was busy dusting some daffodils when she heard that Jesus was coming and went to meet him. 'Here you are, at last,' she said. 'If you'd come when we asked you to, Lazarus wouldn't be dead. Still, you're here now, and God will do anything for you, won't he!'

'Your brother's going to rise to life again,' Jesus said.

'Well, yes,' Martha answered. 'On judgement day.'

'When it comes to things like resurrection and life, I'm the one!' Jesus said. 'You do believe that, don't you?'

'Of course – you're the Messiah, Son of God, the One Who Is To Come, all that kind of thing. Look, just wait here while I fetch Mary.'

Jesus waited, and soon Martha came back with Mary.

'Jesus, if only you'd been here,' Mary cried. 'I know you could have saved him.'

Jesus felt really sorry for Martha and Mary, and when they took him to Lazarus' grave he couldn't help crying himself. Some people standing by noticed. 'See how much he loved his friend!' some of them said.

'Oh, terrific!' scoffed someone else. 'He made the blind see, the lame walk, but where was he when his own friend was dying?'

The grave was a hole in the rock, with a big stone rolled in front of it. 'Take the stone away,' Jesus ordered.

'What!' exclaimed Martha. 'He's been dead four days, and there'll be a terrible smell – if that gets into these clothes I'll never be able to wear them again!'

'Didn't I tell you,' Jesus said, 'that you're going to see God's glory in a big way? Now, just have the grave opened and leave the rest to me.'

The stone was rolled back, and the people all around held their noses as Jesus began his prayer to God. 'Father,' he said, 'thank you for listening to me – well, I know you always do, but I have to say that so people here can hear it because they need a bit of convincing that you sent me – you do understand. Right, here we go then.' And he raised his voice to a great shout. 'Lazarus, come out!'

You could have heard a pin drop! Everyone just held their breath – well, they would, wouldn't they, but it wasn't just because of the smell – and waited to see what would happen next. After what seemed like hours, someone said, 'Hey, someone's moving in there!' And out of the darkness of the tomb came Lazarus, still wearing his grave-clothes but very much alive! Everybody started talking at once, full of amazement at what Jesus had done.

'I know he must have been truly dead,' said one. 'No one who's alive smells like that!'

'Jesus must be someone really special, after all!' said another. 'Maybe we should listen to him more.'

Lazarus was still struggling with the grave-clothes. 'Don't just stand there,' Jesus said. 'Set him free, and let him go – he's got a life to live!'

## Respond to the story

*Discussion*

How do the children think Martha and Mary felt when Lazarus came out?

• Overjoyed?

• Amazed?

• Perhaps just a little scared?

We may not be able to raise the dead, but can we help people in other ways to 'get a life'?

• People who are lonely and need company?

• Children at school who don't have many friends, or who get bullied?

• People who are shy and need gentle friendship to give them confidence?

*Song*

One or more of the following songs might be used here and/or in the all-age worship:

Be still, for the presence of the Lord
Come on and celebrate
Take my hands, Lord
The Spirit lives to set us free
There are hundreds of sparrows
There was one, there were two

*Art and craft*

Prepare a sign saying 'The Crypt' to go over one of the doors leading off the worship area. Plan which door you will use – preferably, if possible, one which faces the congregation as they sit in their seats. You might want to go further and put a complete façade around the door – it's all a matter of what suits you and your resources. Choose someone – a child or an adult – to play the part of Lazarus in the service – someone you feel will do the part well, but without *over*-playing the comedy. See section marked with an asterisk (*) on page 253.

Draw or paint a picture of Lazarus coming out of the tomb.

This is the key picture, but you might want to do others in addition to it, such as:

• Jesus walking toward Bethany

• Martha and Mary talking to Jesus

*Drama*

*See the next page for a dramatised version of the story.*

## Get a life, Lazarus

**Narrator**    Martha and Mary were friends of Jesus, and they lived with their brother Lazarus at Bethany, two miles from Jerusalem. One day, Lazarus was taken ill. At first Martha wasn't too worried.

**Martha**    Trust him to catch a cold just as there's housework to be done!

**Mary**    As far as you're concerned, there's *always* housework to be done.

**Martha**    We can't *all* sit around thinking beautiful thoughts all day, Mary. Oh, don't sit on that cushion – I've only just fluffed it up!

**Narrator**    Before long, though, even Martha was getting worried about Lazarus.

**Martha**    Let's send for Jesus. Now, he'll be hungry when he arrives, so I'd better make a few cakes – about five dozen should be enough.

**Narrator**    Jesus was sad when he heard Lazarus was ill, but he didn't panic.

**Jesus**    We'll go in a couple of days. Peter, will you tell everybody?

**Peter**    You'd be mad to go so close to Jerusalem. You know there are people there who are out to kill you – don't you ever learn?

**Jesus**    What, kill me in broad daylight? Listen, our friend Lazarus has fallen asleep, and we must wake him up.

**Matthew**    You're going to risk your neck to give Lazarus an alarm call? I mean, he's not going to die of too much sleep, now is he?

**Jesus**    Oh, come on, Matthew, d'you have to take everything so literally? He *is* dead, and it's going to take more than an alarm clock to wake him – even if they had been invented, which they haven't. Anyway, stick with me and you'll see something really special.

**Narrator**    The disciples still weren't happy – they still thought it was far too dangerous. But Thomas trusted him.

**Thomas**    Have a bit of faith, you lot! If he's going to die, let's go and die with him – he'd do that much for us.

**Narrator**    Jesus and his friends arrived in Bethany four days after Lazarus died. Martha stopped dusting the daffodils and went to meet him.

**Martha**    At last! If you'd come when we asked, Lazarus wouldn't be dead. Still, you're here now, and God will do anything for you, won't he!

**Jesus**    Your brother's going to rise to life again.

**Martha**    I know – on judgement day.

| | |
|---|---|
| **Jesus** | When it comes to things like resurrection and life, I'm the one! You do believe that, don't you? |
| **Martha** | Of course – you're the Messiah, Son of God, the One Who Is To Come, all that stuff. Look, just wait here while I fetch Mary. |
| **Narrator** | Jesus waited, and soon Martha came back with Mary. |
| **Mary** | Jesus, if only you'd been here, I know you could have saved him. |
| **Narrator** | Jesus felt really sorry for Martha and Mary, and when they took him to Lazarus' grave he couldn't help crying himself. |
| **Bystander 1** | See how much he loved his friend! |
| **Bystander 2** | Oh, terrific! He made the blind see, the lame walk, but where was he when his own friend was dying? |
| **Narrator** | The grave was a hole in the rock, with a big stone rolled over it. |
| **Jesus** | Take the stone away. |
| **Martha** | What! He's been dead four days, and there'll be a terrible smell – if that gets into these clothes I'll never wear them again! |
| **Jesus** | Didn't I tell you that you're going to see God's glory in a big way? Now, just have the grave opened and leave the rest to me. |
| **Narrator** | The stone was rolled back, and the people all around held their noses as Jesus began his prayer to God. |
| **Jesus** | Father, thank you for listening to me – well, I know you always do, but I have to say that so people here can hear it because they need a bit of convincing that you sent me – you do understand. (*Raises voice*) Lazarus, come out! |
| **Narrator** | Lazarus came out, still tangled up in his grave-clothes but very much alive! Everybody was full of amazement about Jesus. |
| **Bystander 1** | He *must* have been dead – no one who's alive smells like that! |
| **Bystander 2** | Jesus must be someone really special, after all! Maybe we should listen to him more. |
| **Jesus** | Set Lazarus free, and let him go – he's got a life to live! |

*The person playing Lazarus will need to either slip out discreetly while the story is being read or wait in the other room for the first part of the service. Have the story read in either dramatised or narrative form and then draw attention to the door. You're going to act out the story now. Call Lazarus to come out, a few times without response. Then turn to the congregation and say you need a bit of help. Could they join in your call? Lazarus could play them along (briefly) by calling out replies such as 'But I've nothing to wear!' and 'Can't I have a shower first?'

When Lazarus emerges, welcome him with applause.

Now you can reflect briefly that many people feel 'entombed' by different things – often a sense of their own unworthiness, or a fear that they will not be welcome or may even be rejected if they venture into places like churches. The church – not just the worship leader or minister! – has a very important role in enabling people to 'come forth' and feel fully a part of this world again.

By this sign, Jesus showed that he is Lord of life and the scourge of death. Perhaps it's not given to many of us literally to bring people back from the grave, but this is a pretty good parallel with it!

MICHAEL FORSTER

## The Grannies sense a touch of mortality

*Characters*   The two Grannies, Moll and Poll, are rather subdued. Recent news has given them a feeling of mortality, which they'd prefer not to experience.

*Scene*   They're sitting at a small table sipping tea. A newspaper lies open on the table.

*Props*   Sombre (dark) clothing with headscarves. Table and two chairs. Teapot and two cups. Large format newspaper.

**Poll**   *(Takes a sip of her tea and then groans)* Ooooh!

**Moll**   Is there something wrong with the tea? *(Strokes the side of the teapot)* It's a fresh brew, best tea leaves and I used the water from my hot water bottle too!

**Poll**   *(Grimaces)* I wondered what the aftertaste was.

**Moll**   *(Purses lips)* Manners, Poll, manners!

**Poll**   Tell that to my feet.

**Moll**   Feet? What have they got to do with anything?

**Poll**   They've been giving me some stick recently.

**Moll**   Well, what can you expect. They've seen some miles, they have.

**Poll**   *(Leans forward and massages a foot)* I was hoping they'd see me through a few more winters, too.

**Moll**   Don't see why they shouldn't. Look after them and they'll look after you.

**Poll**   I'm not sure they're returning the compliment, though.

**Moll**   *(Sips her tea)* Anyway, your feet are the least of your troubles.

| | |
|---|---|
| **Poll** | *(Pauses, sipping her tea. Holds cup slightly away from mouth)* What troubles? |
| **Moll** | *(Taps newspaper)* Read the obituaries recently? |
| **Poll** | *(Pulls a face)* Not quite compulsive reading. |
| **Moll** | The obituaries seem to contain more news about some of our old friends than the rest of the paper. |
| **Poll** | Do I sense a touch of mortality creeping in? |
| **Moll** | A touch? It's more like someone driving a herd of cows through my life. |
| **Poll** | *(Smiles)* And leaving a load of aromatic debris behind? |
| **Moll** | *(Sniffs)* Please, don't be so common. |
| **Poll** | Since when did being 'common' cause you a problem? |
| **Moll** | As long as you don't say 'common as muck' that's all. |
| **Poll** | *(Raises eyebrows)* Would I? |
| **Moll** | *(Taps newspaper again)* Martha Tilbury got her name in the obituaries last week. |
| **Poll** | Martha? Why, she's younger than the both of us! |
| **Moll** | Precisely. |
| **Poll** | *(Takes a sip of tea)* It certainly makes you think. |
| **Moll** | Well, don't think about it for too long or you'll still be in mid-thought when your name appears in the same place as Martha's. |
| **Poll** | *(Shudders)* Ooh, the very thought. |
| **Moll** | Sssh. Leave the thinking for those who've got time on their hands. |
| **Poll** | Like Martha? |
| **Moll** | Surely there's not much life in her thinking-tackle now? |
| **Poll** | Are you implying that death is a sort of breathtaking, final event which is the last day of the rest of your life? |
| **Moll** | Well, it's certainly nature's way of telling you to take things easy from now on. |
| **Poll** | It certainly would cut the cost of your telephone bills. |
| **Moll** | And every other bill for that matter. |
| | *(Poll pauses to sip her tea and stare into space)* |
| **Moll** | Hey! What are you thinking? |
| **Poll** | That when I was young, death was just a distant rumour. |

**Moll**     *(Nods)* And now you realise that it's not a rumour but a certainty?

**Poll**     The only thing in life you can bank on.

**Moll**     *(Shrugs)* I don't see how a bank has anything to do with it. My Mum always used to say that it's no good leaving money behind, someone will only go and spend it. Much better to leave nothing behind and leave them all guessing what you did with your money.

**Poll**     *(Shudders)* Yuck, all this talk of death and our limited mortality makes me feel all cold.

**Moll**     Your temperature will surely depend on whether you're going up *(looks up)* or down! *(looks down)*

**Poll**     I don't like to think about it.

**Moll**     *(Sips tea)* As long as I get a nice cup of tea in the morning, to get me started, I don't mind.

**Poll**     I think death's a little bit more than a blend of tea.

**Moll**     Never underestimate a refreshing cup of tea.

**Poll**     It'd take a damn good tea blend to refresh you after you've got your name in the obituaries.

**Moll**     Steady! Thou shalt not take the name of thy tea blend in vain.

**Poll**     No offence meant, I'm sure.

**Moll**     None taken.

**Poll**     *(Holds teacup in both hands near mouth)* It still makes you think.

**Moll**     Quit with the thinking.

**Poll**     *(Nods towards the newspaper)* Can't help it with the obituary page staring me in the face.

**Moll**     *(Folds newspaper)* Gone but not forgotten.

**Poll**     I hope that's what they say about me when I make the ultimate shopping trip.

**Moll**     That's a nice way of looking at it. *(Sits back and looks up)* Death, one continuous shopping experience. Browsing through the shelves of various purchases we've made in our lives, checking for the bargains, wincing at the over-priced stuff and tut-tutting at the list of additives which added nothing to your life whatsoever.

**Poll**     I wonder whether God's ever thought of a 'buy one get one free' sort of offer.

| Moll | Make a lot of economic sense, that would. Why waste all that hard-earned experience on a youngster. Much better to come to the end of one episode, take a quick sleep, wake up, have a cup of tea and take up where you left off. |
|------|---|
| **Poll** | You could have a sort of reward card that you collect points on. Then you can trade them in for special little items like meeting a tall, dark handsome man with all his own teeth. |
| **Moll** | *(Jerks her head to indicate something behind her)* Obviously didn't have enough points on my card when I came to choose him, did I! |
| **Poll** | *(Takes a sip of tea)* Bargains are difficult to find. |
| **Moll** | I'm not sure I got a bargain, more of a sale of old stock! |
| **Poll** | *(Shrugs)* I think mine was from a closing-down sale. |
| **Moll** | Isn't that what death is, a closing-down sale? |
| **Poll** | I'm not so sure about the sale bit, but closing down seems most appropriate. |
| **Moll** | *(Takes a sip of her tea and sighs)* I sometimes think that certain parts of my body are closing down prematurely. |
| **Poll** | *(Sits back)* You're not going to go into specifics, are you? |
| **Moll** | *(Ignores Poll)* I remember. It was ten years back *(nudges Poll)* you recall, it was when I had that spot of bother with my plumbing. |
| **Poll** | *(Frowns and then raises eyebrows)* Ah, yes, I do remember. You tried all sorts of pills and potions before you plucked up the courage to see Old Doc Rippum. |
| **Moll** | Nothing to do with courage. *(Sniffs)* It was more to do with eliminating all possible alternatives before I troubled the good doctor. |
| **Poll** | If my memory serves me correctly, you didn't use the word 'good' doctor after you went to see him. It was something like . . . |
| **Moll** | *(Interrupts quickly)* . . . nothing of the sort. I was a trifle upset. At my age, having someone suggest that your plumbing problems are nothing more than a simple case of a worn washer, well *(sits haughtily in chair)* I ask you, the impertinence of the man. |
| **Poll** | And did the, er, 'condition' go away? |
| **Moll** | *(Places cup on table, straightens her apron and pats her headscarf)* Not exactly, I simply drink in moderation now. |
| **Poll** | *(Places hands to each side of face in mock surprise)* 'Moderation'! I've never known you to drink, or do anything for that matter, in moderation. |

**Moll**      (*Annoyed*) Excuse me!

**Poll**      That's what you always say just before you fall flat on your face after a tipple.

**Moll**      (*Takes a sip of tea and places cup in saucer, making the cup rattle*) How could you imply such a thing?

**Poll**      Quite easy. I simply state the facts. Anyway, it's a wonder your 'drinking in moderation' hasn't led you to a place in the obituaries.

**Moll**      A little wine for the stomach's sake.

**Poll**      A 'little' wine? I think something more like the deluge that Noah experienced would be a more apt analogy.

**Moll**      You can't talk.

**Poll**      At least there's nothing wrong with my 'washer'.

**Moll**      That may be all that's in working order.

**Poll**      (*Smiles and leans across to pat Moll's hand*) That may be so, but we've still got plenty of life left in the old bones.

**Poll**      You'd better believe it! Let's drink to life, love and gossip.

**Moll**      (*Lifts cup and holds it towards Poll*) Live to gossip.

**Poll**      Love to gossip.

**Moll**      Here's to the future.

**Poll**      (*Lifts cup in the same manner*) Cheers.                    PETE TOWNSEND


## Meditation of Lazarus

It was so weird,
      so unreal.
At least that's how it felt.
And yet it happened!
I'd breathed my last, no question about that.
After those long dark days of sickness,
      the pain growing
      the strength failing;
      after those final terrible hours,
      sweat pouring down my face,
      lungs gasping for air;
      at last came peace,
      darkness closing about me,
      suddenly welcome though it had long been feared.
An end to the struggle,
      the battle nearly over.

For a moment I was a child again, comforted by my mother's embrace,
    a youth running wild as the wind,
    a man setting out afresh on life's great adventure,
    a father, taking my child into my arms.
And then rest.
The light went out,
    the flame extinguished,
    the game completed.
Only it wasn't,
    for suddenly a voice summoned me back to the fray,
    sunshine burst into the tomb,
    and consciousness returned.
No wonder they gasped,
    no wonder they swooned,
    no wonder they wept for joy,
    for I who had been taken from them,
    I who had been dead,
    was alive!
And yes, I thanked him, of course I did,
    once the confusion had cleared anyway,
    but it took a while, I can tell you.
And even now just once in a while
    I wonder if he really did me any favours
    for I know that one day I must face it all over again.
Yet it will be different then,
    very different,
    not just because I've been there before and know there's nothing to fear,
    but because Jesus has shown me
    that death is not so much the end as the beginning.
That's why he raised me from the tomb.
Not just to restore life,
    not simply to defer death,
    but to point to a new birth,
    a resurrection which only he can bring.
He came back too, you know,
    back from beyond the grave.
Three days in his tomb,
    long enough for decay to take hold,
    but he appeared to Mary,
    to Peter,
    to the Apostles,
    to us all.
And we know that even though we die
    one day we shall live
    even as he lives now!

NICK FAWCETT

# Don't be sad – a celebration of life

## Focus

A table or floor display with a Bible open at John 14:1-3; a (paschal) candle; a crucifix or cross.

## Introduction

Jesus knew how it felt to be sad. He experienced the pain and grief we feel when someone we know and love dies. At such times in our lives, Jesus understands and shares those moments of pain in a very special and personal way.

## Penitential reflection

When we turn from God and choose another path
which leads us away from his love:
Father, forgive us.
**Father, forgive us.**

When our words and actions make us unworthy
to be called children of God:
Jesus, forgive us.
**Jesus, forgive us.**

When we forget that we must be ready to forgive,
as we are forgiven:
Father, forgive us.
**Father, forgive us.**

## Scripture

*New Testament reading – adapted from 1 Thessalonians 4:13, 14, 17, 18*

Do not weep for those who have died, or be filled with sadness like those who have nothing to hope for. We believe that Jesus died and rose to new life, and that the same thing will happen to all who believe in him. Take comfort in knowing that everyone who dies in Christ shall rise to new life and be with him for ever.

*Gospel – adapted from John 14:1-3*

Jesus said, 'Do not feel sad and downhearted. Just as you trust in my Father, so you can trust in me. My Father's house has many rooms, and I will make one ready for you. When a place has been prepared, I will come back for you, and we will be together. You already know the way to the place where I am going.'

*Gospel – adapted from John 11:1-45*

Lazarus and his two sisters, Martha and Mary, were very good friends of Jesus. They lived in a town called Bethany, not far from Jerusalem. One day, the sisters sent an urgent message to Jesus, because Lazarus was very ill and close to death. Hearing this message, Jesus said, 'This illness will not bring death for Lazarus, but glory for God and his Son,' and he did not set off immediately, even though he was very fond of Lazarus and his sisters. When Jesus and his disciples arrived in Bethany more than two days later, they found that Lazarus was dead and had already been buried for four days. Martha ran to meet Jesus and said to him, 'Lord, if you had been here, you could have saved our brother.' Jesus said, 'Your brother will live again.' 'I know that on the last day he will come back to life,' she answered. Jesus turned to her and said, 'I am the resurrection and the life. Anyone who believes in me will have eternal life, and he will never die. Do you believe this?' Martha answered him, 'Yes, Lord, because I know that you are the Christ, the Son of God.'

When Jesus saw the great sadness of Martha and Mary and their friends, he wept with love and sorrow. 'Show me where he is buried,' he said. So they took him to the tomb, where Jesus said to them, 'Roll away the stone, and you will see God's glory.'

'Lord,' Martha said, 'Lazarus has been dead for four days and by now he will smell.' Jesus said to her, 'You will see God's glory if you believe in me.' So they did as he said, and, looking up to heaven, Jesus prayed, 'Father, I thank you, for I know that you always listen to me. Let these people see and believe.' Then he called out in a loud voice, 'Lazarus, come out!' To everyone's amazement Lazarus appeared, still wrapped in burial cloths, and walked from the tomb. Many people saw what happened that day, and they believed in Jesus.

## Reflection

Have you ever admired an intricate and detailed piece of needlework or tapestry, and marvelled at the thousands of threads and stitches which together create the picture? If we stand too close to such a piece of work, it can be hard to make out what it is; we need to stand back to appreciate and understand the image before us. If you ever turn such a marvellous creation over and look at the back of the piece of work, you would be equally amazed to see a jumble of intricate knots and loose threads. The whole thing looks a complete mess, and it is almost impossible to guess what the picture on the other side might be.

Life can be compared to such a tapestry, with God the master weaver who is the only one who knows what the final picture will look like. As he busily weaves and helps us to direct the threads of our lives, it is as though we are standing at the back of the tapestry, where we are unable to make out the final picture. We must trust him to direct our efforts, even at times when things seem to be going badly in our lives.

When someone we know or love dies, we can find it difficult to understand why such a sad thing has happened. We are unable to 'see' where it fits into God's plan for the tapestry of life. For a time it can seem that our sadness and grief will stop us from working our part of that tapestry ever again. It is difficult to understand how life goes on as normal, as people around us go about their everyday business, and seem unaware of our heartache and sorrow. Our lives and the lives of those around us can take twists and turns like threads, and we can see no pattern nor make any sense of the direction they sometimes take. We cannot see the final picture which God is in the process of creating.

When someone dies, Jesus understands our feelings of grief, and shares our sadness and loss in a very special way. But, as the readings we have listened to tell us, he gives us hope and the joyful promise of everlasting life with him. Although it is right that we express our sadness when someone dies, it is also good to celebrate their life and to rejoice at their happiness of finding peace with God in the place he has prepared especially for them in heaven.

There they are able to stand on the other side of the tapestry, and see the final picture of God's glory. They will finally be able to understand how the twists and turns in their lives were all part of God's elaborate plan, as the threads of their life become part of his wonderful tapestry.

**Intercession**

With love in our hearts,
let us unite as one family
to ask God for all our needs:

Christ was driven away
by those who did not listen or understand;
may people who are driven from their homes,
their families, and their land,
find forgiveness in their hearts
and comfort in their sorrow.

*Silence*

We pray to the Lord:
**Lord, hear us.**

Christ was betrayed and let down by his friends;
may we be forgiven for the times
when we betray his friendship
and turn our backs on his love
and the love of others.

*Silence*

We pray to the Lord:
**Lord, hear us.**

Christ was imprisoned and tortured
for the sake of goodness;
may all who suffer such cruelty and imprisonment
for just causes
be strengthened by their closeness to God
and our cries for their freedom.

*Silence*

We pray to the Lord:
**Lord, hear us.**

Christ wept at the death of his friend Lazarus;
may the tears of sadness
of those who mourn for a loved one
become tears of joy
with the promise of their resurrection and eternal life.

*Silence*

We pray to the Lord:
**Lord, hear us.**

Christ was laid in the darkness of the tomb;
may those whose lives are overshadowed
by sadness and grief
be enlightened by the knowledge
that Christ shares their sorrow,
and may they draw comfort from his presence.

*Silence*

We pray to the Lord:
**Lord, hear us.**

Knowing that our heavenly Father is listening,
in the silence of our hearts
let us share our own unspoken prayers with him.

*Silence*

Lord God,
we ask you to receive our prayers
and answer them
according to your holy will.
We make these prayers through Christ our Lord.
**Amen.**

### Activities and ideas

- The cross is the most important symbol of the Christian faith. We can look beyond it and see the risen Christ, and be reminded that suffering and death will end in resurrection and new life. Help the children to make bookmarks decorated with a cross. You will need pieces of hessian material or aida fabric cut into bookmark shapes; pieces of squared paper for marking out their designs; darning needles and coloured yarn or fine wool.

- Encourage the children to create a wax and paint picture of someone or some event they especially want to remember. Arrange the children in pairs or small evenly sized groups, and encourage them to spend some time quietly reflecting about the subject of their picture. Then give each child a sheet of white paper and a piece of white candle with which to draw an invisible image. They will need to press down firmly as they draw. When they have written their own name at the top of the paper, ask each child to exchange their paper with another child. They paint carefully over the top of the picture with thin paint. As the paint fails to cover the wax, the picture will emerge. In their pairs or small groups they can share and explain what they have drawn. Their pictures can be used as a display or as part of the central focus.

- Enlarge a suitable line drawing of an image or scene. Using a light pencil, divide the picture into a series of equally sized squares which are numbered in order on the back. (There should be sufficient squares to allow at least one per child.) Cut out the numbered squares. On another piece of paper, draw a grid of corresponding numbered squares and pin or stick this to a suitable surface. Have an assortment of different coloured felt-tip pens for the children to choose from. With reflective music playing quietly in the background, ask each child to come forward and collect a square of paper and some pens. They should then return to their places, and carefully and in silence, colour the side which has no number written on it. They should use as many colours as they like to completely cover all the white paper. When they have completed this task, ask them to check the number of their piece of paper, and then use a small piece of Blu-Tack to stick their individual square on the correspondingly numbered square on the grid. As each child adds a square, a mosaic effect picture of the final image should gradually appear. Using Blu-Tack allows you to rearrange the pictures neatly to create a final image which can clearly be made out. Just as in a tapestry, each person's contribution contributes a vital part in creating the final and complete picture.

- Have some dead leaves scattered around the display. After listening to one of the readings, allow a quiet time for reflection, before inviting the children to collect a leaf in memory of someone who has died. They touch the open Bible with it, before placing it at the base of the candle, which is surrounded by fresh flowers or buds to represent new life.

- Place a tray of soil or compost on the focal display together with a container of seeds which can be easily picked up – nasturtiums or sunflowers, for example. Read the extract from Matthew's Gospel below, and then invite the children to take a seed and push it into the tray of soil, as a symbolic gesture of new life. The tray can later be positioned so that the children can see the seeds growing.

*How does a seed grow? Night and day, while we are asleep and while we are awake, it sprouts and grows; and no one quite knows how. Until finally the crop is ready and the harvest can be gathered in.* (Adapted from Matthew 4:27-29)

## Music
- Be still and know I am with you (LitHON/OS)*

*LitHON/OS – *Liturgical Hymns Old and New/Our Songs*

- I am the Bread of Life (LitHON/OS)
- Walk with me, O my Lord (LitHON/OS)
- Lord of all hopefulness (LitHON/OS)
- Vivaldi: 'Spring' from *The Four Seasons*
- Rodrigo: Second movement (Adagio) from *Concierto de Aranjuez*

KATIE THOMPSON

## Nothing so grave

**Scene**    *Mary and Martha are rushing around the house, busy preparing.*

**Mary**     I'll cook tonight.

**Martha**   You?

**Mary**     Yes.

**Martha**   Cook?

**Mary**     That's what I said.

**Martha**   Are you sure?

**Mary**     I'm offering.

**Martha**   I'm accepting.

**Mary**     Good.

**Martha**   Good. (*Martha goes to the bottom of the stairs and shouts up.*)

Are you awake yet?

**Mary**     Sshh – he's having a rest.

**Martha**   He's been lying down for the last few days. You'd think he'd want to be up and about by now.

**Mary**     I think it's taken a lot out of him.

**Martha**   It's taken a lot out of me, but I'm still keeping going.

**Mary**     I know, but you're different.

**Martha**   What do you mean, I'm different?

**Mary**     He's a man.

**Martha**   Oh yeah.

**Mary**     I think he'll be all right once he's had a rest.

**Martha**   Yeah, I'm sure you're right.

**Mary**     How many are we expecting tonight?

**Martha**   It could be the whole village.

| Mary | You're kidding! |
|---|---|
| **Martha** | I never joke where food's concerned. |
| Mary | But we can't cater for crowds! |
| **Martha** | They may not all come. |
| Mary | I think a load of them went straight off, celebrating. |
| **Martha** | It might just be a few of us tonight, then. |
| Mary | I hope so. |
| **Martha** | So do I. |
| Mary | It's been such a . . . such a . . . such a few days. I just want a quiet meal. |
| **Martha** | With a few friends. |
| Mary | Yeah, and relax, enjoying each other's company and just . . . just enjoy. |

*Mary and Martha smile at each other.*

| **Martha** | Can you believe it? |
|---|---|
| Mary | No. |
| **Martha** | I still think I'm dreaming. |
| Mary | I don't want to wake up if I am. |
| **Martha** | It's not a dream, is it? |
| Mary | No. |
| **Martha** | No, it's not. It's all too real, too incredible, too unbelievable but real, definitely real. |
| Mary | Is this really happening to us? |
| **Martha** | Yeah. |
| Mary | I feel like laughing. |
| **Martha** | I feel like crying. |
| Mary | I feel like dancing. |
| **Martha** | I feel like weeping. |
| Mary | I feel so alive! |
| **Martha** | I felt like I was so dead. |

*They look at each other and laugh.*

| Mary | Like our brother. |
|---|---|
| **Martha** | Good old Lazarus. |
| **Mary** | He was dead, Martha. |

**Martha**    I know.

**Mary**    He was in the tomb for days.

**Martha**    I know.

**Mary**    He did look funny.

**Martha**    What?

**Mary**    Walking about in his grave-clothes.

**Martha**    I don't think he expected to be walking anywhere. Did you?

**Mary**    No. And you thought he'd stink rotten!

**Martha**    He had been in the tomb for four days.

**Mary**    I know – four days!

**Martha**    Four whole days!!

**Mary**    Did you see the look on his face?

**Martha**    I'll never forget it.

**Mary**    When he saw Jesus.

**Martha**    I thought he was going to pass out.

**Mary**    You could say he was somewhat amazed.

**Martha**    We'll never be the same, will we, Mary?

**Mary**    No. No, we won't.

*The two sisters stare at each other.*

**Martha**    Lazarus!

**Mary**    Lazarus!

**Martha**    It's a good job he responded quicker to Jesus!

*They say together*

**Mary**    Lazarus!

**Martha**    Lazarus!

*Freeze.*                                                    TONY BOWER


## You can't keep a good man down

**Official**    This report could finish me off.

**Soldier**    Just look at Lazarus, Sir. He thought he was finished, but he made a comeback!

**Official**    It's stories like Lazarus' that will bury my career. Do you understand?

**Soldier**    Yes, Sir.

**Official**    What can I say about this incident?

**Soldier**    Nothing, Sir.

**Official**    Nothing?

**Soldier**    Yes, Sir. Say nothing. Pretend it never happened. You don't tell anyone, I won't tell anyone.

**Official**    That's a good idea.

**Soldier**    Thank you, Sir.

**Official**    We don't mention it to anyone.

**Soldier**    No, Sir.

**Official**    We'll act like it never happened.

**Soldier**    Yes, Sir.

**Official**    Oh dear.

**Soldier**    What's wrong, Sir?

**Official**    Oh, just all the people who were eye-witnesses who will talk about nothing else for the rest of their lives.

**Soldier**    We could . . .

**Official**    No we could not kill them all!

**Soldier**    Just an idea, Sir.

**Official**    Not a good one. Besides, killing people doesn't guarantee that they stay dead!

**Soldier**    No, Sir.

**Official**    Look at Lazarus.

**Soldier**    Precisely. He couldn't stay dead for more than four days.

**Official**    Exactly.

**Soldier**    We could circulate stories about how all of Jesus' friends were nutters.

**Official**    Nutters?

**Soldier**    Yes, Sir, nutters. Like the woman who dried his feet with her hair. She was a nutter, Sir. Real fruitcake. Barmy as a bat. Lost the plot, didn't even know what day it was. Cuckoo, she was, Sir. Loopy Loo.

**Official**    Shut up! Before you drive me crazy. Let me read the report.

*Freeze.*                                          TONY BOWER

# Holy Week

# Palm (Passion) Sunday

*Jesus is welcomed in Jerusalem, yet comes to offer his life*

(For resources on the Passion of Christ see Maundy Thursday and Good Friday)

## Matthew 21:1-11

*(also Psalm 118:1-2, 19-29; Isaiah 50:4-9; Psalm 31:9-16;
Philippians 2:5-11; Matthew 26:14–27:66)*

### A reading from the Gospel of Matthew (21:1-11)

Jesus and his disciples arrived at Bethphage on the Mount of Olives just outside Jerusalem. He sent two of the disciples to the next village to collect a donkey and her colt.

'If anyone stops you, tell them that they are for me, and will be returned,' he said.

And so it was that the prophecy was fulfilled: 'Tell Zion's daughter: see your King drawing near, humbly riding on a donkey and her colt.'

They brought the animals to Jesus, and put cloaks on their backs so that Jesus could ride on them. When the people heard that Jesus was coming they laid their cloaks on the road before him, and pulled branches off the palm trees to wave in the air. The crowds grew more and more excited, and shouted at the top of their voices, 'Hosanna, Hosanna! Blessed is the one sent by the Lord.'

Excitement filled the whole city, and some people asked, 'Who is this man?'

The people answered them, 'It is Jesus the prophet from Nazareth in Galilee.'

This is the Gospel of the Lord
**Praise to you, Lord Jesus Christ**                                    KATIE THOMPSON

# Introductory material

Lord Jesus Christ,
    we are reminded of how you entered Jerusalem
    to shouts of joy and celebration.
But we remember too how quickly that welcome evaporated,
    how soon the mood of the crowd changed.
Lord Jesus Christ,
    we know all too well that we are not so different –
    our commitment to you so often short-lived,
    superficial, self-centred.
Help us to welcome you into our lives with true gladness,
    and to go on serving you come what may,
    now and always.                                    NICK FAWCETT

# Prayers

## Welcoming the King

Gracious God,
    as we remember this day
        how Jesus entered Jerusalem to cries of celebration,
        help us to welcome him afresh
        into our own hearts and lives.
    Accept the praise and worship we bring you,
        and give us a real sense of expectation
        as we look towards his coming kingdom.
    Hosanna to the Son of David,
        **glory in the highest heaven.**

Gracious God,
    like your people long ago we do not always see clearly,
        our faith shallow and self-centred;
        we do not understand as we should,
        our praise short-lived and superficial.
    But, we ask, take the faith we offer,
        weak though it may be,
        and deepen it through this day,
        so that we may truly welcome Christ as our King,
        and worship him with joyful praises,
        now and always.
    Hosanna to the Son of David,
        **glory in the highest heaven,**
        **now and always.**
        **Amen.**
                                    NICK FAWCETT

## Confession

Lord Jesus Christ,
    you came to Jerusalem and were greeted by shouts of joy,
        welcomed as God's promised deliverer,
        the one he had chosen to rescue his people.
    But when the nature of your kingdom became clear,
        the sort of freedom you offered fully apparent,
        so the response changed.
    The shouts of 'Hosanna!'
        turned to cries of 'Crucify!'
    The hands outstretched in friendship
        became fists curled up in hate.

The declarations of loyalty
    became voices raised in mockery and rejection.
Lord Jesus,
    **have mercy.**

You come to *our* lives
    and *we* welcome you with gladness.
*We* have accepted you as our Saviour,
    the one who sets *us* free.
But we too can so quickly change our tune
    when you overturn our expectations,
    when you do not act as we hope,
    when you turn out to have different ideas from our own.
We, too, even while professing faith
    and going through the motions of commitment,
    can push you aside,
    preferring our own way to yours.
Lord Jesus,
    **have mercy.**

Lord Jesus Christ,
    on this day we are reminded of how easy it is
    to welcome you as King of kings,
    but how hard to follow in the Way of the Cross.
Lord Jesus,
    **have mercy,**
    **for in your name we ask it.**
    **Amen.**

NICK FAWCETT

## Intercession

*Jesus enters Jerusalem as the Prince of Peace, riding on a donkey. At the heart of our rejoicing is the pain he is bound to suffer in redeeming us through unflinching love. Yet we still certainly rejoice, for we know he has won the victory. Jesus is indeed our King.*

Fellow pilgrims, as we welcome Jesus
and hail him as our King, let us offer to God our Father
in prayer the deep concerns and needs
of the Church and of the world.

We bring to your love all who are baptised,
and especially those who have lost their faith
or have stopped praying; may they be brought back
through your love, and put into contact with those
who can guide and reassure them.

*Silence for prayer*

Lord, uphold us:
**give us your strength.**

We bring to your love every meeting, demonstration,
convention and all large crowds; may they be peaceful
and ordered, inspiring those present for good,
rather than inciting them to violence.

*Silence for prayer*

Lord, uphold us:
**give us your strength.**

We bring to your love our own loved ones,
the members of our families, our friends
and especially those from whom we are separated,
either by distance or death;
and all who are missing from their homes;
may your powerful love protect us from all that is evil.

*Silence for prayer*

Lord, uphold us:
**give us your strength.**

We bring to your love those suffering
from incurable or life-threatening diseases;
those who need medical care, but are either too poor,
or live too far away to receive it;
make us more ready to help
with our time, money and influence,
so that unnecessary suffering and death are avoided.

*Silence for prayer*

Lord, uphold us:
**give us your strength.**

We bring to your love those who have died;
may they rest in the light and joy
of your presence for ever.

*Silence for prayer*

Father, may we praise you not only with our voices but
also in the lives we lead.

*Silence for prayer*

Merciful Father,
**accept these prayers
for the sake of your Son,
our Saviour Jesus Christ, Amen.**

SUSAN SAYERS

## A short prayer

Lord Jesus Christ,
    How easy it would have been for you
    on entering Jerusalem
    to have taken the easy way.
With the shouts of welcome still ringing in your ears,
    the hosannas of the crowd
    still fresh in your memory,
    it must have been so tempting
    to give them what they wanted,
    to be the sort of Messiah they hoped you
    would be.
But you soon made it clear, if any doubted,
    that there would be no compromise,
    no watering down of your message
    for the sake of popular acclaim.
You stayed true to your calling
    despite the inevitable consequences.
Lord Jesus Christ,
    we too can try and shape you
    to fit our expectations.
Help us as we recall those last days
    leading up to the Cross,
    to learn what you expect of us,
    and find strength to honour it.

NICK FAWCETT

# All-age-talk material

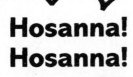

Hosanna!
Hosanna!

What did
the prophecy say about
Jesus riding into
Jerusalem?

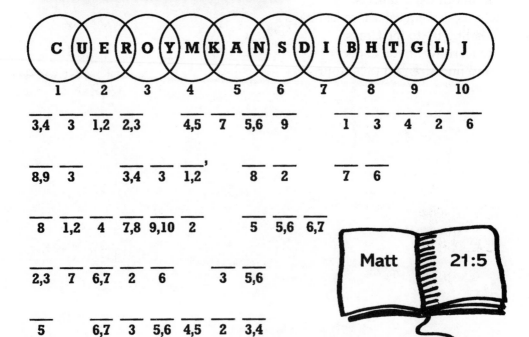

Use the letter code to find out!

C U E R O Y M K A N S D I B H T G L J

1   2   3   4   5   6   7   8   9   10

___ ___ ___ ___   ___ ___ ___ ___   ___ ___ ___ ___ ___
3,4  3  1,2 2,3   4,5  7  5,6  9     1   3   4   2   6

___ ___   ___ ___ ___,  ___ ___   ___ ___
8,9  3    3,4  3  1,2    8   2     7   6

___ ___ ___ ___ ___ ___   ___ ___ ___
8  1,2  4  7,8 9,10 2     5  5,6 6,7

___ ___ ___ ___ ___   ___ ___
2,3  7  6,7  2   6     3  5,6

Matt    21:5

___   ___ ___ ___ ___ ___ ___
5     6,7  3  5,6 4,5  2  3,4

KATIE THOMPSON

Fill the blanks with words from the leaves to see what the crowds shouted

KATIE THOMPSON

Where did Jesus send his disciples to find the donkey and colt?

Follow the letters of the alphabet in order to find the route they took

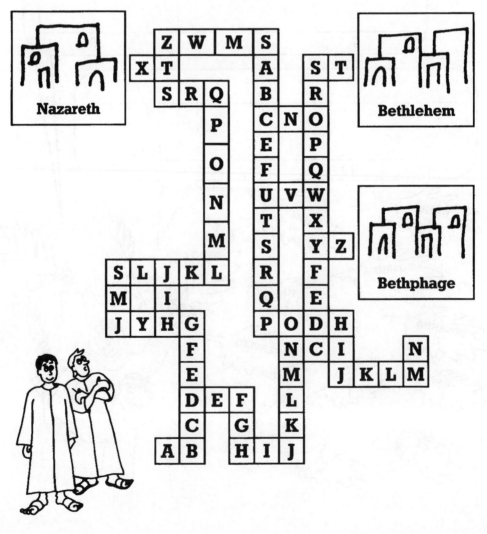

Nazareth

Bethlehem

Bethphage

KATIE THOMPSON

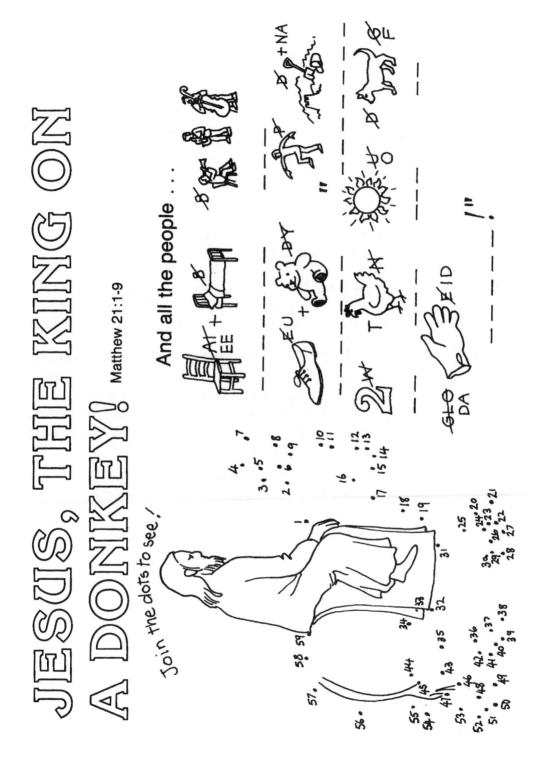

# JESUS, THE KING ON A DONKEY!

Matthew 21:1-9

And all the people . . . .

Join the dots to see!

SUSAN SAYERS

### Read Matthew 21:1-11

In Jerusalem expectations were running high. For the priests and religious leaders it was a time of celebrating the Passover and, possibly, they might at last get their hands on the one person who was a real pain to them: Jesus.

For the ordinary people the Passover was also a time of celebration but their expectations were even higher than normal. They had seen and heard all of the things that Jesus had done recently and they'd heard of his being referred to as the 'Son of David' (see Matthew 20:31). The term 'Son of David' was a title which the Jewish people understood to mean the messianic king, a new ruler who would liberate his people from foreign rule. Even the Mount of Olives was significant as the prophet Zechariah had spoken of the Messiah making a stand there against all of God's enemies (see Zechariah 14:4).

All the evidence pointed to something exceptional, something of the utmost importance. The crowds gathered and welcomed Jesus as he entered Jerusalem on a donkey (a king would ride a donkey as someone who came in peace). Yet within a week this Messiah, the 'Son of David' was dead.

The priests and religious leaders were content. Order had been restored and this nuisance, Jesus, had been dealt with. The Jewish people's hopes had been dashed against the wood of the cross. Expectations seemed to count for nothing where death was concerned.

Just as Jesus had shown time and again, death had no power over him. His mission was to act as the ultimate sacrifice, once and for all, so that the relationship could be finally restored between God and the people. It was obvious that the majority of people hadn't really understood what Jesus had been saying. The freedom he offered and the authority that he'd shown were not to deal simply with Roman rule but to end the rule of evil.

Sometimes our expectations are limited to what we can see immediately in front of us. Perhaps we should try to see things from God's perspective?

PETE TOWNSEND

# Reflective material
### (sketches, meditations and poems)

### Three cheers for Jesus

*(For up to five readers)*

Three cheers for Jesus!
He comes to be our king.
He'll overthrow the tyrants,
    and wealth and freedom bring.
He'll outlaw every evil –
    all pain and fear and greed.
He'll take over the government
    and meet our every need.

Two cheers for Jesus.
He claims to be our king,
    but he's striding through the Temple
    and upsetting everything.
He's scattering our profits
    and the businesses we've made;
    is he really fit to rule us
    if he spoils our holy trade?

One cheer for Jesus.
He came to be our king,
    but now he stands on trial,
    red with the whip's sharp sting.
With crown of thorns they mock him,
    scorned by official power.
He's helpless with authority;
    this cannot be his hour.

No cheers for Jesus.
He's surely not our king.
They've nailed him to a wooden cross
    while people laugh and sing.
The one we thought would save us
    they curse and wound and kill.
Our hopes and expectations
    die with him on that hill.

Now heaven cheers for Jesus.
The world has had its say;
    and God has raised him from the dead –
    there dawns another day.
Disciples stand bewildered
    beside an empty grave,
    but soon they will be cheering too
    for the Christ who came to save.

PETER DAINTY

## If I were a king!

### Aim

To show what good leaders should be like. Christians believe that Jesus is king, but he is very different to other kings.

### Song

Come on, let's celebrate  *or*
Sing hosanna, shout hooray

## Puppet sketch

*(Micky is asleep in his bag, so everyone calls for him. Micky wakes up not knowing where he is.)*

**Micky**     Where am I?

**John**     You're at *(name of venue)*.

**Micky**     I can't be!

**John**     Why?

**Micky**     Because I'm king, that's why.

**John**     A king? Hardly, you're our mate, Micky.

**Micky**     You're joking. Don't say I was only dreaming!

**John**     You were only dreaming.

**Micky**     Oi! I said don't say I was only dreaming. Oh, what a shame. It was a wonderful dream. I – yes, I – was a great, powerful king, dressed in fine clothes and wearing a crown.

**John**     You?

**Micky**     I had lots of servants that I could boss around.

**John**     I bet you enjoyed that!

**Micky**     Servants who did my housework for me. Servants to fan me and keep me cool. Servant girls dropping grapes into my mouth. What a life!

**John**     Dream on!

**Micky**     I intend to! I had a Rolls-Royce to go shopping in, a golden shopping trolley, a bit like a chariot, and adoring crowds waving and bowing to me! No waiting in queues for me, *and* I had millions of bananas. I love being king!

**John**     Micky, kings do more than just boss everyone around all day.

**Micky**     What?

**John**     There's more to being a king than just wearing fine clothes, riding around in chariots and waving to your adoring crowds! It's about wanting the best for your people, making sure they have good homes and plenty to eat.

**Micky**     I'm still tired! I'm going to go back to sleep in my bag and enjoy being a king again. Bye!

**Bible story**

*Matthew 21:1-11*

There's a story about a king in the Bible.

The crowds were waving and cheering, but he didn't have fine clothes, or servants to boss around. He had great power and he used his power for the good of his people. He fed them and healed them.

He wasn't rich – in fact he was poor. He didn't have a horse – he had a donkey! No fine clothes and no crown!

But the people didn't care! They knew he was a true king; a loving, kind king, a servant king. They cheered, they sang, they waved palm branches. A wonderful king.

The King of kings. King Jesus.

**Round-up**

Being a rich and powerful king doesn't mean he's great. He is only great if he treats his people well. Being rich, famous or powerful doesn't make someone great. A great person is someone who is kind and cares for others.

**Prayer**

Lord, thank you that Jesus is a wonderful king; powerful but kind, not rich but generous; a servant king. King of kings. Amen.

JOHN HARDWICK

# Meditation of Simon the Zealot

You should have heard them!
What a noise!
What a sight!
What a welcome!
I'm telling you, I've never seen the like,
    not in all my born days,
    and there's been a few of those.
We've had kings here,
    governors,
    would-be messiahs,
    and they've all had their moments,
    their fans out in force to greet them,
    but nothing like this,
    nowhere near it!
They came in their thousands,
    waiting to meet him,
    the news of his coming having raced before him.
And it wasn't just his followers,
    it was everyone,

men, women and children plucking branches from the trees,
   tearing off their cloaks,
   carpeting the road before him,
   their voices hoarse with shouting.
'Hosanna!' they cried.
'Blessed is he who comes in the name of the Lord!'
It was treason, of course,
   and probably heresy too,
   but no one cared –
   devil take the consequences, this was a time for rejoicing,
   and rejoice we did.
Yet if that was unusual –
   the abandonment,
   the jubilation –
   there were stranger things to follow,
   for just a few days later,
   less than a week in fact,
   the scene was so very different.
The same people by and large,
   once more part of a crowd,
   but this time not love but hatred in their faces,
   not welcome but rejection,
   their waving hands suddenly shaking fists,
   their 'Hosanna to the Son of David'
   all at once 'We have no king but Caesar'.
I wouldn't have believed it possible if I hadn't seen it for myself,
   but the sad fact is I not only saw it,
   in my own way I was part of the whole sorry business,
   for when the crisis came I was found wanting,
   concerned only to save my skin
   with no thought as to his.
It was a chilling lesson,
   and one that I, like so many others, learned the hard way –
   the lesson that it's easy to call someone king,
   much harder to actually serve them.

NICK FAWCETT

# Maundy Thursday

*Jesus offers his all to bring life to all*

(For readings on Gethsemane see Good Friday)

## John 13:1-17, 31-35
*(also Exodus 12:1-4, (5-10), 11-14; Psalm 116:1-2, 12-19; 1 Corinthians 11:23-26)*

### A reading from the Gospel of John (13:33-38)

'I shall not be with you much longer,' said Jesus to his friends after Judas had gone out of the room. 'Love one another – this is my "new commandment". Love one another in the same way as I have loved you. This will be the mark by which everybody will recognise that you are my friends – the way in which you love one another.'

'Sir,' said Peter, 'where are you going?'

'You cannot go with me now where I am going,' said Jesus. 'You will go with me later on.'

'Sir,' said Peter, 'why can't I go with you now? I'll die in your defence.'

'You'll die in my defence?' said Jesus. 'Believe me, before the cock crows, you will say three times that you are no friend of mine.'

ALAN DALE

# Introductory material

What must it have been like to have sat with Jesus in the upper room as he broke bread and shared wine, as he prophesied that one of those sitting there would betray him, and as he spoke of his coming death? What must it have been like to see him wrestling with his inner torment in the garden of Gethsemane, betrayed with a kiss and finally taken off before the Sandhedrin? We know the stories so well that we can read them with barely a flicker of emotion, but if we put ourselves into the shoes of those who lived through these events, we can begin to glimpse something of the pain, the shock and the disbelief they must have faced as the events of that astonishing night unfolded. As we break bread and share wine together this evening, imagine yourself there in that upper room, there in the garden watching with his disciples, there fleeing in haste as the soldiers march him away, and marvel afresh at the selfless love, the astonishing sacrifice, which lies at the centre of it all.

NICK FAWCETT

# Prayers

## Broken for us

Lord Jesus Christ,
    we celebrate today the astonishing truth
        that lies at the heart of this week –
        the fact that you endured the humiliation of Gethsemane,
        the agony of the cross
        and the darkness of the tomb,
        not because you had to
        but because you chose to.
    You gave your life so that we might live.
    You were broken so that we might be made whole.
    **Receive our praise.**

We marvel that, from the beginning of your ministry,
    you knew the fate it would lead to,
    the cost involved,
    and yet you continued undeterred,
        despite ridicule, threats and outright hostility,
        your concern always for others rather than yourself.
You gave your life so that we might live.
You were broken so that we might be made whole.
**Receive our praise.**

We celebrate your awesome commitment,
    your refusal to be deflected from your chosen path.
You could have courted public acclaim,
    seized earthly power
    or secured personal gain,
    but instead you chose the way of humility,
    service and self-sacrifice,
    the lonely path of the cross.
You gave your life so that we might live.
You were broken so that we might be made whole.
**Receive our praise.**

We thank you for your faithfulness to the last,
    conscious of how tempting it must have been
    to save yourself instead of us.
You could have taken a road other than towards Jerusalem,
    walked away from Gethsemane,
    stepped down from the cross,
    but you didn't,
    preferring to put your will second to the will of the Father,
    your immediate future second to our eternal destiny.

You gave your life so that we might live.
You were broken so that we might be made whole.
**Receive our praise.**

Lord Jesus Christ,
    however often we hear it, we never fail to be amazed
        by the magnitude of your love
        and the awesomeness of your sacrifice.
    We deserve so little, yet you gave so much.
    We serve you so poorly, yet your grace is so rich.
    So we come in thanksgiving and celebration
        to offer you our heartfelt worship,
        and to commit ourselves again to your service.
    You gave your life so that we might live.
    You were broken so that we might be made whole.
**Receive our praise.**

For your name's sake.
**Amen.**                                                    NICK FAWCETT


## Prayer of approach

Lord Jesus Christ,
    you invited all who love you,
        all who sincerely desire to be your disciples,
        to share together in this Supper.
    So now we come around this table,
        in fellowship with you,
        with one another,
        and with all your people in every place and time.
    Lord Jesus, as we come to you,
        **so come to us.**

We come to remember your sharing bread and wine
        with your disciples in the upper room;
        a simple expression of fellowship
        with one who would soon betray you,
        one who would deny you,
        and others who would abandon you.
    Lord Jesus, as we come to you,
        **so come to us.**

We come to remember your anguish in Gethsemane
        as you faced the awful, awesome cost of your calling, alone.
    Lord Jesus, as we come to you,
        **so come to us.**

We come to remember your arrest and brutal interrogation,
   your sorrow and humiliation,
   your suffering and death.
Lord Jesus, as we come to you,
   **so come to us.**

We come to remember your quiet acceptance
   of human evil and hatred directed against you,
   you who had done no evil and knew no hate.
Lord Jesus, as we come to you,
   **so come to us.**

Lord Jesus Christ,
   we remember your great love,
      and we marvel at how much you were willing to bear
      for our sakes!
So now we praise, thank and worship you,
   with all our hearts and minds and souls.
Lord Jesus, as we come to you,
   **so come to us,**
   **for your name's sake.**
   **Amen.**

NICK FAWCETT

## Confession – thanksgiving and petition

Lord Jesus Christ,
   we find it hard to walk the Way of the Cross,
      hard to face persecution,
      hard even to risk opposition.
   We want to be popular,
      accepted,
      one of the crowd,
      not different from all the rest.
   **Teach us to follow your way.**

Lord Jesus Christ,
   forgive us all the times
      we have shied away from our responsibilities,
      taking the easy path,
      the way of least resistance.
   **Teach us to follow your way.**

Forgive us that whenever possible
   we have avoided the cost of discipleship,
      serving ourselves instead of others.
   **Teach us to follow your way.**

We thank you for those who have the courage
   to stand up for their convictions,
   and stand out against everything they believe to be wrong.
**Teach us to follow your way.**

We thank you that there are some ready to accept censure,
   even hostility,
   for the sake of what they know to be right.
Give us something of their faith and their courage,
   so that when the moment of challenge comes
   we shall not be found wanting.
**Teach us to follow your way,**
   **for in your name we pray.**
   **Amen.**                                          Nick Fawcett

## Petition

Lord Jesus Christ,
   we will never know just what you felt
      in that week leading up to the cross,
      but what we do know
      is that you were human just as we are,
      experiencing the same emotions that we feel,
      wrestling with the same pressures and temptations.
   And we have little doubt how we would have acted
      had we been in your shoes,
      facing the awful prospect of suffering and death –
      our love of life so great,
      our fear of death so strong.
   Yet though you were tempted like us,
      and though you longed for the cup of suffering
      to be taken from you,
      you stayed true to your calling,
      faithful to the last.
   When we face trials in turn,
      **Lord, deliver us from evil.**

We marvel at the constancy of your love,
   at the fact that though, from the beginning of your ministry,
   you knew what it would cost you,
   still you continued on your chosen path,
   refusing to be deflected from your purpose.
You could have used your powers for your own ends,
   succumbed to the attraction of popular acclaim
   and worldly glory,

and had it been us in your place,
we would probably have done precisely that,
our yearning for acceptance so great,
our fear of rejection so strong.
Yet though you were tempted like us,
and though you longed to see your kingdom
established here on earth,
you stayed true to your calling,
faithful to the last.
When we face trials in turn,
**Lord, deliver us from evil.**

We rejoice that you refused
to compromise your mission in any way,
your thoughts all for others rather than yourself.
While we would have toned down our message,
avoided controversy,
taken the course of least resistance,
you refused even to countenance such an option,
knowing that to do so
would have been to deprive people of your love,
and to dilute the good news you had come to bring.
You healed the sick even on the Sabbath,
you proclaimed forgiveness of sins,
you dined with those deemed the dregs of society,
condemning hypocrisy and corruption,
and overturning the tables of the money-changers in the temple.
We know we would have taken an easier path,
avoiding confrontation wherever possible,
our instinct for self-preservation so great,
our fear of suffering so strong.
Yet though you were tempted like us,
and though you longed for the cup of suffering
to be taken from you,
you stayed true to your calling,
faithful to the last.
When we face trials in turn,
**Lord, deliver us from evil.**

Lord Jesus Christ,
we rejoice today at the wonder of your love,
and we pray for strength to walk in your footsteps,
firm in our faith and true to our calling.
Hear our prayer,
for your name's sake.
**Amen.**                                        NICK FAWCETT

## Intercession

Lord Jesus Christ,
  we are reminded today that you were broken for us,
    that you gladly endured sorrow, suffering and death
    for our sakes.
  You identified yourself with humanity,
    standing alongside the broken-hearted,
    accepting the limitations of life and death.
  So now we pray for all who are broken in body, mind or spirit.
  Lord, in your mercy,
    **hear our prayer.**

We pray for those who are in pain,
    racked by illness and disease,
    physically disabled,
    maimed or injured through war, terrorism,
    disaster or accident.
  Lord, in your mercy,
    **hear our prayer.**

We pray for those who mourn loved ones
    or who face death themselves,
    those tormented by fear or anxiety,
    the mentally ill or handicapped,
    and all who are confused or overwhelmed
    by the complexities of daily life.
  Lord, in your mercy,
    **hear our prayer.**

We pray for those whose spirit
    has been broken in the storms of life –
    overwhelmed by sorrow,
    overcome by disappointment,
    crushed by tragedy.
  Lord, in your mercy,
    **hear our prayer.**

We pray for those whose faith has been battered
    by the harsh realities of this world –
    their confidence shaken,
    their trust destroyed,
    their love grown cold.
  Lord, in your mercy,
    **hear our prayer.**

Lord Jesus Christ,
  who endured such turmoil of mind in Gethsemane,
    whose body was broken on the cross,
    who surrendered your spirit to the Father,
    reach out now in love and compassion
    to all in any such need,
    bringing the assurance of your presence,
    the comfort of your peace,
    and the joy of your love.
  Lord, in your mercy,
    **hear our prayer,**
    **for we ask it in your name.**
    **Amen.**                                                NICK FAWCETT


## Short prayers

Lord Jesus Christ,
  you broke bread, you shared wine –
  with the one you knew would betray you,
  with the one you knew would deny you,
  with those you knew would soon abandon you to your fate.
Despite everything you stayed true,
  freely offering your life.
Lord Jesus Christ,
  you invite us to break bread and share wine,
  even though we too betray you,
  we too deny you,
  we too abandon you time after time.
Despite everything you stay true to us,
  your body broken, your blood shed, for us!
Lord Jesus Christ,
  we praise you and thank you with all our hearts.        NICK FAWCETT


Lord Jesus Christ,
  we are here at your invitation –
  here to share, as so many have shared before us,
  in your supper,
  this simple act which you commanded us to do
  in remembrance of you.
We come, then, to remember –
  to remind ourselves of all you suffered
  to set us free,
  to recall the extent of your love
  and the enormity of your sacrifice.

But we come also to celebrate –
    to rejoice in all you have done for us
    through your death,
    and to thank you for all you go on doing for us
    through what you achieved there on the cross.
Lord Jesus Christ,
    you broke bread,
    you poured wine,
    your body broken,
    your blood shed for us.
Help us, as we eat and drink together,
    to receive you more completely into our hearts,
    to welcome you more fully into our lives,
    and so to represent you more truly
    as your body here on earth,
    until that day when we are wholly one with you,
    and you are all in all.
Amen.                                                          NICK FAWCETT

# All-age-talk material

## Sign of Christ's presence

### Aim

To show that Holy Communion is a special meal which speaks powerfully of everything God has done for us in Christ.

### Preparation

Print the following on separate strips of card:

| | |
|---|---|
| Shrove Tuesday | Pancake |
| Christmas | Christmas pudding |
| Cream tea | Scone, jam and cream |
| Good Friday | Hot cross bun |
| Wedding reception | Wedding cake |
| Picnic | Cakes and biscuits |
| Barbecue | Hot dog |
| Breakfast | Cornflakes |
| Passover Festival | Bitter herbs |
| Garden party | Tea and cucumber sandwiches |
| Birthday party | Jelly and blancmange |
| McDonald's | Hamburger |
| Burns' Night | Haggis |
| Harvest supper | Fruit and vegetables/Bread and wine |

Arrange those in the first column down the left-hand side of a display board. With a piece of Blu-Tack stick the items in the second column around the front of the church where they are visible to all. (If you're feeling adventurous, you might consider offering samples of the items in the right-hand column for volunteers to taste.)

### Talk

Explain that around the church you have scattered the names of different types of food, all of which might be eaten in different places and at different kinds of meals. Invite volunteers to come forward and match the foods to the occasions on the board (as above).

These occasions are all different meals in which we might share at different times. Some are for celebrating; some are about remembering the past; some are simply a way of sharing socially. But how about the two things left over, bread and wine – when might we use these? The answer, of course, is the occasion we call Holy Communion, or Eucharist, or the Lord's Supper. A simple but special meal which is not only a way of sharing together but also a way of remembering and celebrating. And in this week, of all weeks, we remember how that meal started, as Jesus shared his last supper with his disciples.

They had gathered together to share in the traditional Jewish celebration of Passover: a meal and a festival at the heart of the Jewish faith.

> This day shall be a day of remembrance for you . . . When your children ask you, 'What do you mean by this observance?' you shall say, 'It is the Passover sacrifice to the Lord, for he passed over the houses of the Israelites in Egypt, when he struck down the Egyptians but spared our houses.' *(Exodus 12:14)*

For the Jews this was, and is still, a way of remembering and celebrating all God had done for them, most particularly in delivering them from slavery in Egypt centuries before. It is a meal which unites them as individual families and as a nation, in a common faith.

But there, in a simple upstairs room, and an even simpler meal, Jesus gave this festival a new meaning to his followers. Suddenly it spoke not of what God had done centuries before, but of what he was doing there and then among them. And across the centuries since, this meal of bread and wine has spoken to countless people of what God has done and is still doing in Jesus Christ. It reminds us first that Jesus died for our sakes on the cross:

> While they were eating, Jesus took a loaf of bread, and after blessing it he broke it, gave it to his disciples and said, 'Take, eat, this is my body.' *(Matthew 26:26)*

It reminds us also that he rose again and is with us now:

> Then they told what had happened, and how Jesus had been made known to them in the breaking of the bread. *(Luke 24:35)*

And it reminds us finally that Jesus will come again to establish his kingdom and rule the earth:

> I tell you, I will never again drink of this fruit of the vine until that day when I drink it new with you in my Father's kingdom. (*Matthew 26:27*)

A meal can simply be a time for enjoying food, or for sharing; a time for remembering the past, or for celebrating a special occasion. But this meal, though simpler probably than any, says more than all, for it is a testimony to God's love and a sign of Christ's presence.

NICK FAWCETT

# Reflective material
## (sketches, meditations and poems)

### Drama: Jesus on the edge

(Before you begin, make sure the point is driven home that this story, although sad and rather threatening, worked out wonderfully well in the end. But the children won't actually get to it this week.)

**Narrator**   Jesus was very unhappy. He'd just had his last supper with his disciples, and he knew that he was soon going to die. People who hated him were plotting to get rid of him. He trusted his Father God to work things out, but he knew it was going to be very scary and very painful along the way. His disciples followed as he got up from the table and led them to the Garden of Gethsemane. Thomas was worried.

**Thomas**   Jesus seems very thoughtful tonight, James. I get the feeling something really dreadful's going to happen.

**James**   Oh, I wouldn't worry, Thomas. God'll keep us safe – he's good like that – he won't let any harm come to Jesus.

**Thomas**   Well, I don't know. I trust God of course, but I don't think it's quite as simple as that.

**Narrator**   By now, they'd arrived in the garden. They'd never seen Jesus look so upset – and it was Peter's turn to be worried.

**Peter**   If I didn't know better, I'd say he was frightened.

**Jesus**   Peter, James and John, you come with me. The rest of you, sit here while I go and pray.

**Narrator**   Jesus led his three closest friends a little further on.

**Jesus**      This is a very difficult time for me. Will you watch with me?

**Narrator**   Then Jesus went a little further on his own and lay down on the ground to pray.

**Jesus**      Father, this is awful – isn't there some way I can avoid what's going to happen? Isn't there another way? But it's your will that matters, so I'll go through it if I have to.

**Narrator**   He got up and walked back to his three friends, who had fallen fast asleep.

**Jesus**      Oh, Peter, couldn't you manage to stay awake for just one hour, to pray with me? Come on, stay awake – pray that you don't have to go through what I'm going to. I know you mean well, but you're just not strong enough to hack it.

**Narrator**   As he went way, the disciples looked at one another in bewilderment.

**James**      What was that all about?

**John**       I dunno, but I wish we could just go home – it's scary here.

**Narrator**   He was right. It was very dark, with the moonlight casting sinister shadows among the trees – but that was nothing compared with the fear that Jesus was feeling as he lay down again to pray to his Father.

**Jesus**      It's not that I don't trust you, Father, but this is such a terrible thing I'm going to have to bear, and I really wish there was another way. Surely, we can avoid it somehow? Still, it's your will that matters, not mine.

**Narrator**   When Jesus went back to his friends, they were completely out of it – fast asleep and dead to the world. This time, he didn't wake them but went and prayed again – saying just the same as before. The silence was terrible. Although he prayed harder than ever he had prayed in his life, there seemed to be no answer. Just that awesome silence – not even the rustling of the usual wildlife or the movement of the breeze. Nothing. It was as if all creation was holding its breath to see what Jesus would do. Jesus knew what he had to do. But knowing didn't make it easy. For what seemed like hours he lay there on the ground, praying, but all his words seemed just to vanish into the still, horrible silence of the night. Eventually, he got up and went back to his sleeping friends.

**Jesus**      Time to wake up. This is it – I've got to do what God sent me to do. Look, they've come to get me.

**Narrator**  Suddenly, the garden was full of people with swords and sticks, all looking for Jesus. Jesus faced up to them calmly.

**Jesus**  I'm the one you want. Let my friends go.

**Narrator**  Peter wanted to make a fight of it, and pulled out a sword; but Jesus stopped him.

**Jesus**  I've preached love and non-violence all my ministry, and I'm not going to throw all that away just to save my own skin.

**Narrator**  So Jesus was captured and led away, and his friends turned and ran. Jesus had made his choice. He stayed true to God, and true to his own faith. Even as they nailed him to the cross, he prayed for them and kept on trusting God. When he died, some people thought it was all over – but it wasn't. He'd won the battle – he'd kept faith with God even when everything seemed hopeless. And now, God was going to keep faith with him – soon he would be raised to wonderful new life. And that's the story for next week. Let's not miss it!

MICHAEL FORSTER

## Meditation of Peter

It was ready for us, just as he'd said it would be,
   everything arranged,
   everything in its place,
   down to the very last detail,
   as if our arrival there had been planned long before;
   yet – can you believe it? – still the penny didn't drop!
It was only later –
   after we'd shared supper together,
   after his enemies had come for him in the garden,
   after they'd beaten him, broken him,
   nailed him to the cross –
   it was only then that the awesome truth suddenly hit us:
   he *had* planned it! –
   every move, every step, meticulously prepared,
   weeks, months, even years beforehand –
   and our minds reeled at the enormity of it all.
When we'd walked by his side,
   blissfully unaware of anything untoward,
   he'd known that death was waiting for him,
   lurking greedily around the corner.
When we watched as he healed the sick and comforted the distressed,
   his thoughts all for others rather than himself,
   he was aware, nonetheless, of the awful fate in store for him,
   the horror, the hurt, the humiliation.

When we'd accompanied him proudly as he entered Jerusalem,
    basking in his reflected glory,
    revelling in the adulation,
    he'd had one eye already fixed on the days ahead –
    on this last meal we would share together,
    on the darkness to come in Gethsemane,
    on the torture of crucifixion.
Suddenly it all made sense –
    how that stranger had been waiting to meet us inside the city,
    how we'd only to say 'The teacher asks . . .'
    and it was done,
    how we were shown upstairs to that little room
    without any need for explanation.
He'd realised, all along,
    probably from the very beginning,
    that this moment would come,
    that the path he had chosen would lead to suffering and death,
    yet still he carried on,
    undeterred,
    undaunted.
And as that truth dawned on me, a lump came to my throat,
    for he'd done it, willingly, for people like me.
He'd known I would deny him,
    that we'd all fail him in our own way,
    yet it didn't matter,
    still he cared enough to die for us.
He saw us at our worst,
    recognising our deepest weaknesses,
    yet still he walked the way of the cross,
    faithful to the last.
I can't believe it, even now –
    that anyone could love us that much –
    but it's true,
    I saw the proof for myself.
We deserved nothing, as he well knew,
    yet he went to the cross
    and gave everything.

Nick Fawcett

## Meditation of Judas Iscariot

'Do what you have to do,' he told me.
And I realised then, as he looked at me,
    from the expression in his eyes,
    that he knew full well what I'd been up to,
    and understood precisely what I had planned for later that evening.

Call me a fool, but I thought until then I'd covered my tracks,
    played the part of doting disciple to a tee.
And I was right to a point,
    for my fellow apostles fell for it hook, line and sinker.
You should have seen their faces
    when Jesus suddenly turned during supper
    and solemnly announced that one of us would betray him.
'Who is it, Lord?' they gasped. 'Surely not I?'
But they actually believed it might be –
    as much one of them as me.
Not Jesus though –
    I realised the moment he looked at me
    that there was no pulling the wool over his eyes.
He saw through the charade,
    behind the lamb to the wolf,
    beneath the dove to the serpent,
    and suddenly I was ashamed,
    sickened by what I was doing,
    disgusted at what I'd become.
I should have stopped it there and then,
    confessed everything before them all and begged for mercy.
But I didn't.
I was too proud,
    afraid of losing face,
    terrified of what Caiaphas might do to me
    if I failed to deliver the goods.
So I slithered out of the room,
    leaving the rest of them wide-eyed in disbelief.
It still wasn't too late, even then –
    I could have called a halt to the whole business,
    and I only wish I had.
But I didn't –
    I led the soldiers into the garden,
    and greeted Jesus with a kiss –
    the last revolting act of a repulsive evening.
It was bad enough betraying a friend,
    but what made it worse
    was that we'd eaten together such a short time before.
He'd washed my feet,
    shared bread and wine,
    kept faith with me to the very last, despite everything.
If he'd cursed me,
    accused me,
    rebuked me,
    it would have made it easier.

If he'd only shown some sign of resentment,
   maybe then I could have lived with myself,
   knowing he wasn't so perfect after all.
But there was none of that.
A hint of sorrow, perhaps,
   but apart from that, only love,
   compassion, forgiveness.
He knew what was happening, yet it made no difference.
He knew I was leading him to his death,
   and he carried on regardless.
Why?
You tell me!
I only hope he had more idea what he was doing than I had.      Nick Fawcett

## Meditation of Peter

He warned me it would happen,
   told me exactly how it would be,
   but I just didn't believe him.
If he'd said anyone else I'd have thought otherwise –
   I mean you can't trust anyone finally can you, not even your friends?
And, to be honest, I expected a few of them to cave in
   when the pressure was on.
But me, I felt I was different.
It was me after all whom he called to be his first disciple,
   me who realised he was the Messiah
   when the rest were still groping in the dark,
   me he called 'The Rock'.
And I thought I was just that:
   unshakeable,
   firm,
   dependable.
I'm not saying I was better than anyone else,
   just that my faith always seemed stronger.
So I told him,
   confidently,
   proudly,
   'Though all else fail you I will not.
   Lord, I am ready to die for you.'
God, how those words haunt me now,
   how stupid they make me feel.
If only I'd kept my mouth shut,
   if only I hadn't been so full of myself,
   if only I'd had more courage.
We all failed him, all of us in our own way.

They look at me and say, 'He denied him.'
They talk of Judas and say, 'He betrayed him.'
They point at the others and say, 'They abandoned him.'
Well, let them judge if they want to.
Let them imagine they're a cut above the rest;
    I've learnt the hard way that I'm not.                    NICK FAWCETT

## Meditation of one who arrested Jesus

To be perfectly honest, I thought he'd run for it the moment he saw us,
    make himself scarce before it was too late.
He must have seen us coming,
    heard us at any rate,
    what with the noise we made marching into the garden.
He must have known the game was up,
    the writing on the wall,
    long before that so-called friend of his singled him out.
But he just stood there,
    watching,
    waiting,
    almost as though he wanted it to happen,
    as though he was relieved to see us.
Yet it wasn't that simple –
    not that simple at all.
In fact, even now, years later,
    it's still a mystery,
    a puzzle I'm constantly trying to unravel.
You see, in some ways he was just a man, that Jesus,
    like you or me,
    with all the emotions you'd expect to see –
    fear,
    despair,
    hurt.
Yet there was more;
    feelings I hadn't expected to see,
    emotions that made no sense –
    peace,
    assurance,
    expectation.
He looked at that snake Judas,
    and there wasn't hate in his eyes such as I would have felt –
    there was love!

He looked at us,
    and there wasn't that usual mixture of resentment and contempt –
    there was understanding,
    forgiveness,
    even pity.
And when one of his followers tried to make a fight of it,
    whipping out his sword and hacking off one of my men's ears,
    he didn't laugh or gloat –
    he reached out and healed the fellow, right before our very eyes.
I wish we could have more like him, I can tell you,
    a welcome change from the usual rabble we have to deal with.
To be honest I couldn't make out why we were arresting him;
    he seemed harmless enough,
    likeable, in fact,
    not at all the villain they made him out to be.
But orders are orders –
    I was just doing my job, that's all.
And I suppose he must have done something to deserve his fate.
So we marched him away –
    off to Caiaphas,
    off to Herod,
    off to Pilate,
    off to the cross.
He could have run for it, I'm sure of that,
    and when I saw what they did to him, I almost wished he had.
Yet he didn't run, and I don't think he ever would have,
    for looking back it still seems to me, strange though it may seem,
    that it wasn't us in the garden coming for him,
    but he who was waiting for us.                    NICK FAWCETT


## The Choice

Bread of God
    broken for us,
    wine of God
    crushed for us;

Grain ground down
    to give us food,
    grapes destroyed
    to give us drink,

    each dying
    to become
    something greater.

Lord, you gave us
   the pattern of life
   in this bread
   and this wine,
   the ancient message
   that is quickly
   forgotten by
   every generation;
   the law of love
   that was laid down
   before the foundation
   of the world,

   that there is
   no gaining
   without losing,
   no joy
   without pain,
   no singing
   without sadness,
   no light
   without darkness,
   no living
   without dying.

For without breaking
   the bread will be
   locked in the grain,
   without crushing
   the wine will
   stay in the grapes,
   each of us
   must die to become
   something greater.

Bread of God
   broken for us,
   wine of God
   crushed for us

   you gave us
   the pattern,
   you came to show
   us the way

   – but the choice
   is ours.

MARY HATHAWAY

# Good Friday

*The victory of love over evil, suffering and death*

## John 18:1–19:42

*(also Isaiah 52:13–53:12; Psalm 22; Hebrews 10:16-25 or 4:14-16, 5:7-9)*

## A reading from the Gospel of John (18:1-12)

### The Last Days

*In the Garden*         *John 18:1-12*

Jesus left the house with his friends and crossed the Kidron Brook to the other side of the valley. They came to a garden and went inside. They knew it well, for Jesus and his friends had often met there.

Judas knew this, and he led a detachment of Roman soldiers and a company of Jewish police straight to the spot. They were fully armed and carried lanterns and torches.

Jesus stepped out to meet them. 'Who do you want?' he asked.

'Jesus from Nazareth,' they answered.

'I'm the man you want, then,' said Jesus.

At these words, they stepped back and fell on the ground.

'Who do you want?' asked Jesus again.

'Jesus from Nazareth,' they repeated.

'I've told you – I'm the man you want,' he said. 'If it's me you're after, let these men go.'

Peter drew his sword and struck at a slave of the High Priest and cut off his right ear.

'Put your sword up,' said Jesus. 'Do you want to stop me facing what God the Father has set before me?'

The soldiers then arrested Jesus and handcuffed him.

*Before Annas*         *John 18:13, 15-27*

The soldiers took Jesus before Annas, the most powerful man in Jerusalem City. He was not the High Priest of the Jewish people. Caiaphas was the High Priest that year; Annas was his father-in-law.

Now Jesus had a friend whose name we do not know. He was not one of the 'Twelve', but belonged to one of the most important families in Jerusalem; the High Priest knew him well. He was the 'other friend'.

Peter and the 'other friend' followed Jesus along the road. When they got to the courtyard, the 'other friend' went straight in with Jesus; Peter was left standing outside at the door. The 'other friend' came back and had a word with the girl on duty at the door and then took him inside.

'You're one of this fellow's friends, too, aren't you?' the girl asked Peter.

'Not I,' said Peter.

It was a cold night, and the slaves and court officers had lit a charcoal fire. They were standing round it, trying to keep warm. Peter joined the crowd round the fire; he wanted to get warm too.

The High Priest asked Jesus about his friends and what he stood for.

'What I have had to say,' said Jesus, 'I have said openly for everybody to hear. I have talked in the Meeting Houses, and I have talked in the Temple to Jewish people from all over the world. I have not been plotting in back rooms. Why ask me questions now? Ask the ordinary people in the villages and in this city. They heard me. They know what it was I talked about.'

One of the court officials standing near him gave him a slap on the face.

'Is that the way to talk to the High Priest?' he said.

'If I did something wrong,' said Jesus to the officer, 'prove it. If I didn't, why hit me?'

Annas had Jesus handcuffed again and sent to Caiaphas.

Peter was still standing near the fire, getting warm.

'You are one of this fellow's friends too, aren't you?' said some of the men by the fire.

'Not on your life,' said Peter.

Now it happened that one of the court officers standing there was a relative of the man Peter had slashed with his sword.

'I saw you in the garden with him, didn't I?' he asked.

'No, you didn't,' said Peter.

At that moment, somewhere in the distance a cock crowed.

*Before the Roman Governor*                         *John 18:28-31, 33-40; 19:1-16a*

It was now Friday, the day before the Great Feast.

Just before dawn Jesus was marched into the headquarters of Pilate, the Roman Governor.

The Jewish leaders stayed outside the building (it was 'unclean' to them because it belonged to foreigners, and, if they had gone inside, they would not have been allowed, by Jewish law, to take part in the Great Feast). So Pilate came outside.

'What's the charge against this man?' he asked.

'He's a criminal,' they said. 'Would we have brought him here if he wasn't?'

'Well, take him off and deal with him yourselves,' said Pilate. 'You've got your own laws and law courts.'

'But we can't pass the death sentence,' they replied.

Pilate went back into the building and had Jesus brought before him.

'So you're the Jewish King, are you?' he said.

'Are those your own words?' asked Jesus. 'Or are you just repeating what other people have told you?'

'Do I look like a Jew!' said Pilate. 'You've been brought here by your own leaders. What have you been up to?'

'I'm no nationalist,' said Jesus. 'My men would have been out on the streets fighting, if I were – they wouldn't have let me be arrested so easily. My "kingdom" has nothing to do with that sort of thing.'

'So you *are* a "king", then,' said Pilate.

'The word is yours,' said Jesus. 'I was born to defend the truth. Anybody who cares for the truth knows what I am talking about.'

'What is truth?' said Pilate. And with that he went outside again.

'As far as this court is concerned,' he told the crowd, 'there is nothing this man can be charged with. I've been in the habit of setting one prisoner free for you at the Feast. What about letting "the Jewish King" go free this year?'

The crowd broke into a roar. 'Not this man, but Barabbas!'

(Barabbas was one of the terrorists in the Resistance Movement.)

So Pilate had Jesus flogged, and the soldiers – as was often their custom with prisoners – made sport of him. They made a crown out of some thorn twigs and crowned him with it, and dressed him in a soldier's purple cloak. Then they kept coming up to him, saluting him with 'Long live Your Majesty!' and slapping him on the face.

Pilate went out to the crowd again.

'Here he is,' he said. 'I'm going to bring him out to you to make it clear that there is nothing this court can charge him with.'

Jesus was brought outside, still wearing the mock crown and the purple cloak.

'There's the man!' said Pilate.

When the Jewish leaders and their officers caught sight of him, they started shouting.

'The cross! Let's have him on the gallows!'

'Take him and put him on a cross yourselves,' said Pilate. 'He's done nothing this court can deal with!'

'But we've a law of blasphemy,' they answered, 'and by that law he ought to be executed – he claims to be equal with God himself!'

That last sentence frightened Pilate. He went back again into the building.

'Where were you born?' he asked Jesus.

Jesus didn't speak.

'I'm the Governor, you know – why don't you say something?' said Pilate. 'Don't you know I can set you free or have you executed?'

'You would have no power over me at all,' said Jesus, 'if God had not given it to you. The man who handed me over to you is more guilty than you.'

From that moment Pilate made up his mind to set him free.

But the shouting of the crowd went on.

'If you let this man go, you're no friend of the Emperor! Anybody who calls himself a king is an enemy of the Emperor!'

Pilate heard what they were shouting.

He brought Jesus outside again, and took his seat as Governor and Judge at the place called 'The Pavement'. It was now just midday.

'Here's your "King"!' he said.

'Take him away! Hang him on a cross!' the crowd shouted.

'So it's your "King" I'm to hang on a cross?' he asked.

'The Emperor is the only King we've got!' they shouted back.

Pilate handed him over for execution.

*At Skull Hill*                                                                    *John 19:16b-35, 38-42*

The soldiers marched Jesus off, and, with his own cross on his shoulders, he went out of the building to Skull Hill, a place quite near the city. And there they hung him on the cross. Three men were hung on crosses that day – Jesus in the middle, the other two on either side of him.

Pilate had a notice written out in three languages, Jewish, Roman and Greek: JESUS OF NAZARETH, THE JEWISH KING. He had it fastened on the cross. Crowds of citizens read it.

'Don't put the JEWISH KING,' the Jewish leaders protested to Pilate. 'Put – HE SAID HE WAS THE JEWISH KING.'

'It stays as I wrote it,' said Pilate.

When the four soldiers had carried out their orders, they picked up the clothes of Jesus and made four bundles, one for each of them. Then they picked up his tunic. This was one piece of cloth, woven from top to bottom, not made up of several pieces.

'We mustn't tear it up,' they said. 'Let's toss for it.'

That is what they did.

All this time, his mother, his aunt Mary, the wife of Clopas, and Mary from Magdala were standing near the cross itself. Jesus caught sight of his mother – and the friend he loved dearly standing by her side.

'Mother,' he said, 'take my friend as your son.'

'Take my mother as your mother,' he said to his friend.

And from that time, his friend took her into his own home.

'I am thirsty,' said Jesus.

A full jar of sour wine had been put nearby for the guard. The soldier soaked a sponge in it, stuck it on a javelin and put it up to his mouth. Jesus drank it.

'My work is done,' he said.

His head dropped, and he died.

The Jewish leaders did not want the bodies on the crosses to stay there over the Saturday, the Holy Day of the Jews, especially since this was a very important Saturday, the first day of the Great Feast. They asked Pilate to have the men's legs broken to make them die quickly, and then to have the bodies taken away.

This is what the soldiers began to do. They broke the legs of the two men hanging on either side of Jesus, one after the other. They went up to Jesus, but they found that he was already dead. They didn't break his legs, but one of the soldiers jabbed a lance into his side, and water and blood flowed out. (This is what happened; it is the evidence of an eyewitness who can be trusted.)

After all this, two men went to Pilate – Joseph from the village of Arimathea (he was a member of the Jewish Council; he had kept his friendship with Jesus a secret, for he was afraid of what the Council might do) and Nicodemus (who, as we have told, first met Jesus at night).

Joseph asked Pilate to let him take the body of Jesus down from the cross, and Pilate agreed. So his friends came and took his body away, and wrapped it in linen sheets with spices which Nicodemus had brought, more than seventy pounds weight of perfume mixture. (This is the Jewish method of burial.)

There was a large garden nearby. In it there was a new tomb – nobody had yet been buried there.

It was now getting on for six o'clock in the evening, the time when the Holy Day began. The tomb lay near at hand; so they put Jesus there.

ALAN DALE

# Introductory material

Imagine you are one of those in the crowd that has followed the path of Jesus to the place called Golgotha. You have watched thus far in horror, but now you close your eyes, unable to look any more at the scenes unfolding before you, yet you cannot block out the sounds of what is happening; sounds which are equally if not more dreadful. The ringing of the hammer as it drives the nails mercilessly through the flesh of Jesus. The involuntary gasps of agony as the cross is lifted up and those skewered hands and feet begin to tear under his weight. The raucous jeers of the crowd as they gather round to gloat, mingled with the sobs of women close by, their hearts close to breaking. Surely it will be over soon? Nothing can be worse than this! And then it comes, the most terrible, haunting sound of all; a cry of such torment, such desolation, that your blood runs cold: 'My God, my God, why have you forsaken me?' And suddenly you realise, for the first time, just how much this man dying before you has gone through; the full extent of his suffering, the wonder of his sacrifice. Today, as best we may, we stand by that cross again. We listen, we watch, we marvel!

NICK FAWCETT

# Prayers

## Confession – a man of sorrows

Lord Jesus Christ,
>    you know what it is to feel sorrow,
>        for you endured some of the deepest hurt
>        anyone could ever face.

You were betrayed by one of your chosen followers,
    denied by another who you counted as the closest of friends,
    abandoned by those who had followed you
    throughout your ministry,
    and yet still you were willing to give everything for them,
    even life itself.
For all the ways we add to your sorrow,
    **Lord, have mercy.**

Forgive us that we prolong your grief each day,
    betraying our convictions,
    denying our faith through the way we live,
    abandoning your way and rejecting your love.
We are weak and faithless,
    proud, greedy, selfish,
    careless in discipleship
    and poor in our commitment.
For all the ways we add to your sorrow,
    **Lord, have mercy.**

You brought life to the world,
    hope, love and light,
    but you endured the heartbreak of seeing it all rejected,
    the world turning its back on your grace
    and spurning your goodness.
Forgive us that sometimes we do the same,
    keeping you at arm's length,
    resisting your guidance,
    even while we believe we are serving you.
For all the ways we add to your sorrow,
    **Lord, have mercy.**

Lord Jesus Christ,
    you endured pain and humiliation,
        an inner turmoil beyond words,
        and you faced that for *us* as much as anyone.
    You were wounded for *our* transgressions,
        crushed for *our* iniquities.
    You bore the punishment which made *us* whole,
        and by *your* bruises *we* are healed.
    We thank you for the awesomeness of your grace,
        and we acknowledge with shame the poverty of our response.
    Forgive us our failure to honour you as you deserve,
        our inability to love as you have loved us.
For all the ways we add to your sorrow,
    **Lord, have mercy.**

Hear us,
    cleanse us
    and renew us,
    for in your name we pray.
**Amen.**

NICK FAWCETT

## The pain of Christ

Lord Jesus Christ,
    on this day we marvel again at the extent of your love,
        and especially the pain you were ready to face
        so that we might receive life in all its fullness;
        a pain that goes far beyond anything
        we can ever imagine or understand.
    Gracious Lord, for all you willingly endured,
        **we thank you.**

We remember the pain of body
    as thorns were twisted into your head,
    as the lash tore into your body,
    as you staggered under the weight of the cross,
    as nails were hammered into your hands and feet,
    as you writhed in agony,
    waiting for the blissful release of death.
Gracious Lord, for all you willingly endured,
    **we thank you.**

We remember the pain of mind
    as you came to terms with the betrayal of Judas,
    the denial of Peter,
    the faithlessness of your followers,
    and the shouts of 'Crucify!'
    from those who just days before
    had welcomed you as their king.
Gracious Lord, for all you willingly endured,
    **we thank you.**

We remember the pain of spirit
    as you bore the sins of the world on your shoulders,
    as you experienced that dreadful sense of isolation from God,
    as you felt yourself to be abandoned,
    left there to face the awfulness of your fate, alone.
Gracious Lord, for all you willingly endured,
    **we thank you.**

Lord Jesus Christ,
  we can never begin to grasp what you went through,
      nor ever fully appreciate
      the scale of the suffering you endured.
  But we know that yours was a love greater
      than any we can ever show,
      and a sacrifice more costly
      than any we can ever offer.
  Gracious Lord, for all you willingly endured,
      **we thank you.**

Open our eyes to the wonder of this day,
      and help us to respond in the only way we can –
      with heartfelt gratitude,
      with joyful praise,
      and with loving service,
      offered in your name and for your glory.
  Gracious Lord, for all you willingly endured,
      **we thank you.**
      **Amen.**                                    NICK FAWCETT

## Intercession

Lord Jesus Christ,
  broken on the cross,
      tortured there in body, mind and soul,
      you know what it means to suffer.
  So now we pray today for the broken people of our world,
      all those who have experienced something of your pain.
  **Reach out in love, and make them whole.**

We pray for the broken in body –
      those injured in accidents,
      those maimed in war,
      those disabled by disease.
  **Reach out in love, and make them whole.**

We pray for the broken in mind –
      those tormented by fears,
      those wrestling with depression,
      those who have suffered a mental breakdown.
  **Reach out in love, and make them whole.**

We pray for the broken in spirit –
      those whose dreams have been destroyed,
      those whose love has been betrayed,
      those whose faith has been crushed.
  **Reach out in love, and make them whole.**

Lord Jesus Christ,
   you came to make us all whole,
     to mend broken lives,
     to restore broken people.
   **Reach out in love, and make them whole,**
     **for in your name we ask it.**
     **Amen.**

NICK FAWCETT

## Short prayers

Lord Jesus Christ,
   there are many who suffer,
   many who have endured untold agony
   of body, mind and spirit,
   but there are few who do so willingly,
   fewer still who would choose that course
   as their vocation in life.
Yet you came and walked the way of the cross
   with single-minded determination,
   and you gave your life freely,
   so that one day there will be an end
   to all suffering and sorrow,
   a time when all will rejoice
   in the wonder of your love
   and experience the joy of your kingdom.
Until then, Lord, reach out
   into our world of darkness,
   into every place of need,
   and bring the comfort, the strength,
   the peace and the hope which you alone can bring.
In your name we ask it.
Amen.

NICK FAWCETT

Gracious God,
   when you seemed furthest away
   you were nearer than you had ever been,
   when you seemed at your most weak
   you were at your most strong,
   when you seemed overwhelmed by hatred
   you were enfolding all in love,
   when you seemed defeated
   you were victorious.

Gracious God,
  we come to you on this day
  which seemed so full of evil,
  yet which we can call 'Good Friday',
  and we thank you for the proof it brings us
  that no person, no place and no experience
  is outside your love or beyond your purpose.
Receive our praise,
  accept our thanks;
  through Jesus Christ our Lord.
Amen.                                              NICK FAWCETT


Lord Jesus Christ,
  there are no words sufficient
  to express the wonder of your love,
  no deeds sufficient
  to express the enormity of our gratitude,
  but we come asking that you will receive
  our worship, our faith and our lives
  as a token of our thanksgiving,
  and as a sign of our love for you.
Lord Jesus Christ,
  receive this day our heartfelt praise,
  and use us to your glory,
  for your name's sake.
Amen.                                              NICK FAWCETT


# Reflective material
## (sketches, meditations and poems)

### Inner

*(Place a bowl of water in front of you)*

Lord,
  often
  I grouch,
  I moan,
  I groan,
  complain,
  shout,
  mutter,
  mumble,

and, occasionally,
 I have been known
 to utter
 a few
 less than choice comments
 about the way I feel.
*(Dip hand in water. Lift your hand and allow the drips to fall back into the bowl)*
And
 while I'm constantly
 suggesting
 that this isn't the way things should be,
 you're constantly
 reminding me
*(Dip hand in water again and lift your hand)*
 about how much you love me
 and perhaps
 just occasionally
 it might be preferable
 to hear a few less comments
*(Dip hand into the water and then place your hand to your mouth)*
 and allow you
 to refresh
 my aching mind,
 my tired eyes
 and my dulled senses.
Lord,
 creator of life,
 giver of life,
 be with me
 now and for ever.
*(Place both hands into the water, lift them and allow the drops to fall back into the bowl)*
PETE TOWNSEND

## Outer

*(Have a jug of water and several glasses available)*
Lord,
 the voices of the thirsty
 cry out
 as we shield our eyes
 from the biting wind
 and stinging dust
 that attempt to stifle our cries.
*(Give everyone a glass of water)*

Lord,
  your love refreshes, reassures
  that we are never alone,
  never without a hope,
  never without someone
  to walk each step of the way.
*(Take a sip of water)*
Lord,
  take our lives
  and encourage us
  to be as one voice,
  calling in the desert
  to those who thirst
  to come to the one
  who provides
  streams in the barren land,
  which bring life
  where death once prevailed.
Lord,
  let your love flow
  to and through each one of us.

PETE TOWNSEND

I've discovered 'prayer' again.
Not in so many words
but coming to God in my blankness,
waiting to receive
rather than struggle for the right things to say.
This kind of praying is new to me
but it doesn't matter.
I must hang on to the shreds of my faith,
keep going through the crucifying experience –
God is there.
God is with me.
I am not alone.

ELIZABETH RUNDLE

As Jesus died the curtain in the temple split down the middle. The curtain screened the Most Holy Place, where the blood of the sacrifice was poured on the altar once a year, out of the view of everyone except the High Priest. The curtain was a symbol of the power of the High Priest; only he had the authority to go beyond the curtain which separated God and the people.

When Jesus died the curtain ripped from top to bottom. Not only did the torn curtain indicate that the power of the priests had come to an end, but also that

God had made the tear, from the top and not by the people. The sacrifice of Jesus, on the altar of the cross, dealt with sin for all time.

PETE TOWNSEND

## The end? Sacrifice or not?

**Official**  Nothing wrong with that report.*

**Soldier**  No, Sir.

**Official**  Jesus was dead.

**Soldier**  Yes, Sir.

**Official**  We Romans don't mess about.

**Soldier**  No, Sir.

**Official**  We take care of our business.

**Soldier**  Yes, Sir.

**Official**  Efficiency.

**Soldier**  Sir?

**Official**  That's how we run our empire. Efficiency. Efficiency, economy, and . . . everything else which is good about being a Roman.

**Soldier**  Yes, Sir.

**Official**  We don't crucify people for nothing.

**Soldier**  No, Sir. It's usually when people have committed a crime.

**Official**  Yes, well, in most cases that's true. There are always exceptions to rules, aren't there?

**Soldier**  Yes, Sir.

**Official**  Makes life more efficient.

**Soldier**  Yes, Sir.

**Official**  Tidy up loose ends. Make everything nice and neat, keep the wheels of the empire running smoothly.

**Soldier**  Clickety-clack. Clickety-clack.

**Official**  What?

**Soldier**  Chariots, Sir. Clickety-clack. Clickety-clack. That's what they sound like when they are running smoothly. Clickety-clack. Clickety-clack.

*See also Reflective material, 2nd, 3rd and 5th Sundays of Lent

**Official**    You ever been run over by a chariot, soldier?

**Soldier**    No, Sir.

**Official**    You want it to stay that way?

**Soldier**    Yes, Sir.

**Official**    Then SHUT UP!

**Soldier**    Sir!

**Official**    Efficiency. That's my motto. Efficiency.

**Soldier**    I thought that mottoes had more than one word, Sir.

**Official**    I thought we agreed that you were being silent.

**Soldier**    Sorry, Sir.

**Official**    How come there are more pages left in the report? That's not efficient, is it? Bad waste of paper if you ask me. Not very efficient at all.

**Soldier**    Well, Sir. There's a reason for more paper.

**Official**    There'd better be a good reason.

**Soldier**    You may not want to read it, Sir.

**Official**    Of course I do. It wouldn't be efficient if I didn't.

*Freeze.*                                                    TONY BOWER

## Meditation of Annas

He had it coming to him,
    you can't deny it.
We warned him what would happen,
    told him time and again to tone things down.
But would he listen?
Not a bit of it!
He knew our feelings –
    we'd made no secret of them –
    and he knew the risks as well as any.
Many's the time we tried to stone him,
    and we would have done too, but for the crowds.
Yet he kept on preaching,
    kept on violating the Sabbath,
    kept on blaspheming the name of God.
Oh, I know he'd dispute that,
    and no doubt his followers would too –
    come up with some pathetic nonsense to justify his teaching.

Oh yes, I know their sort,
   the most dangerous kind there is, to my mind.
Well, all I can say to them is, be real,
   come down out of your ivory tower.
Maybe he did heal the sick,
   work a few miracles,
   but that's not everything, is it?
What was the cost, that's what I want to know?
What damage did he do to our religion, openly flouting the Law like that?
What effect did he have on temple funds, turning out the traders?
What sedition did he foster, building up expectations of the Messiah?
He could have got us all killed, not just him, that's what gets me;
   the Romans were out to get us, and he must have known it.
OK, so perhaps he did think the next world more important than this,
   that it's better to lose one's life than save it.
But that was *his* problem,
   not ours.
We wanted to live, each one of us,
   priests,
   scribes,
   Pharisees,
   Sadducees.
And we wanted to live well, not with our faces ground into the dust.
It hadn't been easy, but we'd worked hard to get where we were,
   biting our tongues,
   toeing the line,
   swallowing our pride.
And we couldn't let that all be wasted by some lunatic
   with his head in the clouds.
So don't feel sorry for him,
   don't imagine he was hard done by,
   and don't you dare, any of you, point the accusing finger at us,
   suggesting we should feel ashamed of ourselves,
   that somehow we failed.
We had to think of ourselves,
   not to mention our people,
   our country,
   our faith.
We had to put those first,
   ensure we saved them come what may.
So I'm telling you straight, he had to die –
   there was no other way.
I honestly believe that,
   and do you know what?
In a funny kind of way I think he believed it too.       NICK FAWCETT

## Meditation of Pilate

He was different,
   I have to admit it.
Not a bit like I'd expected.
I'd heard the stories, of course.
Who hadn't?
Teacher, miracle worker, Messiah.
But I just thought he'd be like all the others:
   a charlatan out for what he could get,
   or some crazy fanatic who dared imagine
   he could take on the might of Rome.
Give me five minutes and I'll usually break them down.
A good flogging will see to that if all else fails.
Not this one though –
   I tried that,
   I tried everything;
   we gave him the full works.
And still he just stood there looking at me,
   as if I was the one on trial,
   as if he was the one in charge.
He was quite innocent, of course; any fool could see that.
But he wouldn't help himself,
   almost like he wanted to die.
Maybe he knew it was useless,
   that the crowds would never let me get away with it,
   though why they wanted him killed beats me.
I had no choice, that's what I keep telling myself.
It was my duty.
And anyway, it was them, not me, who had the last word.
Yet I can't help thinking I should have done more,
   feeling guilty.
The wife doesn't help, nagging me about him all the time.
Does she think that I can sleep any better than her?
What would she have done in my place?
I washed my hands of him in the end, literally.
But I still feel dirty, as though it's finally down to me.
He was different all right,
   but what sort of man was he?
That's the mystery.

NICK FAWCETT

## Meditation of Barabbas

I still can't believe my luck,
   still, after all this time, can't believe
   that I got off that day scot-free.

What on earth possessed the mob to let *me* off the hook
 and send *Jesus* to the cross? –
 I'll never make sense of it.
All right, so I wasn't a follower of his –
 my way more one of force than persuasion –
 but even I couldn't help being impressed by the man.
He was so clearly innocent, any fool could see that –
 a good man, through and through,
 sincere,
 gentle,
 honest,
 refusing to compromise his convictions
 despite the torment they put him through –
 the very idea of him inciting a revolt frankly laughable.
Yes, maybe he had stirred up the crowd's expectations
 through his signs and wonders,
 allowed them to believe he was the promised Messiah,
 but what of it? –
 he was hardly a revolutionary, was he? –
 not in the sense I wish he'd been, anyway,
 rebellion the last thing in his mind.
I knew it.
They knew it.
So why turn against him?
Why hand him over to the enemy
 to be butchered like a common criminal,
 and let me, a known trouble-maker, wriggle off the hook? –
 it just didn't add up.
Yet that's what they did,
 and the strange thing is
 he made no attempt to defend himself,
 no attempt to expose the ludicrousness of the charges
 or explain the true nature of his claims.
You might almost have thought he wanted to die, the way he acted.
Not that I'm complaining –
 I wouldn't be here now had things worked out differently –
 only I can't help wondering sometimes
 what actually went on that day,
 whether there was more going on than anyone realised,
 some hidden force at work.
It should have been me instead of him,
 anyone rather than a man like that,
 but it wasn't –
 he suffered the punishment I deserved,
 by some strange twist of fate his death buying me freedom.
It's a mystery, isn't it?

NICK FAWCETT

## Meditation of Peter

He was bleeding,
   my friend Jesus,
   skewered to that cross,
   like a piece of meat,
   great drops of blood trickling slowly to the ground,
   from his head,
   from his hands,
   from his feet.
I watched, stricken with horror,
   numbed with grief,
   as the life seeped away.
And I asked myself tearfully,
   angrily,
   why?
Why had God let it happen?
Why didn't he step in and do something?
What was he thinking of?
It seemed criminal,
   a stupid, senseless waste to let such a wonderful man die –
   let alone to die like that!
And for a moment my faith was shattered,
   in myself,
   in God,
   in everything.
But then I remembered his words,
   just the night before when we had broken bread together:
   'This is my blood, shed for you and for many, for the forgiveness of sins.'
And even as I remembered, so that other time came back,
   there by the Sea of Galilee after he had fed the multitude,
   the crowd pressing round him asking for more:
   'Whoever comes to me will never be hungry,
   whoever believes in me will never be thirsty;
   my flesh is true food and my blood is true drink.'
They had been a mystery to me until then, those words,
   hard to stomach, if you'll pardon the pun.
But suddenly, there beneath that cross, I began to understand,
   just a little,
   only the merest fraction,
   yet enough to help me realise it wasn't all in vain;
   that somehow Jesus was hanging there for me,
   for you,
   for everyone.
I still ask why, mind you, and I think I always will,
   for I'll never get that picture out of my mind;
   that picture of Jesus broken on the cross.

Why that way, God, and not another?
Why not something less brutal,
   less awful,
   less messy?
Yet the strange thing is *he* never asked why,
   not once in all the days I knew him.
Oh, he'd have liked there to be another way, of course;
   he didn't want to die any more than the next man.
But he offered his life,
   freely,
   willingly,
   lovingly,
   in the conviction that, through his dying, we might truly live.   NICK FAWCETT

## Meditation of Mary Magdalene

He was gasping,
   his breath coming short and sharp,
   his body contorted in agony,
   and I could scarcely bring myself to watch.
It's a dreadful business, crucifixion, at the best of times,
   even when the poor wretch up there deserves to die,
   but when it's a friend,
   a loved one,
   somebody who's been special to you,
   then, I'm telling you, it's indescribable.
To stand by helpless as the pain takes hold,
   as the muscles tear and the tendons snap,
   as life ebbs out of the body –
   to see the misery,
   the torment,
   the despair,
   and to know it must get worse
   before finally, in the sweet embrace of death, it gets better;
   you just can't imagine what that feels like,
   not unless you've been there.
And we *were* there, more's the pity,
   each one of us enduring our own private hell.
We wanted to run, God knows! –
   to close our eyes and pretend it wasn't happening.
But we couldn't, could we?
For he needed us then more than ever,
   simply to know we were there,
   that we cared,
   that he wasn't alone.

It wasn't much, I grant you,
  the few of us huddled together,
  watching nervously from the shadows,
  fearful of recognition,
  but it was enough,
  one ray of sunshine in a wilderness of darkness;
  for he knew that despite our faults,
  the weakness of our faith and feebleness of our commitment,
  we were risking something,
  sticking our necks out for love of him.
He was gasping,
  and we prayed it wouldn't be much longer
  before release finally came.
But however long it took,
  and whatever it might cost us,
  we were resolved to stay to the bitter end –
  it was the very least we could do.

NICK FAWCETT

## Meditation of Mary, wife of Clopas

It was over,
  finished –
  thirty-three years of life,
  three years of ministry,
  seven days of turmoil,
  six hours of agony,
  finally ended –
  and I couldn't believe it.
Yes, I know that sounds daft, having stood there and watched him die,
  having seen them drive the nails into his hands,
  having watched the spear thrust in his side,
  having witnessed his dying breath.
What else did I expect, you may ask?
What other outcome could there possibly have been?
And I understand all that, for I knew he was dying, of course I did.
Yet when it finally happened,
  when the end came,
  I was numb,
  unable to take it in,
  paralysed with grief.
It just didn't seem possible that this man Jesus,
  whom we'd known and loved,
  whom we'd trusted and followed,
  who had been the very centre of our lives,
  could have been taken from us,

snuffed out, never to be seen again.
It wasn't that he hadn't prepared us,
   you could never accuse him of that –
   he'd spoken of death until we were sick and tired of hearing it.
And we honestly thought we were ready,
   that we'd taken it all in,
   come to terms with the inevitable,
   steeled ourselves to face the worst.
But we hadn't, not when it came to the wire.
The theory was one thing,
   the reality something else.
I realised as we stood there,
   the tears rolling down our faces,
   our hearts torn in two,
   that we'd always expected him in the final chapter to come up smiling,
   put one over on those wretched Pharisees
   and show them who was boss.
But of course it wasn't like that,
   nothing like it at all.
It was over, finished,
   just like he'd said it would be,
   and I couldn't get my head round it,
   couldn't make sense of it whatever.
Yet there's one thing I've held on to since that awful moment;
   one memory which has brought comfort even in the darkest of hours,
   and that is those last words of his,
   that cry he uttered with such dreadful yet confident finality:
   'It is finished,' he shouted.
   'It is finished!'
Words spoken not in sorrow,
   not in anger,
   nor in weary resignation,
   but in a tone of sheer thanksgiving,
   as though somehow even there,
   especially there,
   he had accomplished the very thing he came to do.    NICK FAWCETT

## Jesus – threat to the authorities

The crucifixion of Jesus with two criminals was not a mere coincidence. By positioning Jesus between the two criminals the authorities were attempting to make a statement. First, that Jesus was no more than a common criminal, a thief or con artist. Second, a crown of thorns and a placard declaring him to be a king was intended to imply that he was nothing more than a leader of other criminals, a self-professed lord and liar.

Jesus is mocked by three groups of people. The leaders, or Jewish rulers, mock him with a sense of relief. To them, Jesus posed a threat, a constant thorn in their side who reminded them of their duty to God and to the community. It came as a huge sense of relief to the authorities when Jesus was 'put in his place' and humiliated. It was a public statement that implied Jesus had been judged by the real leaders and found to be a fraud whose followers were nothing more than a bunch of no-hopers.

The soldiers had mocked Jesus by again questioning his ability to do anything about his situation. To the soldiers, a leader was someone to be respected, someone who held authority and whose orders were obeyed. They despised someone who claimed to have authority but who received nothing more than public disgrace.

The two criminals who were crucified with Jesus mocked him because it appeared that he'd been brought down to their level. To be crucified with them meant he was no better than them and was someone who wasn't clever enough, or powerful enough, to avoid the punishment of a common criminal.

Almost immediately the criminals realised that an innocent person was being crucified. One of the criminals understood that Jesus was taking the blame for the crimes of other people.

A little while later a Roman officer began to praise God after recognising that Jesus was everything he claimed to be. And it wasn't long before the authorities realised that their attempt to kill Jesus was nothing more than a fulfilment of everything Jesus had said would happen. Their mockery died as Jesus rose from the dead.

### Why was Jesus considered to be such a threat to the religious authorities?

For a short time the religious authorities welcomed the words that initially John the Baptist and then Jesus used to encourage people to a faith in God. But, it wasn't long before they realised that Jesus considered them, the religious leaders, to be as far from a real relationship with God as anyone else. Even more worrying was the fact that Jesus didn't encourage the people to go through the religious procedures and customs considered so important by the religious leaders. In fact, Jesus pointed out the hypocrisy of the religious leaders who abused their positions of power for their own selfish reasons. Little wonder that the religious leaders thought they'd be better off with Jesus dead.

PETE TOWNSEND

## The prisoners

The scene is a prison cell somewhere east of Skegness. Two prisoners are passing the time away (before it passes away completely) with a bit of chat and the occasional smile. They are feeling less than happy about their predicament but are puzzled by another prisoner who left a few moments ago. Why was he so calm? Why wasn't he terrified at the prospect of being tortured and strapped to a cross? Wasn't he worried about getting splinters? Before they have time to chat any further, a guard comes along to take them on a little walk through the town and up a hill, where they will be given a lift up so that they can admire the view. You never know, they might meet up with that guy they met earlier.

| | |
|---|---|
| *Characters* | Two petty crooks whose expertise and cunning are only rivalled by a bag of jelly babies. |
| *Scene* | Inside a prison cell. Shadows of bars fall across the two prisoners' faces. Sitting nervously, they cast glances about them. Not sure what will happen next they both sit hunched-up. |
| *Props* | Two benches or small seats. Chains around the hands and legs of the crooks. A projector or spotlight to project the shadows of bars. |

**Convict**   (*Looks around nervously. Looks sideways at Villain*) What are you in here for?

**Villain**   (*Doesn't look at Convict*) It's a bit embarrassing really.

**Convict**   You don't look like a bloke who can get embarrassed easily. Not with a haircut like that.

**Villain**   (*Looks at Convict*) You can talk. Looks like you got dressed with whatever you found on the washing line.

**Convict**   (*Sniffs*) I did.

**Villain**   Must have been in a bit of a hurry, then.

**Convict**   I was, mate. Matter of life and death.

**Villain**   (*Folds arms across chest*) Well it certainly is now.

**Convict**   What?

**Villain**   Life and death. I hope you enjoyed what you had because there doesn't seem much hope of extending your life insurance policy.

**Convict**   Insurance salesmen! Bunch of robbers. It's them who should be in here, not law-abiding citizens like me and you.

**Villain**   Not quite law-abiding. Perhaps a citizen who's got a different interpretation of the law to some. A kind of flexible approach. I like to bend it my way.

*Both characters remain quiet for a few moments. In the background can be heard the sounds of shouting, a cell door is slammed shut and chains rattle.*

**Convict**   (*Shakes head slowly from side to side*) So anyway, what are you in here for?

**Villain**   Joyriding.

**Convict**   Joyriding! Is that all? How on earth did you get caught?

**Villain**   Couldn't get the donkey to wake up.

**Convict**   And some early morning guard nabbed you then?

**Villain**   No. I went to fetch some carrots from the local store.

**Convict**   And then you got nabbed? Isn't that breaking and entering?

**Villain**   No, well yes, technically. You see, I suddenly remembered I hadn't had any breakfast, so I munched my way through the fruit section and then moved on to the deli counter.

**Convict**   And then what?

**Villain**   I fell asleep.

**Convict**   And then you felt the long arm of the law prod you into consciousness?

**Villain**   No, it was the storekeeper's wife with her broom.

**Convict**   *(Winces)* Ooh, that could have been nasty. So, how come you got done for joyriding?

**Villain**   I tried to make my getaway on the donkey. *(Faint sound of hooves 'clip-clop' on stone road)* I had to escape.

**Convict**   So would I, mate, with a broom about to interfere with my anatomy. Anyway, that's still not joyriding, merely trying to escape from a severe bout of broomitis.

**Villain**   It's called joyriding when the donkey races off like lightning with me hanging on to its tail. Up-ended six priests, two tax collectors and a soothsayer before they caught me. So, what's your story?

**Convict**   I'm in for domestic violence.

**Villain**   Can't you sort out your domestic squabbles in private?

**Convict**   Wish I could. They put me in here for my own protection. You haven't seen the wife. Muscles the size of temple pillars. Makes me shudder to think. *(Looks nervously around)*

**Villain**   Still, a bit steep putting you in here over a tiff.

**Convict**   That's what I tried to tell them. But some bright spark recognised me from a wanted poster.

**Villain**   What you wanted for then, throwing a tantrum in the bath?

| | |
|---|---|
| **Convict** | I was spotted trying to rob the local tax collector's office. |
| **Villain** | You should have used a look-out. |
| **Convict** | I did. I was told he was the best in the business. |
| **Villain** | Who's that, then? |
| **Convict** | Blind Bartimaeus. |
| **Villain** | But he *is* blind! |
| **Convict** | I just thought it was his nickname. You know, sort of turns a blind eye to things. |
| **Villain** | He definitely did that. |
| **Convict** | Bit of bad luck that, really. |
| **Villain** | Yeah. Still, not so unlucky as the bloke who was in here earlier. |
| **Convict** | Who was that, then? |
| **Villain** | Some religious teacher who got caught up in a bit of politics. |
| **Convict** | Politics. It'll be the death of us. |
| **Villain** | It will, mate, take my word for it. But this bloke, he sounded an OK sort of guy. I heard he was some sort of teacher. Upset a few of the local big noises but his heart was in the right place. |
| **Convict** | Bet he was really narked at being thrown in here and then put on trial. |
| **Villain** | Now, that's the funny thing. He didn't seem to mind, sort of expected it. Didn't hold a grudge. |
| **Convict** | I heard he did a lot of amazing things. Someone told me he even healed Blind Bartimaeus. |
| **Villain** | He'll have to get another nickname now. |
| **Convict** | He might make a better look-out though. |
| **Villain** | Yeah, at least things are looking up for him. |
| **Convict** | I think things will be looking up for us soon. *(Looks in the direction of the light projecting image of prison bars)* |
| **Villain** | Yeah, looking up at a great chunk of wood waiting for our attention. |
| **Convict** | Oh well, beats work. |
| | *Sound of another cell door being slammed and loud footsteps echo along the corridor. A key is heard turning in the lock and a cell door creaks open.* |
| **Villain** | Talking of beating, here comes that guard with the welcoming snarl. |

## Summary

At his trial, Jesus must have felt that the whole world was against him. There were those who openly opposed him and had done everything they could to silence a voice that threatened to disrupt their egocentric lifestyles. There were those people who wanted to dispose of a voice that openly criticised their religious activity (an activity which said more about their devotion to themselves and rituals than their devotion to God). And there were those who wept. They wept because they felt a sense of loss, a sense of defeat and a sense of betrayal. They felt betrayed by those followers of Jesus who faded into the background when things began to get tough. The felt betrayed by their own emotions which had hoped for so much and now saw all their desires crumble under a whip. But the one who was betrayed and had suffered the biting lashes of rejection wouldn't have chosen any other way. This was the way forward, the way chosen by his Father.

The crucifixion was a barbaric form of punishment. The suffering and obvious pain were all part of a process designed to act as a warning to anyone who had thoughts of rebellion against the system.

When the person to be crucified reached the place of crucifixion, the T-shaped cross (there was no extended top piece so that the person had nowhere to rest their head) was placed upon the ground and the person's arms were stretched out across the bar and their hands nailed to the wood. The feet were fastened to the upright. About halfway up the cross was a piece of wood called the 'saddle'. This was designed to take the weight of the victim so they didn't tear their hands from the nails. The 'cross' was then lifted into a socket which kept the person's feet about a metre above the ground.

Dragging the heavy wooden cross through the streets (often going the long way round) and the subsequent nails and lifting into position were excruciatingly painful but not designed to kill the victim immediately. The victim was left to die of a mixture of pain, thirst and starvation.

PETE TOWNSEND

# Easter

# Easter Day

*The victory of love over evil, suffering and death*

## John 20:1-18

*(also Matthew 28:1-10; Jeremiah 31:1-6; Psalm 118:14-24; Acts 10:34-43; Colossians 3:1-4)*

## A reading from the Gospel of John (20:1-9)

Before sunrise on the Sunday morning Mary of Magdala went to the tomb. As she reached the entrance, she saw that the stone had been rolled away and the tomb was empty. She ran to the disciples saying, 'They have taken the Lord from the tomb and we don't know where they have put him!'

Peter and another disciple, John, ran to the tomb and found it just as Mary had described, with the linen burial cloths lying on the ground. The cloth which had been wrapped around Jesus' head lay rolled up separately from the other pieces of cloth. Peter went into the tomb first, followed by John.

Until this moment they had not understood the Scriptures which had said, 'He must rise from the dead.' But now they saw, and they believed.

This is the Gospel of the Lord
**Praise to you, Lord Jesus Christ**                                        KATIE THOMPSON

## A reading from the Gospel of Matthew (28:1-10)

At sunrise on the Sunday morning Mary of Magdala and another woman called Mary went to the tomb where Jesus was buried.

Suddenly the ground trembled violently, like an earthquake; an angel appeared, rolled the stone away from the tomb and sat on it. The angel dazzled like lightning, and the guards at the tomb were frozen with fear.

Then the angel spoke to the women, saying, 'Do not be afraid! I know that you are looking for Jesus who was crucified and buried here, but you will not find him because he is risen, just as he told you. Come and see for yourselves that he is gone! Now you must go to his disciples and tell them that he is risen, and you will see him again in Galilee. Go, and remember everything I have told you.'

Shaking with fear and excitement, the two women hurried from the tomb, and ran to tell the disciples their marvellous news. On the way Jesus suddenly appeared and greeted them with the words, 'Peace be with you!'

The women fell at his feet and worshipped the Lord.

'You have nothing to fear,' Jesus said. 'Tell my disciples to make their way to Galilee where they will see me for themselves.'

This is the Gospel of the Lord
**Praise to you, Lord Jesus Christ**                                        KATIE THOMPSON

# Introductory material

'This is the day that the Lord has made. Let us rejoice and be glad in it.' Words which remind us of the need to let go of the past and embrace the present moment, recognising each day as a new beginning. The theory is excellent, the practice harder, for as the years pass so our ability to bounce back from life's disappointments and look forward with undiminished enthusiasm becomes ever more jaded. Yet if it seems hard sometimes for *us*, how much harder must it have seemed for the disciples of Jesus in the days following his death. How could they recover from that? How could life ever hold any meaning again? Life must have seemed bleak beyond redemption. Until suddenly it all changed! Hope reborn, joy returning as Christ was there once more, risen and victorious. And in that moment they knew it was true; life was beginning again, not just for Jesus but for them all; a fresh start, a new chapter in a story which would have no end. So it is for us – each day, each moment offering a clean break, the past forgotten, the future there for the taking. 'This is the day that the Lord has made. Let us rejoice and be glad in it.'

NICK FAWCETT

'Today is the first day of the rest of your life' – an expression so often used it has become a cliché. But for us as Christians it is a statement that sums up the truth of this day – a truth the Apostles discovered as, huddled behind locked doors, Jesus appeared among them; a truth broken-hearted women discovered as they found the tomb empty and the stone rolled away; a truth countless generations have discovered since as the risen Christ has transformed their lives. For each one suddenly life began again – a clean sheet, a fresh page, a new chapter. Listen to their story, reflect on their experience, and rejoice in the new life God offers to you too.

NICK FAWCETT

# Prayers

### Easter worship

Almighty God,
   with joy and praise,
      **with awe and wonder,**
      with gladness and celebration,
      **we bring our Easter worship.**

   We lift up our hearts,
      **we lift up our thoughts,**
      we lift up our voices,
      **we lift up our souls,**
      recognising afresh all you have done for us in Christ.

We rejoice in the message of this day,
    **the good news at the heart of our faith –**
    light after darkness,
    **joy after sorrow,**
    good after evil,
    **life after death!**

Almighty God,
    speak to us again today
        through all we read,
        **all we hear,**
        all we sing,
        **all we do.**

May the truth of the resurrection inspire us with new hope.
**May the victory of Christ fill us with new joy.**
May the reality of his presence fill us with new faith.
**And so may we serve you with new vigour**
    **to the glory of your name,**
    **through Jesus Christ our Lord.**
    **Amen.**
                                                      NICK FAWCETT

## Thanksgiving – new from old

Lord Jesus Christ,
    this is a season of new beginnings –
        not just your glorious resurrection from the dead,
        but the resurrection of broken dreams,
        crushed hopes,
        shattered faith –
        and we praise you for it.
    Yet it's hard sometimes
        to believe such new beginnings can apply to us,
        that we too can start again.
    We look at our own situations –
        the problems which refuse to go away,
        the mistakes we go on making –
        and we see little prospect of change,
        no reason to believe life can be different.
    But you have promised that we shall be born again,
        that anyone who trusts in you will become a new creation;
        renewed, remade, refreshed through your grace.
    Risen Saviour, conqueror of sin and death,
        **raise us to newness of life.**

Help us to remember that, for your followers,
   there seemed no reason to hope.
They had seen you die,
   and they each knew that, in their own way,
   they had brought you to it,
   not so much through their forsaking you in your time of need
   as in the human weakness and sin which that represented –
   the self-interest,
   the lack of commitment,
   the willingness to compromise that is so characteristic of us all.
They were racked by remorse,
   tortured by guilt,
   all too aware of the limitations of their faith.
Yet you came to them,
   risen and victorious,
   but the same Jesus who had suffered and died,
   and to those same disciples who had failed you so miserably
   you brought new power,
   new purpose.
Risen Saviour, conqueror of sin and death,
   **raise us to newness of life.**

Teach us, however often we might fail,
   never to lose sight of that truth.
Save us from losing our sense of all that you are able to do,
   from growing disheartened,
   disenchanted,
   disillusioned,
   resigned to treading the same old ground
   rather than stepping out into new avenues of faith.
However much it may feel we are getting nowhere,
   however often we may find ourselves
   at what seems like a dead end,
   keep us open to the journey of discovery you hold before us,
   and give us faith to walk with you,
   wherever you would lead us,
   confident of your transforming power in our lives.
Risen Saviour, conqueror of sin and death,
   **raise us to newness of life.**

Lord Jesus Christ,
   this is a time of new beginnings,
   a fresh start,
   a day in which we celebrate the promise of resurrection for all,
   your gift of new life from old,
   and we praise you for it.

Risen Saviour, conqueror of sin and death,
    **raise us to newness of life.**

Hear our prayer,
    for we offer it in your name.
**Amen.** NICK FAWCETT

## Easter thanksgiving and confession

Sovereign God,
    we thank you for the victory we remember this day –
        **the victory of Christ over evil, sin, hatred,**
        **darkness and death.**

So now we come,
    **confessing our many faults,**
    acknowledging our weakness,
    **ashamed of our lack of faith,**
    but also assured of your mercy,
    **rejoicing in your forgiveness,**
    confident of your love,
    **and certain of your renewing, restoring power.**

Sovereign God,
    who makes all things new,
    **fill us now with new faith, new commitment,**
    **new purpose and new life,**
    **through the power of the risen Christ.**
**Amen.** NICK FAWCETT

## Petition and intercession – beginnings from endings

Lord Jesus Christ,
    we remember today how you rose again,
        bringing new beginnings out of what had seemed the end,
        a new chapter in the life of your Church
        which is still being written today.
    We recall how your resurrection changed life for the disciples,
        calling them to let go of the past and embrace the future –
        their role no longer simply to follow but to lead,
        to go out in your risen power and proclaim the good news.
    We know that life must change for us too,
        but sometimes it is harder than we first anticipated,
        moving on a painful business,
        asking more of us than we feel able to give.
    Take all that *has* been
    **and direct all that *shall* be.**

Reach out to all who are finding endings hard to bear.
We think of those reeling from the termination of employment,
   the breakdown of a relationship
   or eviction from their homes.
Take all that *has* been
   **and direct all that** *shall* **be.**

We think of those whose children are leaving home,
   family and friends moving away from each other,
   communities facing the upheaval of change.
Take all that *has* been
   **and direct all that** *shall* **be.**

We think of those coming to terms with unfulfilled ambitions,
   let down by broken promises,
   or overcome by sudden catastrophe.
Take all that *has* been
   **and direct all that** *shall* **be.**
We think of those disabled by disease,
   mourning the loss of loved ones,
   or suffering from terminal illness.
Take all that *has* been
   **and direct all that** *shall* **be.**

We think not only of others but also ourselves.
Show us those areas in our lives
   where it is time to draw a line and move on –
   forms of service which are no longer fruitful,
   activities no longer appropriate,
   dreams no longer viable.
Take all that *has* been
   **and direct all that** *shall* **be.**

Give us the wisdom we need to understand
   when it is necessary to accept change
   and even to welcome it,
   and give us courage then to stride out in faith,
   confident that you will lead us from the old to the new.
Take all that *has* been
   **and direct all that** *shall* **be.**

Lord Jesus Christ,
   remind us again today that endings can lead to new beginnings,
      that from the old, new life can spring,
      and may that confidence touch our lives
      and bring hope to our troubled world.

Receive our thanks for all that *has* been
   **and open our hearts to all that *shall* be.**

We ask it in your name.
**Amen.**                                              NICK FAWCETT


## Intercession – love from hatred

Lord Jesus Christ,
   we thank you for the victory of love over hatred
      that we celebrate in this season.
   We praise you for staying true to your chosen path,
      despite all the malice thrown against you,
      the repeated taunts to put yourself first,
      and the very real temptation you must have felt to do just that.
   Hear now our prayer for the world you gave your life for –
      a world so racked by enmity and division
      and so desperately in need of love.
   Gracious Lord, wherever hatred seems to rule,
      **may love emerge victorious**.

We pray for those whose personal relationships
      have degenerated into hatred –
      scarred by petty grievances and arguments,
      undermined by verbal and physical abuse,
      poisoned by coldness and indifference;
      words spoken to wound rather than woo,
      deeds designed to break down rather than build up,
      all feeling and friendship long since forgotten.
   Gracious Lord, wherever hatred seems to rule,
      **may love emerge victorious**.

We pray for society at large
      where hatred masquerades under a variety of guises –
      prejudice, greed, selfishness, intolerance, ignorance –
      so much that denies, divides and destroys,
      creating a sense of 'them' and 'us',
      the acceptable and the unacceptable.
   Gracious Lord, wherever hatred seems to rule,
      **may love emerge victorious**.

We pray for countries racked by inner tensions
      and at odds with their neighbours –
      torn apart by religious extremism,
      by military dictatorships,
      racial hatred,
      civil war

and abuses of human rights –
lives wantonly destroyed,
families broken,
communities shattered,
nations decimated.
Gracious Lord, wherever hatred seems to rule,
**may love emerge victorious**.

Lord Jesus Christ,
we pray for our world in all its need –
a world of so much hatred,
yet one which you loved so much you were willing to die for it,
and a world which you will never abandon,
no matter how often your love is rejected.
Help us and all people to recognise the folly of our ways –
to understand that violence only breeds more violence,
vengeance more vengeance,
bitterness more bitterness
and hatred more hatred.
Give us the faith and the courage to try another way,
the way you revealed so powerfully
through your life and your death –
the way of love.
Gracious Lord, wherever hatred seems to rule,
**may love emerge victorious**.

We ask it in your name and for your glory.
**Amen.**                                          NICK FAWCETT

## Intercession

*Death cannot hold the Lord of life.*
*New life for him means new life for all*
*who believe in Christ.*

We think of the church celebrating in clusters
and crowds all over the world,
and pray for a deepening of love and faith.
*Silence for prayer*
Lord of life:
**you do all things well**

We remember the areas of the world
where there is conflict and confusion;
and we pray that all may come to know God's love.

*Silence for prayer*
Lord of life:
**you do all things well**

We remember those we have met and talked with
during the week,
and pray for God's blessing on their lives.
*Silence for prayer*
Lord of life:
**you do all things well**

We remember those waiting for surgery,
and those in long-term care,
and pray that God's will
may be beautifully accomplished in their lives.
*Silence for prayer*
Lord of life:
**you do all things well**

We remember those who have died very young,
and those who are finding this hard to accept,
and we pray for God's grace and reassurance.
*Silence for prayer*
Lord of life:
**you do all things well**

We remember the wonder and generosity of God,
his faithfulness and his mercy.
*Silence for prayer*
Merciful Father,
**accept these prayers**
**for the sake of your Son,**
**our Saviour Jesus Christ, Amen.**                    SUSAN SAYERS

## Short prayers

Loving God,
giver of all life and hope,
we praise and thank you this morning
for the wonderful news of Jesus' resurrection,
and for the promise that we too can have new life in him.
We thank you for giving us foretastes of that new life,
here on earth,
and for the promise that we shall share it
in all its wonder and glory in eternity.

Forgive us for the times when we don't trust you enough,
and we shrink back from difficult steps
that you are calling us to take,
and help us to trust in you for hope and renewal,
through Jesus Christ our risen and living Lord.
Amen.                                          MICHAEL FORSTER


Lord God,
    we thank you for this day –
    a day which brought hope after despair,
    new beginnings
    from what had looked like the end of everything.
Teach us that the truth of Easter goes on being true
    today and every day,
    your invitation to start again constantly extended,
    your gift of new life always open.
So, trusting in the future,
    may we rejoice in the present,
    and celebrate each day that you give us,
    through Jesus Christ our Lord.
Amen.                                          NICK FAWCETT


Lord Jesus Christ,
    you met with Mary in the garden,
    bringing laughter after tears;
    you met with women returning from the tomb,
    bringing confidence after confusion;
    you met with Cleopas on the Emmaus road,
    bringing hope after dismay;
    you met with the Apostles
    in a room barred against the world,
    bringing joy after sorrow;
    you met with Thomas, in his disbelief,
    bringing faith after doubt;
    you met with Paul on his way to Damascus,
    bringing love after hatred;
    you met with countless generations
    across the centuries,
    bringing renewal after rejection.
Meet with us now, in this day, this moment,
    bringing light after darkness.
Fill our hearts with the new life of Easter,
    until that day when, with all your people,
    we enter your kingdom

and rejoice in the wonder of your love
for all eternity.
In your name we pray.
Amen.                                                    NICK FAWCETT


Sovereign God,
  you turned the darkest of nights
  into the brightest of days
  through the resurrection of your Son,
  our Saviour,
  Jesus Christ.
Come now into our darkness,
  into the night-time of suffering and sickness,
  of doubt and despair,
  of hurt and heartbreak,
  of injustice and evil,
  of violence and hatred,
  of fear and death.
May your new day dawn here,
  and the light of Christ blaze to your glory,
  as we share his resurrection life,
  and rejoice in the victory he has won.
In his name we pray.
Amen.                                                    NICK FAWCETT


Sovereign God,
  this is the day of victory –
  a day on which we celebrate
  the triumph of good over evil,
  truth over falsehood,
  light over darkness,
  life over death.
This is the day which changes every day –
  which brings joy out of sorrow,
  hope out of despair,
  faith out of doubt,
  love out of hatred.
This is the day which makes every day
  an Easter Day,
  and every moment a new beginning.
Sovereign God,
  receive our praise,
  in the name of the risen Christ.
Amen.                                                    NICK FAWCETT

# All-age-talk material

Read the first part of *Jesus is Risen* (Palm Tree Bible Stories) or tell the story in your own words, acting it out with plasticine models on a tray with a stone 'cave' built on it in a garden.

Sing one of the Easter songs together and give each child a margarine tub with oasis in it, a selection of spring flowers and a tall white candle.

Help them make an arrangement of joy at Jesus being alive for ever. When they have finished, light all the candles, and let the children carry them in procession into the church near the altar.                                    SUSAN SAYERS

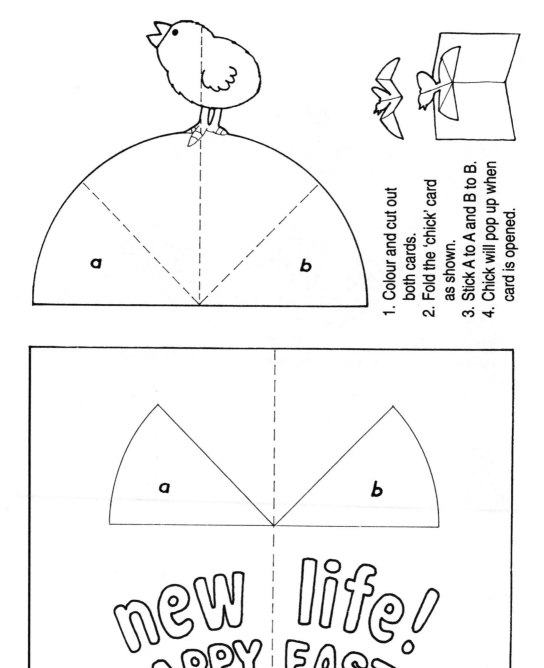

1. Colour and cut out both cards.
2. Fold the 'chick' card as shown.
3. Stick A to A and B to B.
4. Chick will pop up when card is opened.

a

b

a

b

new life!
HAPPY EASTER

Susan Sayers

Jesus is risen from the dead

Stick this message inside card.

HAPPY

EASTER

Fold

Jesus is alive for ever!

SUSAN SAYERS

John 20:9

KATIE THOMPSON

## Strange but true?

Give each member of the group a pen and a piece of paper. Read out each of the following statements and ask them to write whether they think the statement is true or false.

1. St John was the only one of the 12 apostles to die a natural death.
2. A monkey was awarded a medal and promoted to the rank of corporal during World War 1.
3. Sliced bread was patented by a Mrs P. Ride in 1954.
4. An old custom, when drinking, was to throw a pinch of salt over your left shoulder to keep the devil away.
5. The cost of the first pay-toilets in England was one penny.
6. In 1647 the English Parliament abolished Christmas.
7. The word 'Abracadabra', used by stage magicians, was originally intended to cure hay fever.
8. In Victorian times there was a law which prohibited the wearing of a flat cap on a boat.
9. Gabriel and Michael are the only two angels to be named in the Bible.
10. The national flag of Austria was designed by an Irishman.

The answers are: 1. True; 2. True; 3. True; 4. False; 5. True; 6. True; 7. True; 8. False; 9. True; 10. False.

Total the scores and see who was able to make any sense (or good guess-work) of the strange statements. (*Allow 10 minutes for this activity*)

There are many things which appear to be beyond belief, but just because they are slightly strange doesn't mean that there isn't something totally amazing about them.

PETE TOWNSEND

## Read Matthew 28:1-10

The resurrection of Jesus was a major disappointment for all the religious leaders and politicians who thought that they'd got rid of a huge problem. Almost immediately, rumours were spread in an attempt to discredit the eyewitness accounts of those who had seen Jesus buried and those who'd seen him alive again.

The rumours were an attempt to suggest that the people who claimed that Jesus was alive were at best mistaken and at worst desperate frauds.

It was both Mary Magdalene and the other Mary who'd watched Jesus placed into the tomb and the large rock rolled across the entrance. The same two women were the first to discover that the rock had been rolled away and the tomb empty.

Rumours that the tomb had been robbed of Jesus' body were put around despite the tomb being guarded by Roman soldiers who knew they would suffer a severe punishment if they were to fall asleep or desert their duty. More importantly, would anyone have believed that these soldiers would do nothing while the disciples took the body of Jesus away? *(see verse 13)*

Another rumour, which claimed Jesus had merely fainted and then recovered in the cold tomb, ignores the fact that it would take an extremely strong person to roll the rock away from the tomb entrance. This also ignores the fact that Jesus had suffered a beating, whipping, dragged a heavy section of wood around the streets, been nailed to a cross and then had his side punctured by a spear.

The one overriding fact remains that Jesus rose again exactly as he had said he would. Despite the evidence there were plenty of people, and still are, who refused to believe that although it is an absolutely weird thing to happen, Jesus did rise from the dead and appear to hundreds of people.

Although strange to believe, Jesus suffered, died and rose again to fulfil everything that God intended. The facts, hard to believe or appreciate at times, remain that God loves us and went to extreme lengths to make it possible for us to get personal with the Creator.

Read the account of the resurrection again. Ask the group to imagine that they are a group of detectives who are the first to arrive on the scene after the reports of Mary Magdalene and Mary. How would they assess the evidence? What questions would they have asked? What conclusion would they have come to? *(Allow 5 minutes for this task)*

PETE TOWNSEND

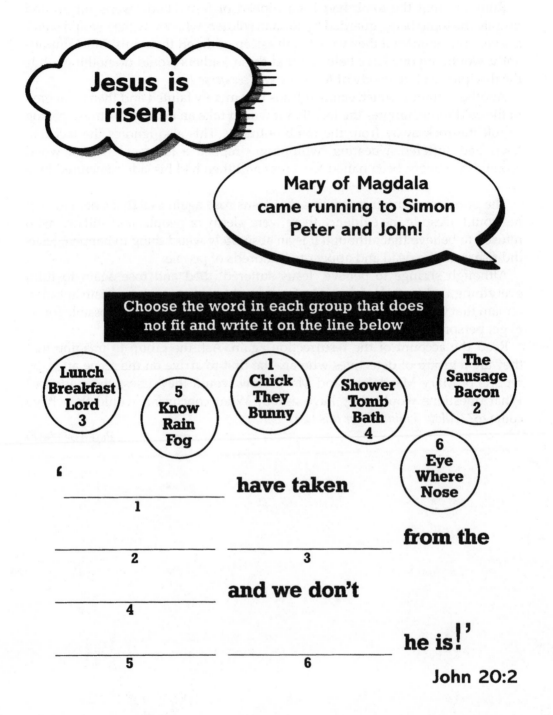

**Jesus is risen!**

**Mary of Magdala came running to Simon Peter and John!**

**Choose the word in each group that does not fit and write it on the line below**

Lunch
Breakfast
Lord
3

5
Know
Rain
Fog

1
Chick
They
Bunny

Shower
Tomb
Bath
4

The
Sausage
Bacon
2

6
Eye
Where
Nose

'_____ have taken
        1

_____     _____ from the
      2                    3

_____ and we don't
      4

_____     _____ he is!'
      5                    6

John 20:2

The two disciples ran to the tomb! What did they see when they got there?

Use the code cracker to find out!

## CODE CRACKER

D (1)　E (3)　I (5)　B (7)　S (9)　O (11)　H (13)　G (15)　R (17)
U (2)　N (4)　L (6)　T (8)　F (10)　A (12)　Y (14)　C (16)　P (18)

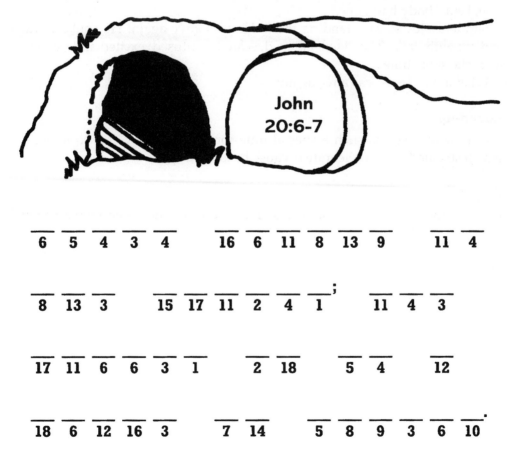

John 20:6-7

$\overline{6}\ \overline{5}\ \overline{4}\ \overline{3}\ \overline{4}$　$\overline{16}\ \overline{6}\ \overline{11}\ \overline{8}\ \overline{13}\ \overline{9}$　$\overline{11}\ \overline{4}$

$\overline{8}\ \overline{13}\ \overline{3}$　$\overline{15}\ \overline{17}\ \overline{11}\ \overline{2}\ \overline{4}\ \overline{1}$;　$\overline{11}\ \overline{4}\ \overline{3}$

$\overline{17}\ \overline{11}\ \overline{6}\ \overline{6}\ \overline{3}\ \overline{1}$　$\overline{2}\ \overline{18}$　$\overline{5}\ \overline{4}$　$\overline{12}$

$\overline{18}\ \overline{6}\ \overline{12}\ \overline{16}\ \overline{3}$　$\overline{7}\ \overline{14}$　$\overline{5}\ \overline{8}\ \overline{9}\ \overline{3}\ \overline{6}\ \overline{10}$.

KATIE THOMPSON

## Bible story

### John 20

I wonder if you've been really upset, confused and overjoyed all in the same day.

It must have been like that for Jesus' friends. They had seen him taken, beaten and put to death. They were deeply upset and wept! They were scared, probably hiding in a house behind closed doors.

Suddenly there was a loud knocking at the door! 'Who's there?' they asked.

'Mary!' came the reply. 'He's gone!'

'Who's gone?' they asked.

'Him!'

'Him who?'

'Jesus!' Mary told them.

'We know,' said the friends, 'we saw him die!'

'I went to the tomb, but his body has gone!' wept Mary.

Peter and John raced to the tomb. It was true. Jesus' body had gone like Mary had said! His grave clothes were there, but Jesus' body was gone! The two of them were very upset and confused as they explained to the others that it was true, Jesus' body had gone.

Suddenly Jesus was standing there. He was alive again! He spoke to them and ate with them. They were amazed, scared, confused, excited and overjoyed all at the same time.

What a day. Jesus was alive again!

## Round-up

This is why Easter is such a special time for Christians. A time to remember why Jesus died and to celebrate because he is alive again.

## Prayer

Lord, thank you for this wonderful story. Help us to understand what Easter is really all about. Amen.

JOHN HARDWICK

# The angel's message

When the Sabbath had ended, Mary of Magdala and another woman called Mary made their way to the tomb.

**Use the picture clues to spell out another name for a tomb**

KATIE THOMPSON

As the women
ran to tell the disciples,
whom did they meet?

Solve the clues to find the answer.
The first letter of each clue will spell out the person's name!

## CLUES

1. The first month
of the year

2. These are laid by hens

3. A creature with its home
on its back

4. A device for keeping
the rain off

5. Something you find
at the beach

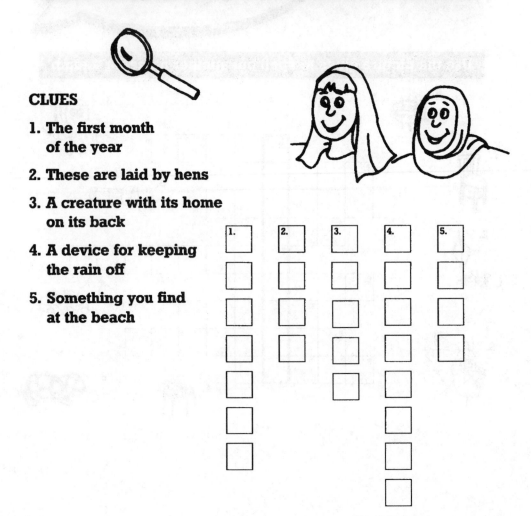

KATIE THOMPSON

**Suddenly the ground shook and an angel appeared and rolled away the stone!**

**Use the code to find a description of the angel in Matthew 28:3**

 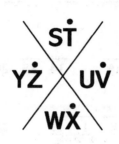 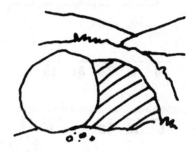

KATIE THOMPSON

Then the angel gave them an important message

Use the code to find his words

| A | B | C | D | E | F | G | H | I | J | K | L | M | N | O | P | Q | R | S | T | U | V | W | X | Y | Z |
|---|---|---|---|---|---|---|---|---|---|---|---|---|---|---|---|---|---|---|---|---|---|---|---|---|---|
| 1 | 2 | 3 | 4 | 5 | 6 | 7 | 8 | 9 | 10 | 11 | 12 | 13 | 14 | 15 | 16 | 17 | 18 | 19 | 20 | 21 | 22 | 23 | 24 | 25 | 26 |

'

10 5 19 21 19    9 19    14 15 20    8 5 18 5

6 15 18    8 5    8 1 19    18 9 19 5 14 !

8 5    9 19    7 15 9 14 7    1 8 5 1 4

15 6    25 15 21    20 15    7 1 12 9 12 5 5 ,

**Matthew 28:6-7**

## An astonishing comeback!

### Aim

To bring home the awesome and astonishing truth of Jesus' resurrection from the dead.

### Preparation

This talk focuses on people and places that have made surprising comebacks having been written off as past history, or having lost something of their past glory. Examples are given below, but these date quickly and you will need to add questions of your own, drawing on recent news (in the world of sport, pop music and cinema, for example). There is no need to prepare any visual material for the talk, though you may find it useful to display the names of places or people who have made an astonishing comeback.

- Which two countries were among the first to regain their identity from the old Soviet Union a few years ago?
  (Latvia and Lithuania)

- Which heavy metal pop group split up several years ago but then reformed with old and new members?
  (Status Quo)

- Which Victorian garden has been carefully restored by the National Trust after years of neglect?
  (Biddulph Grange)

- Which Scottish TV series about a doctor was remade a few years ago, many years after the original series?
  (Dr Finlay)

- What form of transport is running again in Manchester years after it was scrapped?
  (Tram)

- Which Royal home was badly damaged by fire several years ago but has now been fully restored?
  (Windsor Castle)

- What farm animal is once again a common sight, having nearly been lost to our country altogether?
  (Jacob sheep)

- Which Midlands city and cathedral was rebuilt after being almost totally destroyed during the Second World War?
  (Coventry)

- What famous feature of York Minster was lovingly remade, having been destroyed by fire?
  (Rose Window)

- Which football team plays at The Valley, having returned there after years away from the ground during which time the club almost became extinct?
(Charlton Athletic)
- Which well-loved British boxer made numerous comebacks, finally becoming world heavyweight champion?
(Frank Bruno)

### Talk

Tell the congregation you have prepared a quiz about people, things and places which have made surprising comebacks.

Each of these people, things or places seemed for a time to have reached the end of their useful lives, either having finished their careers or having been so badly damaged as to be beyond repair. All were written off as belonging to the past, has-beens which had had their day. But all, in different ways, made unexpected comebacks, finding a new lease of life, each with a fascinating story to tell.

Yet none of those stories, extraordinary though they may be, are as amazing or wonderful as the event we celebrate today – the resurrection of Jesus! He too, like all of these, seemed to belong to the past. He was dead and buried, and, as far as his enemies were concerned, his life over. But, just in case, they took steps to ensure there was no way he could come back, dead or alive:

> The chief priests and the Pharisees gathered before Pilate and said, 'Sir, we remember what the imposter said while he was still alive, "After three days I will rise again." Therefore command the tomb to be made secure on the third day, otherwise his disciples may go and steal him away, and tell the people, "He has been raised from the dead," and the last deception will be worse than the first.' Pilate said to them, 'You have a guard of soldiers; go, make it as secure as you can.' So they went with the guard and made the tomb secure by sealing the stone. *(Matthew 27:62-66)*

And having done that, not only his enemies believed they could forget him; his friends thought so too. They believed it was all over, his life at an end, the only thing left to console them being memories of times past. But then Mary, Peter, and the rest of the disciples came to realise how mistaken they were.

> He is not here; for he has been raised, as he said. Come, see the place where he lay. *(Matthew 28:6)*

> They departed quickly from the tomb with fear and great joy, and ran to tell his disciples. And behold, Jesus met them. *(Matthew 28:8)*

Jesus had come back, just as he promised he would! He was alive! And not just picking up where he left off, but victorious over death and evil, returning to give new life to his followers!

There are many astonishing comebacks in the list we looked at earlier, comebacks which left those who witnessed them shaking their heads in astonishment, but none is anywhere near so amazing or half as wonderful as the resurrection of Christ we celebrate today.                                    NICK FAWCETT

# Reflective material
## (sketches, meditations and poems)

## Forward to new life

Not everyone liked Jesus. There were some people who liked to think they were important, and they were afraid Jesus might get to be more important than they were. There were other people who didn't like what Jesus said. 'He wants us to be friends with bad people,' they would say, 'and with people who have skin diseases and horrible things like that.' So one day, some of these people (who thought they were good, but were really not very nice at all) took Jesus to court and said untrue things about him. They even managed to frighten the judge, so that he wanted to get rid of Jesus and sentenced him to death.

After Jesus died, the bad people thought they'd won. 'That will teach people not to interfere in our religion,' said Jerry, one of the religious leaders.

'Yes,' said another, 'and it will stop all that stuff about God loving everybody – so now we can go on saying that God only loves people like us, and Jesus won't be here to argue about it.'

'I think we've done a good day's work, getting rid of him,' said Jerry.

What they didn't know, of course, was that they hadn't got rid of him at all! Jesus was killed on the Friday. Nothing happened on Saturday, because that was the rest day and people weren't allowed to work. Then on the Sunday, Mary Magdalene said to her friends, Joanna and another Mary, 'Let's go to Jesus' grave.'

Joanna wasn't sure. 'The authorities didn't like Jesus,' she said. 'Won't they be watching his grave to find out who his friends were?'

The other Mary said, 'They probably know about us, anyway. I agree with Mary – we should go and have a look.'

So there they were, very early on Sunday morning, going along to the grave where Jesus had been buried. When they got there, they found that the grave was empty. Then they found someone waiting there, who said, 'It's no good looking for Jesus here – he's alive again, so what would he be doing in a grave?'

Well, Joanna and Mary were terrified! They didn't know what was going on, but they knew they didn't like it very much! So they ran off and didn't dare tell a single person what they had seen.

Mary Magdalene stayed, though. What was said hadn't sunk in and she was still wondering what to do when she thought she saw the gardener. It was not really light yet and she couldn't see very well, but she thought he looked like quite a kind person. So she said to him, 'I've come to find the grave where they buried Jesus, but it's empty. What have you done with him?'

The man said to her, in a very familiar voice, 'Mary!'

It was Jesus! He was alive again! Mary called out, 'Teacher!' and went to grab hold of him, but Jesus stopped her.

'Don't cling on to me,' he said. 'You can't just hang on to the past. We've got new things to do, now!'

'What shall I do, then?' asked Mary.

'Go and find the others,' said Jesus, 'and tell them that I'm alive.'

'Shall I bring them back here?' asked Mary.

'Oh no!' replied Jesus. 'Don't do that. I'm not going to hang around in this place for ever – I've got work to do.'

'So where will they find you?' asked Mary.

'Where they always have,' said Jesus, 'out in the world. Wherever people are, there they'll find me.'

So Mary went running back and told the disciples what Jesus had said. 'He's alive,' she said, 'and no one's ever going to be able to kill him again. He's going to be here for ever, even when we can't see him, and he'll never leave us.'

And do you know, she was quite right.

MICHAEL FORSTER and SIMON SMITH

## The burial

Jesus is not buried by his enemies,
    but by his friends –
    not by Caiaphas and Pilate,
    but by Joseph and Nicodemus;
    not by atheists and unbelievers,
    but by those who love him.
It is his followers who seek
    to lay him reverently to rest.

They bury him deep
    under mountains of tradition,
    safely entomb him
    in the narrow coffin of religion.
They wrap him up tight
    in the protective shroud of dogma,
    preferring funereal ritual
    to resurrection joy,
    and a dim religious light
    to the eye-stinging brightness
    of God's good morning.

The tears are genuine,
    and the precious ointment of fine words,
    preserving the fragrant memory
    of a mummified saviour.
But the heavy stone
    they roll across the tomb
    is the stone of fear –
    fear of the living God.

God-in-a-box
   is not as disturbing
   as God in the world.

Yet they may as well try
   to bury the wind,
   for he is free and alive,
   and his devoted guardians
   cannot hold him down,
   however grave their intentions.                    PETER DAINTY

## Tell the story: Passion and Resurrection narratives

*(See page 362 for a dramatised version of this story.)*

### King of Life and Love

This is the story of how Jesus won the greatest battle in history. He didn't use guns, or swords, or anything like that, and to be honest it didn't even look, at first, as if he *had* won. But let's begin the story.

The trouble with Jesus was that he couldn't be fooled. He knew that the religious leaders weren't as perfect as they pretended to be, and when he was around other people saw it too. And that made him dangerous.

'We've got to get rid of him,' said Caiaphas, the high priest. 'He's asking too many awkward questions, and giving the people funny ideas – all that stuff about love and peace. He's a real troublemaker.'

'Got to make it look legal, though,' warned Annas, Caiaphas' father-in-law. 'We can't just bump him off – let's get the authorities to sentence him to death.'

So they got some soldiers and took Jesus to the Roman Governor, Pontius Pilate.

'He's a really dangerous man,' Caiaphas said. 'He wants to overthrow the government. He claims to be our king, and he tells people to break the law.'

Pontius Pilate saw through it straight away. 'You're just jealous of him,' he said. 'I'm going to let him go.'

Caiaphas was ready for that. 'I tell you, he's a rebel,' he said. 'And if you let him go you're no friend of the Emperor's.'

Pilate went pale. He wasn't the Emperor's favourite person as it was, and he didn't want any more trouble.

'Put him to death,' Caiaphas insisted. 'Crucify him.'

Pilate really hated Caiaphas, so he decided to make fun of him. 'You want me to crucify your *king*?'

'He's not our king,' Caiaphas retorted. 'He just says he is. The only king we've got is the Emperor.'

Pilate smiled. He'd tricked Caiaphas into saying what no good priest would ever have said. Good Jews knew that the only king they had was God – and certainly not the Roman Emperor. But then, bad people will sometimes say almost anything to get what they want.

Well, to cut a long story short, Pilate eventually gave in and had Jesus crucified. But he couldn't resist poking fun at the priests while he was doing it. He had Jesus dressed like a king in a bright purple robe, and had a crown made of horrible sharp thorns put on his head. Then he put a big notice on the cross saying, 'The King of the Jews'.

'He's not our king!' Caiaphas fumed. 'He just said he was! We'd never have a pathetic king like that!'

'Never mind,' said Annas. 'People are soon going to see Jesus for the fraud he really is. All that talk about love and peace – just wait until they drive the nails into him, and he starts cursing and swearing the way people always do. Everyone will know then that *he's* the hypocrite, not us.'

As the soldiers drove in the nails, Jesus shouted out – but it wasn't what Annas had expected. What he shouted was a prayer. 'Father God, please forgive them all – they don't know what they are doing!'

Caiaphas was horrified. 'People are going to love him even more now!' he complained. '*We* might have won the court case, but *he's* won the people's hearts.'

For once, Caiaphas was right. Jesus *had* won the people's hearts. He'd also won the most important battle – between good and evil. Whatever they did, Jesus couldn't be made to say bad things or stop loving them. In that way, he'd won. And that's one reason why the day he died came to be called '*Good Friday*'. But that wasn't the end. There was even better to come.

On the Sunday morning, some women went to visit Jesus' grave. Caiaphas had had it sealed with a big stone and guarded by soldiers because of some fantastic idea he'd got about Jesus' friends stealing his body. But as the women approached, the soldiers had gone and the grave – a big hole in the rock – was standing open with the stone rolled to one side.

While the women were wondering what to do next, a man in white clothes appeared beside them.

'Why are you looking for Jesus here?' he said. 'He's alive. No, really – alive. Go and tell his disciples that God has raised him back to life just the way he promised.'

Suddenly it all fell into place! Of course! This is what God had promised would happen – and they were the first ones to hear about it! The women ran to tell Jesus' friends, and before long everyone was talking about the good news. Caiaphas might be high priest, and Pilate might be governor – and they might have the power to kill people they hated. But there was only one true king – the one who had the power of life and love. And now they knew that that true king was Jesus!

## Drama: King of Life and Love

**Leader**   This is the story of how Jesus won the greatest battle in history. He didn't use guns, or swords, and to be honest it didn't even look, at first, as if he *had* won. But let's begin the story.

| Narrator | Jesus couldn't be fooled. He knew that the religious leaders weren't perfect as they pretended, and when he was around other people saw it too. And that worried Caiaphas, the high priest and his father-in-law, Annas. |
|---|---|
| Caiaphas | We've got to get rid of Jesus. He's asking too many awkward questions, and giving the people funny ideas – all that stuff about love and peace. He's a real troublemaker. |
| Annas | Got to make it look legal, though. We can't just bump him off – let's get the authorities to sentence him to death. |
| Narrator | So they got some soldiers and took Jesus to the Roman Governor, Pontius Pilate. Caiaphas got his word in first. |
| Caiaphas | He's really dangerous – wants to overthrow the government. He claims to be our king, and tells people to break the law. |
| Narrator | Pontius Pilate saw through it straight away. |
| Pilate | You're just jealous of him. I'm going to let him go. |
| Caiaphas | He's a rebel. If you let him go you're no friend of the Emperor's. |
| Narrator | Pilate went pale. He wasn't the Emperor's favourite person as it was, and he didn't want any more trouble. |
| Caiaphas | Put him to death. Crucify him. Nail him to a cross until he dies. |
| Narrator | Pilate really hated Caiaphas, so he decided to make fun of him. |
| Pilate | You want me to crucify your *king*? |
| Caiaphas | He's not our king – just says he is. The only king is the Emperor. |
| Pilate | (*Aside*) Nice one! They've never admitted *that* before! |
| Narrator | Well, to cut a long story short, Pilate eventually gave in and had Jesus crucified. But he couldn't resist poking fun at the priests while he was doing it. He had Jesus dressed like a king in a bright purple robe, and had a crown made of horrible sharp thorns put on his head. Then he put a notice on the cross: 'King of the Jews'. |
| Caiaphas | He's not our king! He just said he was! We'd never have a pathetic king like that! |
| Annas | People will soon see Jesus is a fraud. All that talk about love – when they drive the nails into him, and he starts cursing the way people always do, everyone will know *he's* the hypocrite, not us. |
| Narrator | As the soldiers drove in the nails, Jesus shouted out. |
| Jesus | Father God, please forgive them – they don't understand! |
| Caiaphas | (*Horrified*) People are going to love him even more, now! *We* might have won the court case, but *he's* won the people's hearts. |

| | |
|---|---|
| **Narrator** | For once, Caiaphas was right. Jesus *had* won the most important battle – between good and evil. Whatever they did, Jesus couldn't be made to say bad things or stop loving them. In that way, he'd won. And that's one reason why the day he died is called '*Good Friday*'. But that wasn't the end. There was even better to come. On the Sunday morning, some women went to visit Jesus' grave. |
| **Mary** | How are we going to get past the soldiers? |
| **Salome** | Soldiers? |
| **Mary** | Caiaphas had some fantastic idea about Jesus' friends stealing his body, so he put a guard on the tomb. |
| **Other Mary** | Well, they're not there now. |
| **Salome** | (*Mockingly*) Perhaps something frightened them off. |
| **Other Mary** | Look – the tomb's open – the stone has been rolled away! |
| **Narrator** | Suddenly, an angel appeared beside them. |
| **Angel** | Why are you looking for Jesus here? He's alive. No, really – alive. Go and tell his disciples that God has raised him back to life just the way he promised. |
| **Narrator** | Suddenly it all fell into place! Of course! This is what God had promised would happen. The women ran to tell Jesus' friends, and before long everyone was talking about the good news. Caiaphas might be high priest, and Pilate might be governor – and they might have the power to kill people they hated. But there was only one true king – the one who had the power of life and love. And now they knew that that true king was Jesus! |

MICHAEL FORSTER

## The Resurrection convergence

If Jesus did not rise from the dead, then there is no good news. Evil would have triumphed, and we could all end up on a cross for all God cared, and that would be that. Where does the evidence for the Resurrection come from?

It is not a case of a fable that grew and grew in the telling. There are several independent sources of witness to the fact of Jesus' being risen. There is the version of Mark, which is repeated by Matthew and Luke. Then Matthew has his own independent version of what happened, and Luke too has his own version which does not come from Mark. There is the version of John's gospel, and the further version in that gospel which stems from John's disciples.

The evidence from Paul in his First Letter to the Corinthians dates from only three years after the Resurrection itself. He tells the Corinthians that the truth about Jesus' death and Resurrection which he handed to them about AD 48 was like a deposit held in a bank, since Paul himself was taught it fifteen years earlier, neither more nor less than the original message. Perhaps even closer to the events themselves are the speeches of Peter written out in Luke's Acts of the Apostles, speeches which may date from the very year of the Resurrection. They use language and terminology that had gone out of date by the time Luke finally wrote that book. Then, too, there is the fact that Paul can write to churches all over the Mediterranean, knowing that they believe all he believes.

Each of these sources agrees on the basic message, and the apostles were so sure the Resurrection appearances were from God that they were willing to die for the truth of them.

GERALD O'MAHONY

## Dead and Alive Again

*Based on the Passion and Resurrection Narratives*

**Narrator**  Not everyone liked Jesus. Some people liked to think they were important, and were afraid Jesus might get to be more important than they were. Others didn't like what Jesus said. So one day, some of these people (who thought they were good, but were really not nice at all) said horrible things about Jesus and had him killed. Jesus' enemies thought they'd won. What they didn't know, of course, was that they *hadn't* got rid of him, at all! Jesus was killed on the Friday. Then on the Sunday, Mary Magdalene and her friends had an idea.

**Mary**  I'm going to Jesus' grave. I want to put some flowers on it. Coming, Joanna?

**Joanna**  I'm not sure. Won't the people who killed Jesus be watching his grave, to find out who his friends are?

**Mary**  So what? They know about us, anyway.

**Joanna**  I suppose you're right, Mary – I'd like to go.

**Narrator**  So they went together but when they got there, they found that the grave was empty. They were very puzzled.

- They *scratched their heads*
- They *wrung their hands*
- They *peered all round*

Then they noticed a stranger waiting there.

**Stranger**  It's no good looking for Jesus here – he's alive again, so what would he be doing in a grave?

**Narrator**  Joanna was terrified! She didn't know what was going on, but she knew she didn't like it! So she ran off, but Mary Magdalene stayed. What was said hadn't sunk in, and she was still wondering what to do when she thought she saw the gardener. It was not really light yet, and she couldn't see clearly.

| Mary | Excuse me, I've come to find Jesus' grave. |
|------|---------------------------------------------|
| **Jesus** | Mary! |
| **Narrator** | It was Jesus! He *was* alive again! Mary went to grab him, but Jesus stopped her. |
| **Jesus** | Don't cling on to me! You can't just hang on to the past. We've got new things to do, now! Go and tell the others that I'm alive. |
| **Mary** | Shall I bring them back here? |
| **Jesus** | Oh no! I'm not going to hang around in this place for ever – I've got work to do. |
| **Mary** | So where will they find you? |
| **Jesus** | Where they always have – out in the world. Wherever people are, there they'll find me. |
| **Narrator** | So Mary ran back and told the disciples what Jesus had said. |
| **Mary** | He's alive, and no one's ever going to be able to kill him again. He's going to be here for ever, even when we can't see him, and he'll never leave us. |
| **Narrator** | And d'you know, she was quite right.          MICHAEL FORSTER |

## What a day

*Theme: Easter*

### Aim

To show why Easter is so special to Christians. A sad time, a confusing message, yet a time of rejoicing and celebration.

### Puppet sketch

| John | *(to Micky)* I hear you had quite a day yesterday. |
|------|----------------------------------------------------|
| **Micky** | You can say that again! I was so excited that I woke up really early and dashed into Mum and Dad's room. But they told me to go back to bed. Had they forgotten? |
| **John** | Forgotten what? |
| **Micky** | Don't you start! Later, I went downstairs to collect my post, but there was none for me. Had everyone forgotten? |
| **John** | Forgotten what? |
| **Micky** | There were no cards, no smiling faces, and worst of all, no presents! I thought they loved me! I almost cried! Had they forgotten? |
| **John** | Forgotten what? |

**Micky**   Then we went to Grandma's! I went inside the house when . . .

**John**   Surprise! *(both look happy)*

**Micky**   Exactly! Balloons, streamers, cheering, presents! All my family and friends!

**John**   Yep! A surprise birthday party.

**Micky**   They hadn't forgotten after all. I was so happy I almost cried.

**John**   Gosh, twice in one day.

**Micky**   Yep, I had been really sad, then I was really happy! What a day! I must go, more presents to open!

JOHN HARDWICK

## Meditation of Mary Magdalene

I was shattered at the time,
    inconsolable.
It was as though the bottom had fallen out of my world
    and there was nothing left to live for.
How could they do that to him, I asked myself?
How could they destroy someone so loving and gentle,
    so caring,
    so good?
Yet they had.
I'd seen it myself,
    I'd watched as he drew his last agonised breath;
    and it was dreadful,
    more terrible than I can ever describe.
It wasn't just the pain he went through, though that was awful enough;
    it was the isolation of it all –
    standing there before Pilate, alone,
    forsaken by his friends,
    one man against the might of an empire;
    groaning under the lash of the whip, alone,
    no one to offer him comfort,
    no one to bathe his wounds;
    hanging upon that cross, alone,
    crying out in such heart-breaking anguish,
    as though he were separated not just from us but from God himself.
I felt at the time I would never forget it,
    that the memory would haunt me for the rest of my days.
And so it would have,
    unquestionably,
    were it not for what came after.

It was all so unexpected –
    suddenly, in the nightmare of my grief, a ray of sunshine,
    and then joy, immersing me in its light.
One moment despair,
    then the stone rolled away,
    the tomb empty,
    the mysterious stranger appearing from nowhere,
    and that familiar voice speaking my name.
One moment tears,
    the next laughter.
One moment death,
    the next life.
And now my heart dances with delight.
I still can scarcely take it in though;
    sometimes I have to pinch myself to be sure it's not all a dream.
But no, it's true.
He died yet rose again!
He was killed yet conquered death!
He lived and lives again!
I really thought that life was over,
    not just for him but for me.
But I was wrong, wasn't I?
For it wasn't over;
    it was only just beginning.

NICK FAWCETT

## Meditation of Peter

He was back!
Back in the land of the living,
    just when we'd given up hope!
Three days it had been,
    three days of dark despair as slowly the truth sank home –
    our Lord, laid in a tomb,
    dead and buried,
    never to walk this earth again.
We couldn't believe it at first,
    none of us,
    even though we'd seen it for ourselves.
We expected to wake up any moment to find it was all a dream,
    a dreadful mistake that had somehow taken us in.
But as the numbness passed, so the reality hit us,
    and the pain began in earnest.
It was an end to everything –
    our plans,
    our hopes,
    our dreams.

There was nothing left to live for,
    that's how we felt –
    we'd pinned our hopes on him,
    and he was gone.
Only he wasn't!
He was there,
    meeting Mary in the garden as her heart broke beside the tomb.
He was there,
    on the Emmaus road as two followers trudged slowly home,
    their world in tatters.
He was there,
    speaking to Thomas, breaking through his disbelief!
He was there,
    standing among us in the upper room!
He was back in the land of the living,
    and suddenly so were we –
    faith rekindled,
    hope renewed,
    joy reborn,
    life beginning again!
                                                    NICK FAWCETT


## Meditation of John

One look, that's all it took!
One look,
    and I knew beyond all doubt that God was at work,
    that Jesus was alive!
I should have known it sooner, of course,
    for he'd told us what to expect often enough,
    but when the hammer blow fell
    we simply couldn't see beyond it,
    tears blinding our minds as well as our eyes.
It was when Mary came bursting in,
    beside herself with excitement,
    that the mist started to clear,
    that his words about death and resurrection
    came flooding back,
    rekindling a flame that had all but been extinguished.
I ran then as I've never run before,
    hope lending wings to my feet,
    heart pounding within me,
    not just from the exertion
    but from the emotion that had taken hold of me,
    the curious mixture of fear and exhilaration.

I wanted so much to believe it was true,
　　only I was afraid it might be some cruel hoax
　　or fancy of the imagination,
　　a trick of the mind or, worse still, of our enemies.
But when I went in to the tomb
　　and found the abandoned grave clothes,
　　then I knew,
　　and my spirit soared in jubilation.
He was not there:
　　he had risen just as he promised,
　　death not able to have the final word.
And suddenly everything fitted into place,
　　the heartache, the hurt, the humiliation –
　　it was all meant to be,
　　all a part of God's sovereign purpose!
Where we had seen darkness, he had brought light!
Where there had been death, now there was life!
Everything was turned around,
　　transformed,
　　renewed,
　　sharing in the wonder of resurrection.
One look, that's all it took –
　　one look, and life was changed for ever!

NICK FAWCETT

# Additional Easter Material

*Second week of Easter*
**John 20:19-31**
*Personal encounters with the risen Christ; faith and doubt*

*Third week of Easter*
**Luke 24:13-35**
*Jesus on the Emmaus Road opens the Scriptures*
*and is recognised in the breaking of bread*

## A reading from the Gospel of John (20:19-31)

Late on the Sunday evening the disciples sat huddled together, feeling sad and afraid. The doors of the room were locked, to stop the Jews finding them.

Suddenly, Jesus appeared in the room with them and said, 'Peace be with you.'

They were amazed when they saw him and could hardly believe their eyes. But Jesus showed them the wounds in his hands and where his side had been pierced by the sword, and they were filled with joy and wonder.

Once again Jesus said, 'Peace be with you.' Then he breathed on them, saying, 'The Holy Spirit has been given to you. Whatever you choose to forgive will be forgiven. Whatever is not forgiven by you will remain unforgiven.'

The disciple called Thomas was not with the others when Jesus appeared to them. When they told him that they had seen Jesus, he scoffed at them and said, 'Unless I see for myself the wounds in his hands and his side, I will not believe you.'

Several days later, when Thomas was with the other disciples, Jesus appeared to them again, and greeted them with the words, 'Peace be with you.' Turning to Thomas he said, 'See and touch the wounds in my hands; feel the wound in my side and doubt no more.'

Thomas fell to the ground and said, 'My Lord and my God.'

Jesus said to him, 'Because you have seen you now believe, but blessed are those who have not seen and yet believe.'

Only some of the marvellous things which Jesus did and which were witnessed by his disciples are written down in this book. These have been recorded so that you might believe in Jesus, as the Christ, the Son of God, and through that faith and belief in him you may have life.

This is the Gospel of the Lord
**Praise to you, Lord Jesus Christ**                                    KATIE THOMPSON

### A reading from the Gospel of Luke (24:13-35)

On that same Sunday morning two disciples of Jesus were making their way to a village called Emmaus, a short distance from Jerusalem. They were totally miserable as they talked about the events of the past days, and the death of Jesus.

As they walked, Jesus himself joined them, but they did not recognise him.

Jesus asked them, 'What are you talking about together?'

One of them, called Cleopas, answered, 'Surely you must have heard about what happened to Jesus of Nazareth! He was a powerful prophet who was handed over to the chief priests, and the Roman governor who had him crucified. We believed that he was the Saviour sent by God. All this happened more than two days ago, and we have heard this very morning that his body is missing from the tomb where they laid him. Some of the women claimed that an angel told them that Jesus has risen and is alive, but we are not sure what has happened.'

Jesus said to them, 'Do you not believe what the prophets have foretold?' He began to explain to them the prophecies about himself in the Scriptures.

When they arrived at Emmaus, Jesus seemed to be travelling further, but because it was late in the day the disciples asked him to stay and share a meal with them.

When they were at supper Jesus took some bread, blessed it, broke it and gave it to them. At that moment they saw clearly that the stranger was in fact Jesus, but he had already disappeared from their sight.

'Of course it was the Lord,' they said. 'Remember how our hearts seemed to burn as he shared the Scriptures with us. How could we have been so blind!'

At once they returned to Jerusalem and found the other disciples gathered together and filled with joy, because Jesus had appeared to Simon.

'Yes, he is risen,' they said. 'We knew him in the breaking of the bread.' And they began to tell the others what had happened that day on the road to Emmaus.

This is the Gospel of the Lord
**Praise to you, Lord Jesus Christ**                                    KATIE THOMPSON

# Introductory material

'I believe in God, the Father Almighty, creator of heaven and earth. I believe in Jesus Christ, his only Son, our Lord.' The opening words of the Apostles' Creed, which across the centuries have been accepted and repeated as a summary of the faith of the Church, the essentials of Christian belief. And probably most of us most of the time would be happy to add our voices alongside those who have gone before us. Most, but not all, of the time – because for virtually every one of us there are times when we find ourselves wrestling with doubts; a multitude of questions which unexpectedly thrust themselves upon us, disturbing our peace and even threatening to undermine our faith completely. To make things worse, such moments are often compounded by a sense of guilt, a feeling that we are wrong and even sinful to entertain such thoughts. The result can be a lonely struggle in the wilderness, crushed by a sense of isolation, failure and shame. Yet if we look at the Scriptures we see there that doubt is not as uncommon as we might at first imagine. Alongside the glowing testimonies of faith, there are also several examples of those whose faith was tested to the limit; those who were not quite so sure and who found themselves struggling to keep going. Who can forget the words of the father who came to Jesus seeking help for his son: 'I believe; help my unbelief'; or the words of Thomas: 'Unless I see the mark of the nails in his hands, and put my finger in the mark of the nails and my hand in his side, I will not believe.' Even Jesus himself apparently faced a time when for a moment he seemed to question his ability to continue: 'Father, if you are willing, remove this cup from me; yet, not my will but yours be done.' Doubt may come to us all, however secure in faith we appear to be. Do not fear it, for it is not something to be ashamed of. Believe, rather, that God is able to take and use your questions to lead you into a deeper understanding of his purpose and a richer sense of his love. Do that, and you will discover that doubt is not the opposite of faith, but for many of us an essential part of the journey of discipleship.

NICK FAWCETT

# Prayers

## Easter praise

Living God,
  we thank you for this day of praise and celebration –
    a day of hope after despair,
    joy after sorrow,
    life after death –
    **a day to lift up our hearts**
    **and to offer you our praise!**

Loving God,
  we remember today all you have done for us
    and for all the world –
    your great victory over sin and death,
    **your triumph over everything that keeps us from you**
    **and prevents us living the life you want us to lead.**

Saving God,
  we join this day with your Church in every age
    to bring our Easter worship –
    to acknowledge you as a God of love and power,
    **to welcome Christ as our living Lord.**

Sovereign God,
  **breathe new life into our hearts this day.**
  **Fire us with renewed confidence and enthusiasm.**
  **Fill us with resurrection power,**
    **and grant that we might meet and walk with Christ,**
    **offering him our joyful faithful service**
    **this and every day,**
    **for his name's sake.**
  **Amen.**                                              NICK FAWCETT

## Easter victory

Loving God,
  we praise you once more for the good news of Easter,
    the triumphant message of resurrection –
    new hope,
    new joy,
    new life!
  Christ is risen,
    **he is risen indeed!**

We praise you for what we see in the Easter stories –
    your love that could not be kept down,
    your purpose that could not be defeated,
    your goodness that could not be destroyed.
  Christ is risen,
    **he is risen indeed!**

Teach us that what was true then is true now –
    that resurrection is not just about life after death
    but about constant new beginnings,
    the way you are able to transform every part of our lives,
    the way you are always bringing renewal –
    and may that truth inspire us
    to keep on following you
    not only through the good but the bad.
  Christ is risen,
    **he is risen indeed!**

When life seems hard,
    when we feel overwhelmed by trials and temptations,
    when faith seems to fly in the face of reason,
    assure us once more that your love will not be overcome.
  Christ is risen,
    **he is risen indeed!**

When our work seems to bear no fruit,
   when our efforts go unrewarded,
   when our hopes remain unrealised,
   teach us that your purpose will ultimately be fulfilled.
Christ is risen,
   **he is risen indeed!**

When the innocent suffer,
   when goodness is rejected,
   when evil appears victorious,
   teach us that right will finally emerge victorious.
Christ is risen,
   **he is risen indeed!**

Loving God,
   grant to us the deep inner assurance
     which only Easter can bring –
     that whatever life brings,
     whatever we face,
     however things may seem,
     your will shall be done and your kingdom come.
Christ is risen,
   **he is risen indeed!**
**Thanks be to God!**
   **Amen.**
                                                       NICK FAWCETT

## Thanksgiving – triumph from tragedy

Lord Jesus Christ,
   we thank you for the great message of Easter –
     your awesome triumph over the forces of darkness
     and the power of evil.
We thank you that, in what the world counted defeat,
   you won the greatest of victories;
   that what looked to be a disaster
   proved to be the most glorious of conquests.
In the valley of sorrow and suffering,
   in the shadow of death,
   you have demonstrated that God is present,
   working out his eternal purpose.
**For that glorious truth, we thank you.**

We thank you that women arriving at the tomb
   found their tears turned to laughter,
   that disciples on the Emmaus Road

found confusion turned to faith,
that Apostles trembling behind locked doors
found despair turned to confidence,
that your people across the centuries
have found sorrow turned to joy.
Time and again you have repeated the Easter miracle,
supremely demonstrating your purpose
in the face of events which seem to contradict it.
In the valley of sorrow and suffering,
in the shadow of death,
you have demonstrated that God is present,
working out his eternal purpose.
**For that glorious truth, we thank you.**

We thank you for our own experiences of your resurrection power –
occasions when we have cried out
from the depths of our beings,
called to you from the pit of despair,
and discovered not only that you can lift us out,
but that you were there with us in our need,
holding our heads above the water,
and using our experience of adversity
to deepen our faith and broaden our understanding.
In the valley of sorrow and suffering,
in the shadow of death,
you have demonstrated that God is present,
working out his eternal purpose.
**For that glorious truth, we thank you.**

We thank you for the assurance that nothing in heaven or earth
can separate us from your love,
that no situation, however dreadful it may seem,
is finally beyond your power to redeem,
and we rejoice that you hold a kingdom in store for us
where all this world's trials and tragedies will be no more;
where we shall dwell for ever in the light of your presence.
Take, then, the changes and chances of this life,
and help us, whatever we may face,
to trust that your purpose will triumph over all.
In the valley of sorrow and suffering,
in the shadow of death,
you have demonstrated that God is present,
working out his eternal purpose.
**For that glorious truth, we thank you.**

**Amen.**                                                          NICK FAWCETT

## Petition – the continuing reality of Easter

Sovereign God,
    we thank you for the realities of Easter
        which we continue to celebrate today,
        realities that make such a difference to life –
        the victory of good over evil,
        love over hate, life over death;
        the turning of weakness into strength,
        fear into courage, doubt into faith;
        a new beginning where it had seemed like the end,
        new hope where there had seemed despair
        new confidence where there had been confusion.
**Teach us to live each day as your Easter people.**

Sovereign God,
    we thank you that Easter
        is not just about events long ago,
        but about life now,
        not just about others, but about us,
        not just about one thing, but everything!
**Teach us to live each day as your Easter people.**

Help us, we pray, to live each day in the light of Easter,
    with its joy bubbling up in our hearts,
    its laughter shining from our eyes,
    and its message always on our lips.
So may others, seeing the difference it has made to us,
    discover the difference it can make for them.
**Teach us to live each day as your Easter people,**
    **to the glory of your name.**
    **Amen.**
            NICK FAWCETT

## A short prayer

Gracious God,
    we come today confessing our faith
    in your love,
    your goodness,
    your purpose.
We acknowledge your greatness,
    we rejoice in your mercy,
    and we thank you for the many blessings
    you have showered upon us.
But we come today also confessing our doubt –
    the many things we don't understand,
    the statements of faith which don't make sense,

the events of life which seem to contradict
everything we believe about you.
Gracious God,
there are times when we are sure
and times when we are uncertain;
times when we feel ready to take on the world
and times when faith hangs by a thread.
Give us sufficient trust in you
to acknowledge all such feelings openly,
and sufficient humility
to offer each to you honestly in prayer.
Save us from taking refuge
in hollow words or empty ritual,
but teach us to face the challenges life brings
and to work through our faith
in the light of them,
so that, having been tested,
it may grow the stronger,
able to face all and still to stand,
through Jesus Christ our Lord.
Amen.                                          NICK FAWCETT

# All-age-talk material

## The Resurrection

Beforehand cut a rough circle shape from a very large carton (such as will hide a small child). This represents a gravestone. Also cut a number of teardrop shapes out of paper and leave one of these on each row before the service. Just before the talk secrete a small child behind the card gravestone, holding a bunch of spring flowers.

First talk about times when we have been disappointed with a present or a treat, and how let down and rather flat we feel. The disciples must have felt like that on Good Friday when Jesus, their master and friend had been killed.

Sometimes we feel disappointed with God, too. Perhaps he doesn't answer our prayer for someone we love to get better, or perhaps things aren't working out for us in the way we hoped they would. Ask people to find the teardrop on their row and, as they pass it along to the aisle, to look at it and think of their own personal disappointments or regrets. Have a couple of people to collect the teardrops in a basket and walk up in silence to lay them at the foot of the cross. In a way, that's what was happening as Jesus hung dying there.

But Jesus couldn't be bound in death, and on the third day the cave entrance was found rolled away and Jesus was alive. At this point, roll the card stone away and the small child jumps up, holding a bunch of flowers, which s/he gives out to people all over the church.                    SUSAN SAYERS

## I believe

Begin by passing round a 'feeling' bag with a couple of objects inside it, such as a sieve and a marble, for instance. Each child has a turn to feel the bag and guess what the objects are, but the guesses aren't shared until everyone has had a go.

Then each one says: 'I believe there's a . . . in the bag.' Take the objects out to see who's right, and talk about how they didn't know for sure what was there until they saw it, but they could believe it by using clues, such as what it felt like.

Display a large sign: 'I believe Jesus is God's Son.'

How do we know?

Have we actually seen him?

What clues do we use, then?

Talk about the record of his friends in the Bible, the way Jesus helps us to be kind when we feel like being nasty (so long as we ask him); the way he helps us through sad or painful times; and the happy feeling we have when we enjoy the lovely world with him.

Then read the Thomas section of *Jesus is Risen* and give the children a picture of this to colour, with Thomas's prayer on it. Encourage them to use this prayer themselves in church or at home.

SUSAN SAYERS

## Read John 20:19-31

As Jesus appeared to the disciples, he greeted them in a traditional Jewish way: 'Peace to you.' Peace was not quite what the disciples felt at that moment in time. They'd locked themselves in the room for fear of the Jewish leaders.

After greeting them again, just in case they'd not understood the first time, Jesus then tells them that he's going to send them OUT! Just what the disciples wanted to hear!

Firstly, Jesus told the disciples that he was sending them, just as the Father had sent him to preach the good news to everyone.

Secondly, Jesus wasn't sending them out to face the world alone, he gave them the Holy Spirit who would enable them to carry on where Jesus had left off.

Finally, he gave them the authority, and power, to forgive anyone's sins. This wasn't a simple throwaway line that was said as an afterthought. Jesus gave the disciples the ability to forgive sins because he, Jesus, had become the ultimate sacrifice and paid the price of sin for all time.

As a result of the disciples being sent out, and communicating the good news of Jesus, we too have the opportunity of accepting Jesus as God's son, who has made it eternally possible for us to be free from the effects of sin, and become part of the family of God.

PETE TOWNSEND

John 20:19

KATIE THOMPSON

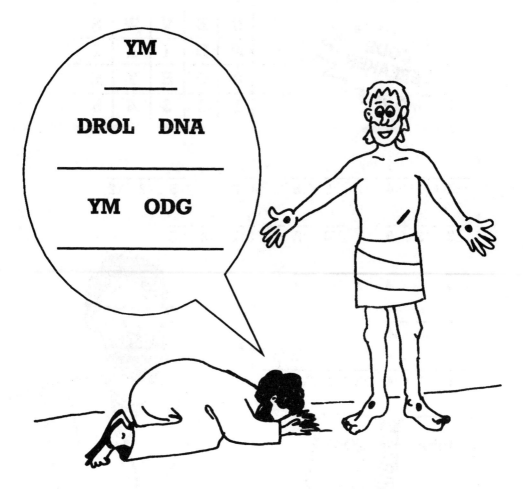

John 20:28

KATIE THOMPSON

The disciple called Thomas was not there when Jesus appeared. He would not believe what the other disciples told him!

Use the code breaker to find his words

CODE BREAKER

| △ | U | E | V | W | S |
|---|---|---|---|---|---|
| ○ | N | D | I | L | I |
| □ | B | O | H | T | E |
|   | 1 | 2 | 3 | 4 | 5 |

'
△1 ○1 ○4 △2 △5 △5   ○3   △5 △2 △2

□3 ○3 △5   △4 □2 △1 ○1 ○2 △5

○3   △4 ○3 ○4 ○4

○1 □2 □4

□1 △2 ○4 ○5 □5 △3 □5 !'

John  20:25

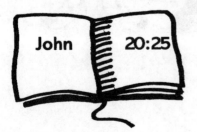

KATIE THOMPSON

**Luke 24:13-35**

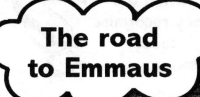

# The road to Emmaus

Two disciples of Jesus were on the road to Emmaus when another traveller joined them

Find which route will take them to Emmaus

KATIE THOMPSON

Fit the numbered words in place to reveal the answer!

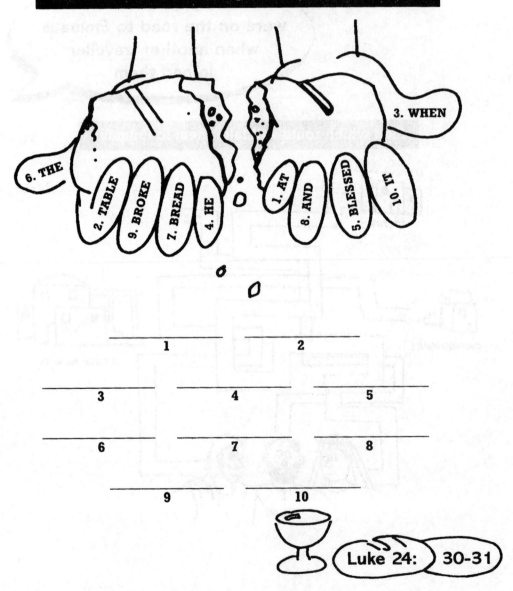

Luke 24: 30-31

KATIE THOMPSON

> **Sadly they told the traveller all about Jesus of Nazareth, and how he had been put to death**

**Use the code to see who the traveller was and what he talked about**

|   | A | B | C | D | E | F | G |   |
|---|---|---|---|---|---|---|---|---|
|   | H | I | O | R | X | E | K | H |
|   | J | C | A | L | N | P | D | I |
|   | M | T | B | U | S | F | W | J |

A,I  F,H  E,J  D,J  E,J        F,H  E,H  F,I  D,I  C,I  B,H  E,I  F,H  G,I

C,I  D,I  D,I        B,J  A,H  F,H

E,J  B,I  D,H  B,H  F,I  B,J  D,J  D,H  F,H  E,J

C,I  C,J  C,H  D,J  B,J        A,H  B,H  A,J  E,J  F,H  D,I  F,J

KATIE THOMPSON

# Reflective material
## (sketches, meditations and poems)

## Meditation of Andrew

We've seen Jesus!
No, don't laugh,
   we've seen him, I tell you!
We made the mistake of dismissing it ourselves,
   scoffing when the women came racing back wild-eyed with excitement.
'Pull yourselves together!' we told them,
   'for God's sake calm down!'
We couldn't believe he was alive,
   refused to accept it could possibly be true.
And when they admitted they couldn't be certain,
   that they'd only seen the empty tomb rather than Jesus himself,
   then we looked for some simpler explanation,
   an answer more in line with common sense.
Even when Mary returned, tears of joy in her eyes,
   even when the two from Emmaus spoke of having seen him,
   we wouldn't accept it, certain that we knew best.
It's understandable, I suppose;
   I mean, you'd think twice, wouldn't you,
   if you'd seen your best friend murdered,
   sealed in the tomb,
   only to be told he'd been spotted down the street?
And anyway, we didn't want to build our hopes up.
We were still reeling from the shock, the horror, the sorrow of it all.
Yet if I'm honest there's more to it than that,
   for most of all our pride was hurt.
If he was alive, we reasoned, then why hadn't we seen him?
Why should Mary,
   or those two disciples,
   or anyone else come to that,
   have seen him before we did?
We were his chosen disciples,
   we the ones who'd given up everything to follow him,
   we those who had taken all the risks –
   so if he had risen surely we'd have known?
It's awful, I know, but that's the way we saw it
   until he finally appeared to us.
We should have remembered, of course, what he'd said so often,
   how the first will be last,
   the least greatest;
   but we still had much to learn
   and were too full of ourselves by half.

Anyway, there we were,
   huddled together in that upstairs room,
   arguing about what it all meant,
   when there he was,
   standing among us,
   arms outstretched in welcome.
Where he came from or where he went after I've no idea.
I only know that it was him –
   Jesus –
   and that he was alive,
   wonderfully,
   amazingly,
   gloriously,
   alive!

NICK FAWCETT

## Meditation of Thomas

I wanted to know, that's all,
   to see for myself if it could possibly be true –
   was that so awful?
Remember, we'd *all* doubted at first,
   when the women came back that morning,
   dismissing their story of the empty tomb as so much nonsense,
   so why point the finger at me,
   as though *I* questioned and *they* didn't?
All right, the situation had changed since then, I accept that,
   for they all claimed to have seen him in the meantime,
   and not just them, but others,
   each adamant the Lord had risen,
   yet as much as I wanted to believe it, I simply couldn't,
   not unless the proof was spelt out for me in black and white.
That was me all over, I'm afraid,
   the way I'd been since a boy,
   struggling to accept anything I couldn't touch for myself
   or see with my own eyes,
   and I'd said as much to Jesus before he died,
   that day he spoke about his Father's house,
   and his going there to prepare a place for us.
'Believe in God,' he'd said,
   'believe also in me.'
A wonderful promise, yes,
   only to me he was talking in riddles,
   and I made no bones about it:
   'Lord, we do not know where you are going.
   How can we know the way?'

He wasn't angry with me,
  though he could have been,
  for after all that time, all he'd said, I should have known,
  just as I should have understood
  he would rise from the tomb and return among us.
He'd spoken of it, often enough,
  done his best to prepare us not simply for his death
  but his resurrection to follow,
  but, as so often happens, we dwelt on the bad
  and forgot the good,
  unable to see beyond the demands of the present moment.
So despite it all I refused to believe,
  convinced there were still too many questions
  and not enough answers.
And I'd be doing that still,
  still wondering if it ever could be,
  but for his grace.
For suddenly he was there again, standing among us,
  arms outstretched in welcome,
  those pierced hands reaching out to me, Thomas,
  and I knew I'd been wrong –
  he was alive, just as they'd said,
  risen and victorious –
  and I knelt down in worship,
  my heart overflowing with thanksgiving,
  for he'd come, despite me,
  despite my lack of faith –
  though I had doubted him,
  still he believed in me!                      NICK FAWCETT

# Ascension

# Ascension Day

*Jesus returns to the Father in glory*

## Acts 1:1-11

*(also Daniel 7:9-14; Psalms 47, 93; Ephesians 1:15-23; Luke 24:44-53)*

### A reading from the Acts of the Apostles (Acts 1:1-11)

In the first part of my work, Your Excellency, I have told the story of Jesus – all he began to do and say. I bring this to an end by telling you what orders he gave to his friends on the day when he was taken up from us. After his death, for a month or more, he showed himself alive again to his friends and talked to them about God's Way. While he was with them, he told them not to leave the city.

'You must wait here,' he said, 'until God gives you his power, as he has promised to do and as I have told you. John the Hermit baptised people with water; before long God will give you his own power in your hearts.' Jesus and his friends were together on the hill called 'Olive Orchard'.

'Lord,' they asked him, 'will you now make the Jewish people a free nation again?'

'That's God's business!' said Jesus. 'It's not your business to ask "How long are we going to be an occupied country?" or "When shall we be free?" You will be given God's own power when his spirit comes into your hearts; and then *your* business will be to go all over the world to tell everybody what you know about me. You must start here in this city first of all, go out into your own homeland, and then right to the very ends of the earth.'

With these words, Jesus was hidden by a cloud and they saw him no more.

ALAN DALE

# Introductory material

How many of you would read a novel only to put it aside without reading the last page? Or how many would do a jigsaw puzzle and leave out the last piece? Unthinkable, surely? And yet there is a sense in which we as Christians can do something similar when it comes to Ascension. We celebrate the birth of Jesus, we mark the time he spent in the wilderness, his triumphant entry into Jerusalem, the last supper he shared with his disciples, his death and resurrection, not to mention the giving of his Holy Spirit. But Ascension all too often is the poor relation of the Christian Year, celebrated by the few rather than the many. Yet to ignore the message of this day is to content ourselves with an unfinished, incomplete Gospel, for Ascension reminds us that Jesus is greater than we can ever begin to imagine – one with God himself, before all, over all, and in all.

NICK FAWCETT

# Prayers

## Praise – the King of kings

Lord Jesus Christ,
>we worship you today as the Lord of lords and King of kings.
>We bring your our praise,
>>we offer our homage,
>>we dedicate our lives to your service.
>Blessing and honour and glory and might are yours, O Lord,
>>**this day and for evermore!**

>We acknowledge you as sovereign over life,
>>the Lord of creation, through whom all things were made,
>>and in whom we live and move and have our being.
>Blessing and honour and glory and might are yours, O Lord,
>>**this day and for evermore!**

>We acknowledge you as sovereign over death,
>>the risen Lord who triumphed over the grave,
>>the resurrection and the life.
>Through you the door to eternity has been opened,
>>the path to your everlasting kingdom.
>Blessing and honour and glory and might are yours, O Lord,
>>**this day and for evermore!**

>We acknowledge you as sovereign over evil,
>>the crucified Christ who nailed our sins to the cross,
>>who defeated the powers of darkness,
>>who conquered hatred with love.
>Blessing and honour and glory and might are yours, O Lord,
>>**this day and for evermore!**

Lord Jesus Christ,
>we acknowledge you as sovereign over all,
>>Lord of space and time,
>>ruler of the ends of the earth,
>>enthroned in splendour at the right hand of the Father.
>Blessing and honour and glory and might are yours, O Lord,
>>**this day and for evermore!**

>**Amen.**                                        NICK FAWCETT

## Ascension confession

Lord Jesus Christ,
>we remember today
>>how your apostles stood gazing into heaven,

troubled and confused,
fearing they had lost you,
struggling to make sense of their experience.
**Open our eyes to your glory.**

We remember how in the days following your Ascension
they remained hidden behind locked doors,
bound by the weakness of their imagination,
tied down by the feebleness of their vision,
restricted by the smallness of their faith.
**Open our eyes to your glory.**

Instead of worshipping you
as King of kings and Lord of lords,
they thought you had gone from them.
Instead of rejoicing at your exaltation,
they felt they were separated from you once again.
**Open our eyes to your glory.**

Despite what they had been told,
they looked still for the man they knew and understood,
the man who had walked the streets of Nazareth,
who had talked with them beside the sea of Galilee,
who had suffered and died for them in Jerusalem.
**Open our eyes to your glory.**

But you showed them that Jesus was greater
than they had begun to imagine –
not bound by space and time,
nor tied down to one particular place,
nor restricted to one particular people,
but ascended to your side
and one with you for all eternity.
**Open our eyes to your glory.**

Lord Jesus Christ,
forgive us that all too often
we make the same mistake as the apostles –
we expect you to fit in with our own expectations,
we assume we know all there is to know about you,
we settle for a comfortable, cosy picture of you
that offers much and asks little;
and when that way of thinking
is challenged or threatened,
we are puzzled,
suddenly overcome by a multitude of questions.
**Open our eyes to your glory.**

Forgive us that our horizons have been too narrow,
  our sights set too low,
  our expectations too limited.
**Open our eyes to your glory.**

Help us to glimpse the wonder of who you are
  and the untold possibilities of all you can do,
  catching our breath in awe
  and captured by a new vision of your kingdom.
**Open our eyes to your glory,**
  **for we ask it in your name.**
  **Amen.**                                              NICK FAWCETT


## Intercession – the Servant King

Lord Jesus Christ,
  Ruler of all,
    Servant of all,
    we pray again for the kingdoms and rulers of this world,
    that those in positions of authority
      may use their power in the service of their people
      and for the good of all.
Servant King,
  **may your love reign supreme.**

We pray for those who take counsel together on behalf of nations,
  all those who carry the responsibility of leadership.
Grant them wisdom in all their decisions,
    humility to listen to the point of view of others,
    courage to stand up for what is right,
    and a determination to work for justice and peace.
Servant King,
  **may your love reign supreme.**

We think of our own country,
    and we pray for the royal family and especially our Queen,
    thanking you for the example she has given,
    the dedication to duty she has shown,
    and the commitment to our nation she has displayed
    throughout her rule.
Grant to her,
    and to her successor when the time comes,
    your guidance, discernment, strength and inspiration.
Servant King,
  **may your love reign supreme.**

We pray for our government and members of Parliament,
 giving thanks once more for the service they give.
Guide them in their discussions and decisions,
 and give them a proper sense
 of the responsibility entrusted to them.
Help them to work not just for personal or party interest
 but for the good of all.
Servant King,
 **may your love reign supreme.**

We pray for all who strive to build a fairer society
 and a better world –
 those who campaign against poverty, injustice and exploitation;
 who work for peace and reconciliation;
 who offer healing to body, mind or spirit;
 who serve the needy.
Encourage them in their work,
 support them in adversity,
 provide the resources they need,
 and make known your love through their ministry.
Servant King,
 **may your love reign supreme.**

Lord Jesus Christ,
 we pray that your kingdom may come,
 despite everything that seems to fight against it;
 a kingdom in which the first are last and the last first,
 in which everything that frustrates your purpose
 and denies your love is defeated,
 and in which all people live together in justice and harmony.
Servant King,
 **may your love reign supreme.**

We ask it for your name's sake.
**Amen.**                                               NICK FAWCETT

## Short prayers

Lord Jesus Christ,
 you were brought low,
 yet you have been lifted high.
You were the servant of all,
 yet you are above all and beyond all.
You were despised and rejected,
 yet your name is exalted above all names.

You were fully human,
   yet you are divine.
You were taken into heaven,
   yet you are here by our sides.
You are higher than our highest thoughts,
   greater than our minds can ever grasp.
So, with all your people in every age,
   we bow before you and confess you as our risen Saviour,
   the King of kings and Lord of lords,
   to the glory of God the Father.
Amen.                                                      NICK FAWCETT


Lord Jesus Christ,
   you are greater than we can ever imagine,
   before all,
   beyond all,
   in all,
   over all.
Forgive us for losing sight of your greatness,
   for underestimating the breadth of your love
   and the extent of your purpose,
   for tying you down to the things of earth
   rather than opening our hearts
   to the kingdom of heaven.
Broaden our vision,
   enlarge our understanding,
   deepen our faith,
   kindle our imagination,
   that we may glimpse your glory,
   and work more faithfully for your kingdom.
In your name we ask it.
Amen.                                                      NICK FAWCETT

# All-age-talk material

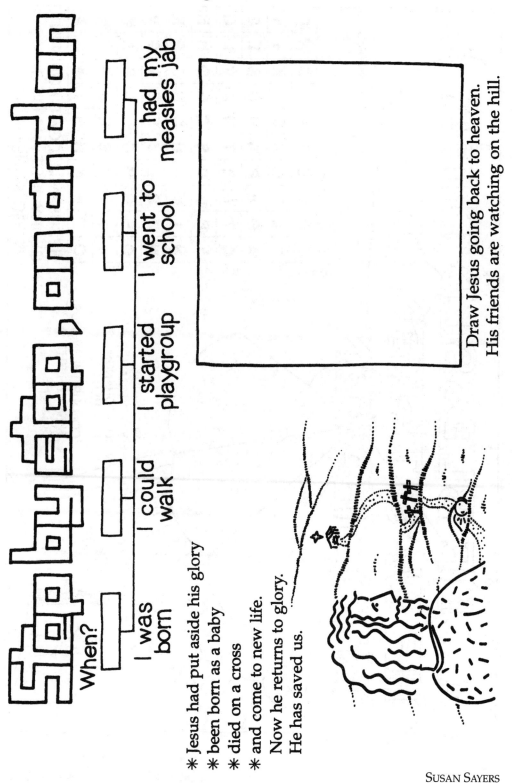

**Step by step, on and on**

When?

I was born

I could walk

I started playgroup

I went to school

I had my measles jab

* Jesus had put aside his glory
* been born as a baby
* died on a cross
* and come to new life.
Now he returns to glory.
He has saved us.

Draw Jesus going back to heaven.
His friends are watching on the hill.

SUSAN SAYERS

AS HE BLESSED THEM
HE WAS TAKEN UP
INTO HEAVEN

Luke 24:50-53

| C | O | M | E | A | F | I | Q | W | R |
|---|---|---|---|---|---|---|---|---|---|
| Y | L | X | G | X | S | A | K | I | T |
| A | O | E | P | W | H | D | S | L | G |
| O | T | U | B | T | N | J | V | L | U |
| Y | B | M | D | S | C | G | O | H | N |
| H | I | M | U | U | O | R | F | E | K |
| N | Z | S | L | J | Y | E | V | G | V |
| Q | E | C | M | O | L | A | S | A | W |
| J | I | T | S | E | J | R | U | W |   |
| O | T | P | N | H | N | I | A | G | A |

'JESUS WILL COME AGAIN IN GLORY JUST AS YOU SAW HIM GO TO HEAVEN.'

W – WHITE
Y – YELLOW
O – ORANGE
R – RED

COLOUR THE WORDS
IN ANY BRIGHT
COLOURS

SUSAN SAYERS

In an effort to steer clear of false impressions, we sometimes avoid teaching children about heaven. Today is a good opportunity to put that right. Start with a game. In a box have slips of paper which describe things in terms of other things:

- a bit like an orange but not so sweet, and coloured yellow;
- a kind of chair which has no back;
- a tall sort of cup;
- a wax stick that you can burn slowly; etc.

Point out that if you had not known before what a lemon was, you would have a better idea now, but not an exact idea until you actually saw a lemon yourself. Show them one. And similarly with the other items described.

It is the same with heaven. Pictures and words in the Bible give us clues but no more.

Show a large round poster with these words written all round the edge:

Then make a collection of words inside the circle which give us an idea of what heaven is like:

- happy
- beauty
- peace
- joy
- no worry
- Daddy finds you when you were lost
- like when you give Nana your best drawing and she's very pleased
- like when your friends ask you to join in their game, etc.

Stress that these are only clues, but try to show them some idea of what being with Jesus means in feelings they can understand, rather than looking at the idea of 'place'.

Let the children decorate the words with lovely bright colours and patterns and if possible display the poster in church.

SUSAN SAYERS

# Reflective material
## (sketches, meditations and poems)

### Meditation of James

We stood there, speechless for a moment,
   struck dumb by the enormity of it all,
   for he was gone,
   plucked away from before our very eyes
   and, quite simply, we were lost for words,
   stunned into silence.
It wasn't the first time, you see;
   we'd lost him once already –
   watched in horror as he was nailed to a cross, sealed in a tomb,
   and we'd been devastated,
   convinced we could never bounce back from such a blow.
We wouldn't have, either,
   not by ourselves,
   but suddenly he was back,
   there in the garden,
   there on the roadside,
   there in the upper room –
   our Lord, alive, risen, victorious,
   death unable to hold him!
I just can't tell you how wonderful that was,
   how our hearts skipped and our spirits soared
   each time we saw him.
We felt certain nothing could ever again destroy our happiness,
   for he had taken on the last enemy
   and emerged triumphant!
Life, all at once, pulsated with promise,
   no problem too great for us,
   no challenge too daunting,
   for, with Christ by our side, what had we to fear?
Yet suddenly, as we stood there that day gazing into heaven,
   he was by our side no longer,
   and for an awful moment
   it seemed as though all our hopes had disappeared again,
   vanishing with him like a bubble on the wind.
Only, of course, this time was different,
   for we'd made time to listen,
   paid heed to his warnings,
   and we understood that, as he had departed,
   so finally he would return.
You should see us now,
   our faith, if anything, stronger today than it's ever been!

We've spoken more boldly and witnessed more powerfully
    than I thought possible –
    preaching the word,
    healing the sick,
    renewing the weak,
    uplifting the broken-hearted,
    carrying the good news of Jesus far and wide.
And I'll tell you why:
    because his going that day
    has somehow brought him closer than he's ever been before,
    filling our whole being – body, mind and soul –
    transforming our every thought and word and deed.
He's here,
    he's there,
    he's everywhere,
    no person beyond his love,
    no situation beyond his purpose,
    for he has not simply risen,
    he has ascended –
    Jesus, the man who lived and died amongst us,
    who shared our flesh and blood,
    one with the Father,
    Lord of lords and King of kings,
    nothing in heaven or earth able to separate us
    from the wonder of his love.
And sometimes when I think of all that means,
    once more I'm struck dumb,
    stunned into silence by the enormity of it all,
    for it's wonderful, isn't it? –
    almost too wonderful for words!

NICK FAWCETT

# Order of service

## Ascensiontide

Ascension Day invariably falls on a Thursday, at the end of the 'great forty days', but while this provides a fitting culmination to the Easter celebrations, it tends to fall a bit flat liturgically by coming in the middle of the working week. From an ecumenical viewpoint, the non-conformist Churches in general tend to make less of it than Anglicans and Roman Catholics, for both of whom worship would normally be eucharistic, but the inevitably lower midweek attendance might be offset by extending an invitation more widely to other traditions. However, a service on the seventh Sunday of Easter is likely to be a more practical ecumenical option, so this outline uses the *Songs of Praise* format.

This is a time in the Christian year when hymns and songs for a wide range of seasons and themes are suitable, which gives plenty of scope to those invited to choose one. Experience suggests that hymns of praise and rejoicing are among the most popular, followed by those in a more devotional style. Ideally the choices should be explained by those who've made them, which can be done very effectively (and more briefly!) by using an interviewer to elicit information.

While an informal feel is a great asset to this kind of service, a basic structure is necessary to hold it all together, and the spontaneity of the contributions is ideally offset by slightly more formal elements. Prayer which everyone present can join in will both draw worshippers together and provide a fixed point to which everyone can relate, and a Bible reading also gives the necessary common focus. The interviews/explanations preclude the need for any other spoken input, but they should be separated into blocks of two or at most three so that the overall impact is not that of a lengthy sermon! Musical resources may restrict the choice of hymns – modern worship songs with a syncopated blues or jazz rhythm can sound distinctly odd on an organ, while *Jerusalem* would require a virtuoso worship group! Clearly those invited to participate should be given as free a choice of hymns or songs as possible, but the suggestions below might serve as a guideline.

### Opening response

We have a great high priest
who has passed through the heavens,
Jesus, the Son of God.
**You are worthy, O Lord our God,**
**to receive glory, honour and power.**

God raised him from the dead
and seated him at his right hand
in the heavenly realms.
**You are worthy, O Lord our God,**
**to receive glory, honour and power.**

Therefore God exalted him to the highest place
and gave him the name above all other names,
that at the name of Jesus every knee should bow.
**You are worthy, O Lord our God,**
**to receive glory, honour and power.**

### Hymn

At the name of Jesus (HON 46)*

### Confession

Lord Jesus Christ, King of Glory,
you left your home in heaven

*HON – *Hymns Old and New*, Kevin Mayhew Publishers

to share our earthly life
and die for us on the cross.
We are sorry we have not loved you
with all our heart.
In your mercy,
**forgive and help us.**

You rose from the grave
as victor over sin and death.
We are sorry we have not lived
in the light of eternal life.
In your mercy,
**forgive and help us.**

You ascended into heaven,
where you reign for ever with the Father.
We are sorry we have not always
acknowledged you as our king.
In your mercy,
**forgive and help us.**
**Make us joyful in worship**
**and obedient in service,**
**to the praise and glory of your name. Amen.**

### Absolution

Almighty God,
Father of our Lord Jesus Christ,
pardon and deliver you from all your sin,
that you may live in the light of his presence,
walk with him by faith
and reign with him in glory,
through Jesus Christ our Lord. Amen.

### Interviews/testimonies

### Hymns or songs

*Chosen from:*

He is exalted (HON 203)
Majesty (HON 327)
Rejoice, the Lord is King (HON 432)
The head that once was crowned with thorns (HON 480)

### Reading

Acts 1:1-11 or
Ephesians 1:15-23

**Prayer**

We ask you, Lord God,
Father of our Lord Jesus Christ,
for the gift of your Spirit,
to reveal him to us,
that we might know him better;
to open our eyes,
that we might see his light
and know the hope we are called to;
to open our hearts,
that we might receive the riches
of his grace and power,
available to all who believe,
through Jesus Christ our Lord. Amen.

**Interviews/testimonies**

**Hymns or songs**

*Chosen from:*

Hail the day that sees him rise (HON 191)
Jesus shall take the highest honour (HON 278)
The Lord is King! (HON 485)
You are the King of Glory (HON 570)

**Reading**

Matthew 28:16-20 or Luke 24:44-53

**Prayer**

Lord Jesus,
to you has been given all authority
in heaven and on earth.
Yours is the name above every other name,
the name to which the greatest
and the least will bow.
In your name
may we go out together from here
to obey the great commission
which you give to all who follow you:
to make disciples among all the peoples
of the world,
to baptise them in the name of the Trinity,
and to teach them to obey
your commands and will.

And in going out
may we know the reality of your promise
to be with us always,
until the end of time itself. Amen.

### Interviews/testimonies

### Hymns or songs
*Chosen from:*

A man there lived in Galilee (HON 3)
From the sun's rising (HON 150)
God forgave my sin (HON 167)
We have a gospel to proclaim (HON 532)

### Intercessions

We pray to our Saviour Jesus,
enthroned on high as King of kings,
saying, Lord of glory,
**hear your people's prayer.**

Jesus, King of kings,
you are worthy to receive glory and power,
for you created all things.
Restore and heal your creation,
spoiled by human selfishness and greed.
May we show your love and care
in all our relationships,
with our world and with all people . . .
Lord of glory,
**hear your people's prayer.**

Jesus, Lord of lords,
you are worthy to receive wisdom and might,
for by your blood you have purchased for God
people from every nation and race.
Restore and heal the nations of the world,
torn apart by hatred and violence.
May we demonstrate your righteousness
and justice . . .
Lord of glory,
**hear your people's prayer.**

Jesus, Sovereign over all,
you are worthy to receive honour and praise,
for you have made us a kingdom of priests
to serve our God.

Restore and heal your Church,
troubled and weakened by divisions
and disunity.
May we set aside our differences,
recognising that we are one in you . . .
Lord of glory,
**hear your people's prayer.**
**As we kneel before your throne**
**in praise and adoration,**
**we offer ourselves to you,**
**in the name of Christ our Lord. Amen.**

**Our Father . . .**

### Hymn

Crown him with many crowns (HON 103) or
Christ triumphant (HON 81)

### Final prayer

In our worship and witness
**may we know God's presence.**

With our families and friends
**may we know God's love.**

In our living and moving
**may we know God's peace.**

In our hearts and minds
**may we know God's blessing,**
**now and for evermore. Amen.**

STUART THOMAS

# Pentecost

# Pentecost Sunday

*The gift of God's promised Holy Spirit*

## Acts 2:1-21

*(also Numbers 11:24-30; Psalm 104:26-36, 37b; 1 Corinthians 12:3-13; John 20:19-23 or 7:37-39)*

## A reading from the Acts of the Apostles (Acts 2:1-11)

The disciples had gathered together in Jerusalem to celebrate the Feast of Pentecost and to wait for the Holy Spirit that Jesus had promised to send.

One day, as they were praying together, the room was suddenly filled with the sound of a powerful wind which roared through the house. Then, what looked like small tongues of fire appeared and spread out to touch each one of them. So it was that they were filled with the Holy Spirit.

At once, in their excitement, they rushed outside to tell everyone what had happened to them. As they began to speak, they were amazed to find that everyone listening to their words could understand them! People from different regions and countries were astounded to hear these men preaching to them in their own native languages.

This is the Word of the Lord
**Thanks be to God**                                          KATIE THOMPSON

## A reading from the Gospel of John (20:19-23)

Late in the evening the disciples sat huddled together, feeling sad and afraid. The doors of the room were locked, to stop the Jews finding them.

Suddenly, Jesus appeared in the room with them and said, 'Peace be with you.'

They were amazed when they saw him and could hardly believe their eyes. But Jesus showed them the wounds in his hands and where his side had been pierced by the sword. They were filled with joy and wonder.

Jesus said to them, 'Peace be with you. Just as my Father sent me, so I am sending you.'

Then he breathed on them, saying, 'The Holy Spirit has been given to you. Whatever you choose to forgive will be forgiven. Whatever is not forgiven by you will remain unforgiven.'

This is the Gospel of the Lord
**Praise to you, Lord Jesus Christ**                          KATIE THOMPSON

# Introductory material

One moment confusion and the next certainty; one moment doubt and the next faith; one moment despair and the next hope; one moment fear and the next confidence. All of this goes some way to describing what happened on that extraordinary day of Pentecost recorded in Acts, chapter 2. But exactly what was going on? And how did those people directly affected make sense of their experience? In this service today we look at some of those whose lives in contrasting ways were transformed by the gift of the Holy Spirit – the Spirit that is equally able to transform our lives in turn.

NICK FAWCETT

# Prayers

## The omnipresent Spirit

Holy Spirit,
    we rejoice that, as you came to the Apostles
        on that day of Pentecost,
        so you keep on coming to us today;
        making yourself known in different ways,
        at different times
        and in different places,
        but always there,
        constantly moving in our lives.
For your presence at work within us,
    **we give you our praise.**

You come when we are most aware of our need –
    bringing comfort in times of sorrow,
    courage in times of fear,
    peace in times of trouble
    and hope in times of despair.
For your presence at work within us,
    **we give you our praise.**

You come when we forget our need of you –
    challenging,
    searching,
    refining,
    cleansing;
    inspiring us to greater vision and renewed commitment.
For your presence at work within us,
    **we give you our praise.**

You come to us in power –
  releasing unimagined potential,
  imparting unexpected gifts,
  cultivating undreamed-of fruits.
For your presence at work within us,
  **we give you our praise.**

You come to us in quietness –
  coaxing us to new initiatives,
  nurturing confidence
  and deepening our faith.
For your presence at work within us,
  **we give you our praise.**

Holy Spirit,
  we welcome you again –
  opening our minds to your guidance,
  our hearts to your love
  and our lives to your purpose.
Breathe upon us,
  fill and enthuse us,
  and send us out in the service of Christ.
For your presence at work within us,
  **we give you our praise.**

In his name we pray.
**Amen.**                                  NICK FAWCETT

## Intercession – the transforming Spirit

Holy Spirit,
  coming as wind and fire,
    free and irrepressible,
    we pray today for all who long for change
    and for all who fear it.

We think of the poor and the hungry,
    the homeless and the refugee,
    the sick and the unemployed,
    the downtrodden and the oppressed –
    these, and so many others, who yearn for a new beginning,
    an opportunity to start afresh.
May their prayers be answered and their dreams realised.
As you came at Pentecost,
    **come again today.**

We pray for those who see change as a threat –
    a sweeping-away of everything that is tried and trusted,

and the imposition of unknown challenges
and an uncertain future.
May they rest secure in the knowledge that,
whatever else may change,
you will remain constant.
As you came at Pentecost,
**come again today.**

Holy Spirit,
coming gently as a dove,
we pray for all who long for peace,
and all who have lost sight of what peace really means.
We think of those in homes racked by tensions,
families split by petty disputes,
communities scarred by prejudice and intolerance,
and countries torn apart by war.
May dialogue triumph over confrontation,
and unity replace division.
As you came at Pentecost,
**come again today.**

We pray for those who fill their lives with noise or activity,
afraid of facing themselves in a time of quiet reflection,
attempting somehow to mask their sense of emptiness;
and we pray, too, for those who seek fulfilment
in that which can never finally satisfy –
wealth, possessions, power, success.
May they discover the secret of true contentment,
the peace that passes understanding which only you can give.
As you came at Pentecost,
**come again today.**

Holy Spirit,
you changed the lives of the Apostles
and of countless people through history,
just as you are changing our lives in turn,
each renewed through your sovereign power.
Come now and change our world in all its need,
so that it may enjoy hope and peace,
healing and harmony,
and so that all may come to a saving knowledge
of Jesus Christ our Lord.
As you came at Pentecost,
**come again today.**

We ask it for his name's sake.
**Amen.**                                                         NICK FAWCETT

## Short prayers

### Prayer of Petition

Lord,
    it is hard to share our faith with a few,
    let alone many.
When we listen to your call
    to be witnesses to the ends of the earth
    we feel that the task is hopelessly beyond us,
    our resources feebly inadequate to meet the challenge.
Yet that is to view things from our perspective
    rather than yours,
    for you do not leave us dependent on our strength
    but rather equip us with the power of the Holy Spirit
    who is able to work in ways far exceeding our expectations.
Move within us,
    as you have moved in your people across the centuries,
    and teach us to trust you for the help we need,
    when we need it.
In the name of Christ we pray.
Amen.

NICK FAWCETT

Living God,
    we remember today
    how you transformed the lives of the Apostles,
    how, through the breath of your Spirit,
    you turned their fear and uncertainty
    into a confidence which knew no bounds.
Come to us now, through that same Spirit.
Take our weak and hesitant faith
    and fill us with unshakable trust in your purpose.
Take our stumbling discipleship,
    and grant us energy and enthusiasm
    to proclaim the gospel through word and deed.
Take our fear and anxieties,
    and give us courage
    and your peace which passes understanding.
Take our gifts and talents,
    and use them in the service of your kingdom.
Living God,
    help us to remember today
    not simply all you did *once*,
    but to rejoice in all you are doing *now*,
    and all you shall continue to do
    through your Holy Spirit.
In the name of Christ we ask it.
Amen.

NICK FAWCETT

# All-age-talk material

## Read Acts 2:1-21

Each day our actions, from morning to night, depend upon having energy. Initially, we need the physical energy to propel ourselves (or crawl) out of bed, amble to the bathroom, show our face at the mirror and then slither downstairs towards a bowl of cereal. After that the whole day is one chaotic jumble of movement which, hopefully, results in performing the right actions at the right time.

However, although we require our physical energy to move around, we are also totally dependent upon other forms of energy to help us complete both simple and complex tasks throughout each day.

Simple functions, such as heating water, light, communication, each require an energy form to work. This energy isn't a secret or hidden power source. We know of its existence, we understand, basically, how it is made and how it works, and we know of its effects on our daily lives. The energy is something we usually take for granted and simply expect it to be there when we need it. But, when that energy source isn't available, even for a short time, we feel isolated, frustrated and deprived.

In the reading, we find the Lord's followers meeting together in Jerusalem not really sure what the future held for them. They had no idea how they could fulfil what Jesus had asked them to do when he told them, 'Go to the people of all nations and make them my disciples, baptise them in the name of the Father, the Son and the Holy Spirit' (see Matthew 28:19).

Without warning, and totally unexpected, on the day of Pentecost, the Lord's followers were given an energy source which would give them the power to perform all that Jesus had asked of them. The Lord's followers, and countless others, now knew that God was going to be with them wherever they went. They knew they could depend upon God, that he keeps his promises and that he wouldn't ask them to do anything without giving them the right power source.

This same power source also provides us with the strength that we need to work through the questions and hassles that confront us each day.

PETE TOWNSEND

## Symbols of the Spirit

### Reading

Acts 2:1-13

### Aim

To demonstrate that the symbols we used to describe our experience of the Holy Spirit each convey an important truth, but none can express what is finally beyond words.

## Preparation

Reproduce the weather symbols below.

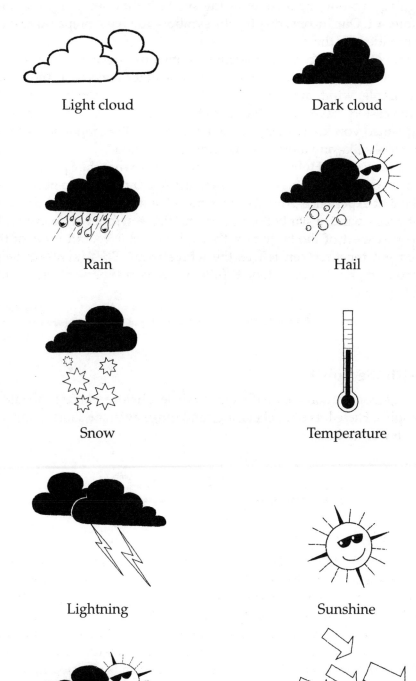

Light cloud

Dark cloud

Rain

Hail

Snow

Temperature

Lightning

Sunshine

Sunshine and showers

Gales

**Talk**

Explain that you want today to think about symbols, and to help you do that you are going to show them some of the symbols they see every day on the weather forecast. One by one, display the symbols you have prepared and ask if anybody can identify them.

With some of the symbols the meaning is obvious. We only have to look at them to tell straightaway what they mean. But other aspects of the weather, like, for example, wind, are more difficult to portray. It's the best symbol the weather forecasters have been able to come up with so far, and once you've seen it explained you know next time what it means. We cannot actually show what wind looks like any more than we can temperature.

And so it is with the Holy Spirit. We do not know what the Spirit looks like, where it is or what it is doing, but we experience it in our lives and need symbols to describe that experience. And the three most commonly used are the dove, a symbol of peace; wind, a symbol of power; and fire, a symbol of cleansing. Each points to one aspect of the Holy Spirit's work in our lives, but none of them, even when put together, can tell us the whole truth. These symbols help us glimpse the truth, but to understand it fully we need to experience the reality of the Spirit for ourselves.

NICK FAWCETT

## Filled with the Spirit

Protect the demonstration area with a groundsheet before starting the talk, just in case of spills. Have lots of buckets, jugs and mugs available, some empty and some with water in them.

Begin by explaining that all these represent people who go to church and are Christians. Sometimes, sadly, people may know all about Jesus, when he lived and what was and wasn't written about him, what everything in church is called and so on, but they are empty inside (tip the jug up). If anyone goes to them for a drink of God's love (try it), the person needing the drink will go away thirsty – they won't be able to get refreshed or comforted or healed or loved because the person they thought could help them is all dried up inside.

Let's try another Christian. (Try another container.) That's much better – this Christian is full of the loving Spirit of God so the thirsty person will come into close contact with God's love through them.

Look at all the different shapes of containers. We don't have to be a special shape of Christian to qualify. We may be simple or dramatic (choose containers to emphasise this), tall or short, Evangelical or Catholic. God is delighted to pour his Spirit into all of these, but one thing is necessary for all of us: we need to go to the source to be filled. We need to tell God that we want him to fill us with his living Spirit, and when he starts to, we need to keep ourselves open so that he can. He may fill us full in a rush, or he may gently fill us bit by bit; however he chooses to do it will be the very best way for us.

SUSAN SAYERS

The Holy Spirit gives life. Colour the flames to bring this picture to life!

# I will pour out my Spirit. (Joel 2:28)

The Holy Spirit helps us to understand things more clearly. So use the key below to colour this picture and discover a message.

1=Blue    3=Red    5=Green
2=Brown   4=Pink   6=Light Brown or
                    Yellow

## WORDSEARCH

Find the following words in the grid below: COMMUNICATE, WAITING, FIRE, WIND, NEW LIFE, SPIRIT, POWER, PROMISE, GOOD NEWS, JESUS, BROKEN BARRIERS.

```
G O O D N E D S P I R C
N M B A R R I E R S O O
I M R O M I S E P U K M
T U O M M U N I C S E M
I N K G O O R N E E N U
A I E W I I N D O J E N
W I N D T X G O O D N I
N C W E P R O M I D E C
E W S N W L I F E N W A
E R B A R R I E D E S T
W I L N D P R O M I S E
L I F F E F I R E W O P
```

MICHAEL FORSTER

**The Spirit gave them the courage to share the Word of God with everyone!**

Find the words of Jesus, using the key

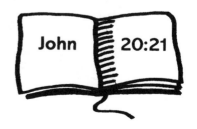

John 20:21

KATIE THOMPSON

come, Holy Spirit

come, Holy Spirit

come Holy

1. Colour the flames.
2. Cut out and staple to fit head.

SUSAN SAYERS

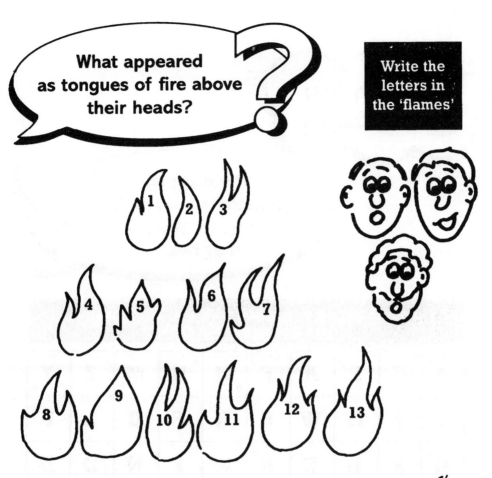

**What appeared as tongues of fire above their heads?**

Write the letters in the 'flames'

1. The first letter of 🌳
2. The first letter of ✋
3. The fourth letter of 🦋
4. The first letter of 🏠
5. The second letter of 🏢
6. The third letter of 🍂
7. The first letter of 🪀
8. The fourth letter of 👓
9. The second letter of 🕷
10. The second letter of 🧷
11. The second letter of 🚙
12. The second letter of 🚲
13. The fourth letter of ⛺

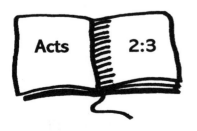

Acts   2:3

KATIE THOMPSON

## The coming of the Spirit

The disciples had gathered together in one room. What did they hear?

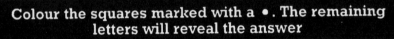

Colour the squares marked with a •. The remaining letters will reveal the answer

| A | C | E | A | F | G | H | M | Z | Y |
|---|---|---|---|---|---|---|---|---|---|
| J | P | O | W | E | R | F | U | L | P |
| O | S | L | E | R | W | I | N | D | D |
| P | F | R | O | M | S | L | O | N | R |
| D | A | E | H | E | A | V | E | N | S |

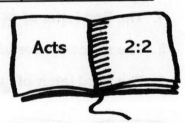

Acts 2:2

KATIE THOMPSON

# Reflective material
## (sketches, meditations and poems)

## Do not underestimate the wind

How the wind blows!
   sweeping the grass,
   tossing the trees,
   hurrying from nowhere to nowhere;
   turning, twisting,
   and then returning
   in a flurry of nothingness;
   movements without purpose
   and without pattern.

And yet the wind roars
   and can ravage the defenceless earth.
Trees are torn up,
   buildings destroyed,
   floods let loose, and people can be tossed
   like matchsticks into the air.

Do not underestimate the wind.

So is the Holy Spirit of God,
   sweeping unseen across
   the uplifted faces of the nations;
   moving in ways
   beyond our understanding.
Who would not smile
   at children trying to catch
   the wind in their hands?
Yet we try to confine him
   in flurries of words
   that disperse
   into nothingness.

But he is the all-powerful God,
   surging through history,
   piercing dark clouds
   of sin, ignorance and fear.
He tosses aside the strong and wise
   like fallen leaves,
   and lifts up the weak,
   the foolish and the lost.

He blew across the void
  before time was,
  and will again
  when time is no more.

Do not underestimate the Holy Spirit of God.                    MARY HATHAWAY


## Drama: The Spirit comes to those who wait

**Narrator**    You know, I never could work out what those people did in my back room. Oh, I'm Zedekiah, by the way, landlord of the Harp and Halo tavern in Jerusalem. Most people just call me Zed – because I snore a lot. Anyway, this bunch of people used to rent one of my rooms every weekend. They seemed a really odd lot to me, I don't mind telling you. Their leader was a man called Peter, and even he didn't seem to know what they were doing, but he had some really weird ideas, I can tell you.

**Peter**    Well, we're just waiting, that's all.

**Zed**    Waiting for what?

**Peter**    We don't know, but we'll know when it happens. Jesus told us to wait.

**Zed**    Seemed potty to me. Oh, yes, and that was the other thing – this Jesus guy. Now, we all knew Jesus was dead, see – he'd been publicly executed weeks before, and we'd all watched him die. Well, with no telly we have to get our entertainment somehow. But these friends of his were saying he'd risen from the dead and gone back to heaven to be with God.

**Peter**    He's going to come back one day, and we've all got to make sure everyone's ready when he does. That's why we're waiting here – for him to give us the power.

**Zed**    Well, it seemed to me they were quite capable of telling a tall story without any help from God's office, but they were harmless enough and they paid the rent, so I let them sit in my upstairs room to wait for whatever-it-was – and whenever I had a few spare minutes I'd find an excuse to go and visit them. So there we all were, this one day – Pentecost it was, which is our harvest festival, and you usually expect people to get a bit carried away then. But this wasn't hysteria, this was real – I was there, and I know. Thomas noticed it first.

**Thomas**    Hey, just listen to that wind.

| | |
|---|---|
| **Zed** | He was right – we could hear this roaring, rushing sound just like the big winds that come in off the desert – but Philip noticed that it was different. |
| **Philip** | Something creepy's happening. We can hear the wind, but nothing's being blown around. |
| **Mary** | I think this is it. I don't know what 'it' is, but it's definitely it! |
| **Zed** | Women! I ask you! But then, Mary Magdalene had always seemed a bit sus, to me. Trouble is, she turned out to be right, in the end. |
| **James** | Don't panic! Don't panic – the room's on fire! |
| **Zed** | James was in a right old state – but, to give him his due, it *was* pretty scary. There seemed to be flames all around us, touching each of the people there, but nothing was burning. And still we could hear that strange wind that no one could actually feel. Peter flipped completely. |
| **Peter** | Yippee! It's happened! We've got the Power! The power of the Holy Spirit! Let's go tell everybody about Jesus. |
| **Zed** | And he was gone – just like that. Just like Peter, actually – he never did stop to think. I tried to talk some sense into them, though. 'You just can't go out there spreading your stories,' I said. 'You need to think, plan, devise a corporate strategy. You've got to identify your consumer base.' But no one was listening. They'd all gone rushing out into the street. Well, I knew they were barking, but I really had to go and see what happened next – so I followed them outside. The first thing I heard was a couple of Cypriot wine merchants talking. |
| **Cypriot 1** | It's amazing! These are such ordinary people – I mean, they're just so, well, common, really. So how come they can talk to each of us in our own language? |
| **Cypriot 2** | They're drunk, that's all it is! |
| **Zed** | I was just going to point out that if getting drunk made you fluent in five languages, most of my customers would earn a fortune as interpreters, but Peter got in first. |
| **Peter** | Come off it! At this time of day? This is God's Spirit, not something out of a bottle – and it's being poured out on the whole world just as the prophet said it would be. |
| **Zed** | Well, there was no holding them after that – soon everyone was hearing about Jesus. Even I ended up believing in him – just don't tell Peter, or I'll never hear the end of it. |

MICHAEL FORSTER

## What it means to believe

So much faith is backward looking, like digging out old photographs from the attic; a clutching at snapshots and searching for the glow of comfort from a romanticised past.

At Pentecost the world shakes, the verbs turn, the present lives; and a future, free from old and weary repetitions, becomes possible.

Now with you . . . will be in you. New meanings emerge. New discoveries are being made. New communities are born. New behaviour is practised. New worlds of truth and understanding and beauty are given.

We, both material for the working, and the stumbling apprentices . . . he, the disturbing Creator.

PATRICK WOODHOUSE

## True direction

The Holy Spirit of God flows in a certain direction, from the Father to the Son first, then from the Son back to the Father. God the Son who is 'light from light' receives light and then reflects it back. In our own world of the adopted children of God, the Spirit has to come to us before we can reflect it back to God and before we can imitate it by showing God-like love for our fellow human beings. We have to breathe in the breath of God before we can breathe it out . . .

I often use a metre or so of hosepipe to illustrate the change Jesus made, from the Old Covenant to his New Covenant. Hold the pipe with a loop at the top (∩) and to get water through the pipe it has to be pumped up; this shows how great effort must be made to climb up towards God before God's love comes back to the one who worships. It is like trying to breathe out before ever breathing in. Time and time again the prophets before Jesus show God saying, 'If you keep my rules, I will be your God; but if you fail, I will desert you', or words to that effect. It all depends on human effort.

But Jesus turned the whole idea on its head. The best illustration of Jesus' way would be to turn the hosepipe upside down (U) with the loop at the bottom. God pours in the love from above, and by the grace of God it flows up again on the other side. This can be shown to work as a model: pour water in at one end and it comes out at the other, all by itself! Such is a life lived always in gratitude for the love of God ever coming down. The power of love-in-return is all God's, not ours.

GERALD O'MAHONY

## Winging, soaring, swooping Spirit of God

Holy Spirit of God,
winging, soaring, swooping,
filling to the brim
each cup held up
in faith-filled expectation.

Work your wonder in me.
Fill me to the brim
with your blessings,
so that I may go out from here
in Jesus' name
to be a blessing to others.
In God's name I ask it.
Amen.

SUSAN HARDWICK

## Wait for the Power

The friends of Jesus were wondering what to do. Jesus had gone back to heaven, and left them to carry on his work, but he'd told them not to start straight away. 'Stay in Jerusalem,' he had said, 'until you get the power you need.' So they were waiting, all together, in a meeting room.

Peter was getting impatient, though. 'It's all very well,' he said, 'but the city is full of people. We shan't have another chance like this for nearly a year. We should be telling people about Jesus.'

'Jesus told us to wait,' said Matthew, who used to be a tax collector before he met Jesus. 'I know all about that – people used to keep me waiting for months.'

'It's no good, anyway,' said James. 'The visitors are from all over the world – we'd need to know dozens of different languages if we were going to tell them about Jesus.'

'Let's be honest,' said Thomas. 'We don't really want to go out there, anyway. There are people out there who want to kill us, and I'm too young to die – come to think of it, I always will be.'

As usual, Thomas was the most honest one of the group; he was saying what the others were afraid to say. And as usual, he got into trouble for it.

'I'm not afraid of anyone out there!' said Peter. 'I'll soon show them . . .' But his voice tailed off – petered out, you might say – because he'd remembered how he used to say that to Jesus, but when it actually came to it he'd lost his nerve. It was easy to talk big among friends, but very different to have faith, and be brave, when things got dangerous!

The question was, how were they ever going to get the courage to do Jesus' work? They had seen him several times after he had risen from the dead, and yet they still seemed to be frightened of being killed themselves. How could that ever be changed? No wonder they were a little bit glum!

Just as they were beginning to get desperate, and thinking what dreadful, useless disciples they were, they heard a strange sound. 'Close the window, Andrew,' said John. 'Sounds like the wind's getting up.'

'It's already closed,' said Andrew.

'Well, you didn't do it properly,' grumbled Peter. 'That's the trouble with you – you can't be trusted.'

'Ooh! Look who's talking!' said Andrew, and he would have said a lot more but Thomas stopped him.

'It's not the wind,' he said. 'I can hear it, but I can't feel any draught at all. Something funny's going on here.'

All the disciples sat very quietly and listened. Sure enough, the noise got louder and louder, but they couldn't feel any breeze. Thomas was just thinking that it was a bit like the burning bush – when Moses had seen the flames but the bush didn't actually burn – when he noticed something else.

'Hey, Peter!' he said. 'Your hair's on fire!'

'Don't be daft!' said Peter. 'I'd know if my hair was on fire. You're the one who's got that problem.'

Then they realised that there seemed to be flames over everybody's head. 'It *is* like the burning bush!' thought Thomas. 'Something special's happening.'

'Come on!' shouted Peter. 'Let's go outside and . . .' But he was too late. They'd gone. They'd unbolted the door and gone rushing out into the street and started telling everyone that Jesus was alive – and all of a sudden they were language experts! Andrew was speaking in Persian to a group of carpet merchants, while John had cornered a couple of soldiers and was talking in Latin, and Thomas – who had always doubted the importance of learning languages – was busy winning an argument with some philosophers, in Greek.

Then Peter realised what he was doing. 'This is silly,' he thought. 'We could get ourselves into serious trouble doing this.' He realised he was still quite frightened, but then he thought, 'Well, some things are worth getting into trouble for – and there's nothing more important than doing this.'

That morning, thousands of people heard the good news that Jesus was alive. The religious authorities didn't like it. 'What will happen to all our power and our privileges,' they asked, 'if ordinary people start being listened to?' So they went around saying that Peter and his friends were drunk.

'Do me a favour!' laughed Peter. 'At this time of the morning? This is the power of God at work, but you're too bothered about yourselves to recognise it.'

Then the disciples realised that this was the 'power' Jesus had promised them. They knew there would still be hard and dangerous times ahead, because Jesus had told them that, too. But they knew it was worth it. Now they understood that, whatever happened, Jesus would always be with them and God wouldn't let their lives or their work be wasted.

Now that's what I call power!

MICHAEL FORSTER and SIMON SMITH

## The power of the Spirit

Who can stand the wind,
  the wind of the Spirit?
No cosmic force
  can his strength withstand.

For with one breath of God
   the vastness of infinity
   rolls up like a plaything
   and drops into his hand.

Who can stand the fire,
   the fire of the Spirit,
   the lightning of God
   striking us within?
Pure joy of heaven,
   burning through our darkness,
   white fire of God,
   a holocaust for sin.

Who can stand the healing,
   the healing of the Spirit?
Who will ask for wholeness
   if it means his fire within?
Bowing to his power,
   acknowledging his greatness,
   letting in the light
   to cauterise our sin?

Do you want a part
   just a part of the Spirit?
Can we say to God,
'We'll have the joy and peace
   but keep the wind and fire –
   why, they might consume us!
Don't disturb our comfort,
   tell the storm to cease!'

Do you want the glory,
   the glory of the Spirit,
   the pure and brilliant beauty
   that's cleansed and free from sin?
Then yield yourself to burning,
   to blasting and to breaking,
   for through these storms alone
   comes gloriousness within.

So do you want the whole,
   the whole of the Spirit?
We must have him in completeness
   or we have him not at all!
For he is fully God,
   he cannot be divided –
   are you sure you want to risk
   answering his call?

MARY HATHAWAY

# Trinity

# Trinity Sunday

*The inexpressibly awesome nature of God – Father, Son and Holy Spirit*

## Isaiah 40:12-17, 27-31
*(also Psalm 8; 2 Corinthians 13:11-13; Matthew 28:16-20)*

### A reading from the Gospel of Matthew (28:16-20)

Then the eleven disciples went to Galilee to the mountain where Jesus had told them to go. When they saw him, they worshipped him; but some doubted. Then Jesus came to them and said, 'All authority in heaven and on earth has been given to me. Therefore go and make disciples of all nations, baptising them in the name of the Father and of the Son and of the Holy Spirit, and teaching them to obey everything I have commanded you. And surely I am with you always, to the very end of the age.'                    NIV

# Introductory material

We are here today on Trinity Sunday, a day which perhaps captures the imagination less than any other in the Christian year, and to a point that is understandable, for rather than historical events this date in the calendar is concerned with abstract doctrine which has perplexed theologians and ordinary believers alike across the centuries. Yet complex though the issues may be, we do well to reflect on them, for this should be a day which captures the imagination like no other, reminding us of the sheer breathtaking reality which we describe as God. We try to pin that reality down as best we can; to talk about our experience in terms of God the Father, the Son and the Holy Spirit, but we are always at best simply grasping at the truth, for, as the prophet Isaiah reminds us, God's ways are not our ways, neither are his thoughts our thoughts. Thank God for this day which reminds us of this simple inescapable fact, and use it to deepen your faith and enrich your experience of his living, loving, and transforming presence.

NICK FAWCETT

# Prayers

### Trinity approach

Great and wonderful God,
   with awe and wonder we come to you.

   You are greater than our minds can fathom,
     more powerful that we can ever imagine,
     beyond our highest thoughts,

Lord of space and time,
  ruler over all.
Sovereign God,
  **receive our worship.**

You love us with a fierce and total love,
  valuing us for who and what we are,
  caring enough to call us your children,
  providing each day our every need,
  guiding us throughout our lives.
God the Father,
  **receive our worship.**

You have shared our humanity,
  identifying yourself wholly with our world,
  experiencing first-hand our joys and sorrows,
  decisively demonstrating your love in action,
  showing us the way of service.
God made flesh,
  **receive our worship.**

You are with us each and every day,
  constantly by our side,
  working in us and through us,
  teaching, guiding, encouraging,
  leading us to new experiences of your love.
Mighty and mysterious God,
  **receive our worship.**

Give us this day a sense of your greatness
  and your gentleness;
  a glimpse of your otherness
  and your nearness;
  an awareness of your eternal purpose that spans creation
  yet includes us all, here and now.
Great and wonderful God, Father, Son and Holy Spirit,
  **receive our worship, in Jesus' name.**
  **Amen.**

NICK FAWCETT

## The God who is here, there and everywhere

God beyond us,
  God with us,
  God inside us,
    **we worship you.**

God outside us,
   God among us,
   God within us,
      **we praise you.**

God above,
   God beside,
   God below,
      **we thank you.**

God the Father,
   God the Son,
   God the Holy Spirit,
      **we honour you.**

God of past,
   God of present,
   God of future,
      **we bless you.**

God of here,
   God of there,
   God of everywhere,
      **we salute you.**

God of majesty,
   God of love,
   God of power,
      **we acknowledge you.**

Loving God,
   Father, Son and Holy Spirit,
      for all you are,
      all you do,
      all you mean,
      **we give you our thanks,**
      **and offer our worship,**
      **in the name of Christ.**
      **Amen.**

NICK FAWCETT

## Confession – bringing our faults

Sovereign God,
   all loving,
      all gracious,
      all powerful,
      you deserve our praise.
Mighty God,
   ever faithful,
      ever near,

ever active,
you deserve our worship.
Eternal God
all goodness,
all mercy,
all truth,
you deserve our thanks.
Father, Son and Holy Spirit,
**hear our prayer.**

You are greater than our minds can grasp,
yet you have revealed your glory.
You are before all, above all, beyond all,
yet you lived and died among us.
You are at work in every situation and circumstance,
yet so often we fail to recognise your presence.
For our narrowness of vision,
our feebleness of faith,
our spiritual blindness,
forgive us, O Lord.
Father, Son and Holy Spirit,
**hear our prayer.**

You are there watching over us, day after day.
You are here by our sides, until the end of the age.
You are here within, now and always.
For our rejection of your care,
our forgetfulness of your presence
and our stifling of your movement,
forgive us, O Lord.
Father, Son and Holy Spirit,
**hear our prayer.**

Accept now our worship, for all its weakness,
our discipleship, for all its frailty,
and our service, for all its limitations.
Speak to us this day,
so that we may experience more of your love,
reflect more of your goodness
and live with more of your power,
Father, Son and Holy Spirit,
**hear our prayer.**

And to you, the one God,
be glory, praise and honour,
today, tomorrow and for evermore.
**Amen.**                                          NICK FAWCETT

*The God we worship is Father, Son and Holy Spirit. The qualities of God are revealed in the three persons of the Trinity, and in us, too, when we found our lives on him. Filled with his life, the Christian community will be enabled to show the love of God, the grace of Jesus and the fellowship of the Holy Spirit.*

Gathered together in the love and fellowship of God,
let us speak to our Father of our cares and needs.

We pray for the work of your Church
in suburbs, cities, slums and villages all over the world,
especially where there is violent opposition,
complacency or apathy;
that all who work in your name
may be blessed and encouraged,
so many may find peace in your love.

*Silence for prayer*

Abba, Father:
**hear your children.**

We pray for the world; for all areas
in which there is a breakdown of communication
between individuals, groups or nations;
may your unifying love draw people together,
helping them to find shared interests to build on,
rather than dwelling on hurtful divisions.

*Silence for prayer*

Abba, Father:
**hear your children.**

We pray for a greater love and fellowship amongst us
here in this parish and in our families;
live in us, Father, and make us more ready
to respond and forgive, to help and to listen.

*Silence for prayer*

Abba, Father:
**hear your children.**

We pray for the homeless
and those living in crowded, inadequate
accommodation; those living alone and isolated;
for the hungry and malnourished;
may your love, working through us, your body,
reach those in desperate need and give them new hope.

*Silence for prayer*

Abba, Father:
**hear your children.**

We pray for those who have travelled through death
to eternity; may they live in your peace
and joy for ever.
Rejoicing in your strength, love and fellowship
we offer you our thanks and praise.

*Silence for prayer*

Merciful Father,
**accept these prayers**
**for the sake of your Son,**
**our Saviour Jesus Christ, Amen.**                    SUSAN SAYERS


## Short prayers

Mighty God,
   beyond all space and time,
   greater than our minds can fully grasp,
   ruler over all that is and has been and shall be,
   we worship you.
We worship you as the God
   made known to us in Christ,
   a God all good and wholly other,
   and yet a God who loves us
   as a father loves his children.
We worship you
   as the God we experience within us,
   the God who fires our imagination
   and sets our hearts aflame
   through the Spirit of Christ.
Mighty God,
   help us to catch a sense of your greatness,
   opening our hearts and minds to your presence
   made known through Father,
   Son and Holy Spirit.                    NICK FAWCETT


Gracious God,
   there are some experiences
   which we cannot put into words
   however hard we try –
   moments of joy, love, awe, hope, beauty
   and so many more.
Yet though these may defy expression,
   they are no less real;
   on the contrary they are often more real
   and special than any.

So it is with our experience of you.
Together with your Church across the ages,
    we strive to articulate our faith,
    to describe somehow
    everything that you mean to us –
    your awesome sovereignty,
    your unfailing care,
    your intimate closeness,
    your presence within –
    yet the language we use
    seems hopelessly inadequate.
Father, Son and Holy Spirit,
    three in one and one in three.
It makes no sense according to human logic,
    yet we know it to be true,
    not in our minds but in our hearts.
And so we rejoice,
    and acknowledge you as our God
    in joyful worship,
    one God, world without end.
Amen.                                                        NICK FAWCETT

# All-age-talk material

## Read 2 Corinthians 13:11-13

What is the definition of a friend? Would you agree that a friend is: 'Someone who you're not embarrassed to be yourself with?' or could it be: 'Someone who makes me feel totally accepted?'

Friendship is one of the greatest gifts anyone can give to another person. There are possibly many people who we might consider to be 'sort of' friends or just acquaintances, but friends who you can rely on whatever the situation, are often few and very precious.

Often friendship develops over a long period of time, where you slowly get to know each other and become confident in sharing little bits about yourself. There are always those people who will listen to what you have to say and then, before you know it, every single detail is broadcast on the evening news!

Friends are people who you are not afraid to make a mistake in front of. They are the sort of people who will support you and stick up for you against all the odds. Friends should be the type of people who won't be afraid to be honest with you, such as when you say: 'Do I look OK wearing this?' and they reply: 'Erm, you sort of look like something that should be entered for a dog show!'

To have a real friend, and to be a real friend to someone is something that is extremely precious. It helps get us through stages in our life that are tough and best not faced alone. Being friendly to other people is also an encouragement and helps to make them feel accepted and not as if they've just arrived from some distant planet.

Paul's final greetings to the Corinthian church encourages honesty, openness, acceptance and kindness. These are all traits that we should encourage in each other and especially with those people who we consider to be real, close friends.

PETE TOWNSEND

## Bigger than you think!

### Readings

Isaiah 40:21-24; 55:8-9

### Aim

To show that God is greater than we can ever begin to imagine, defying adequate expression, but that through the doctrine of the Trinity we glimpse his wonder a little more clearly.

### Preparation

It is possible to deliver this talk without visual aids, but printing and displaying the questions and choice of answers listed below makes much more of an impact. The real answer in each case is given in brackets but this should not be displayed until *all* the questions have been answered.

### Talk

Tell the congregation you have prepared a challenging brain-teaser for them; a quiz all about astonishing facts. Ask the questions below, and invite members of the congregation to decide which they think is the correct answer. After taking a few answers each time, ask for a show of hands as you call out each answer. Don't give any hint at this point as to what the right answer is. You will probably find that one or two people quickly realise the point of the quiz, but continue anyway until you have asked all the questions.

1. How old is the earth?
   40,000 years old? 4 million years old? 1,000 million years old?
   (4,600 million years old)

2. How far is the earth from the sun?
   1,000 miles? 40,000 miles? 100,000 miles?
   (93 million miles)

3. How many species of bird are there in the world?
   400? 1,000? 6,000?
   (8,600)

4. How high is the world's tallest building?
   300 feet? 800 feet? 1,200 feet?
   (Shanghai World Finance Centre – 1,508 feet)

5. What is the speed of sound?
   200 mph? 400 mph? 600 mph?
   (760 mph)

6. How much does an African elephant weigh?
   50 stone? 190 stone? 375 stone?
   (787 stone)

7. What is the length of the world's longest river?
   800 miles? 1,999 miles? 3,007 miles?
   (Nile – 4,145 miles)

8. How much rain falls each year in the wettest place in the world?
   91 inches per year? 167 inches per year? 201 inches per year?
   (Buenaventura, Colombia – 265.47 inches)

9. What is the span of the Humber Bridge?
   1,234 feet? 2,065 feet? 3,980 feet?
   (4,626 feet)

10. What area does the Pacific Ocean cover?
    90,000 square miles? 250,000 square miles? 49,650 square miles?
    (63,800,000 square miles)

If it hasn't already become apparent, ask what was wrong with all of the answers you gave the congregation to choose from. The answer, of course, is that they were all too small!

Each of the answers was probably far bigger than expected. But if we can think too small here, the prophet Isaiah warns us how easily we can do the same in our understanding of God:

> Have you not known? Have you not heard? Has it not been told you from the beginning? Have you not understood from the foundations of the earth? It is he who sits above the circle of the earth, and its inhabitants are like grasshoppers; who stretches out the heavens like a curtain, and spreads them like a tent to live in; who brings princes to naught, and makes the rulers of the earth as nothing . . . My thoughts are not your thoughts, nor are your ways my ways, says the Lord. For as the heavens are higher than the earth, so are my ways higher than your ways, and my thoughts than your thoughts. *(Isaiah 40:21-24; 55:8-9)*

This is the God who is greater than we can ever begin to imagine. And that is what Trinity Sunday reminds us of – the fact that God is bigger than we think: both one person and three: God the Father, God the Son, and God the Holy Spirit; above us, beside us, within us, yet finally beyond us. Lose sight of those three persons and our picture of God is distorted. Hold on to them all, and we catch just a glimpse of the God who, as Paul wrote in his letter to the Ephesians, 'is able to accomplish abundantly more than we can ask or imagine, to him be glory in the church and in Christ Jesus to all generations, for ever and ever. Amen.' *(Ephesians 3:20-21)*

NICK FAWCETT

# Jesus told them . . .

'Go make disciples of all nations'

Can you fit his words into this puzzle?

F

G

Matt 28:19

KATIE THOMPSON

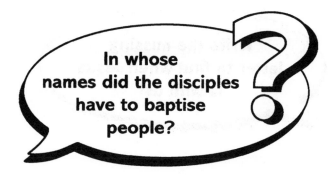

In whose names did the disciples have to baptise people?

**Add or subtract words and letters to find the answer!**

🌻 – LOWER + 🛁 – B + 🍐 – PA

_ _ _ _ _ _

☀ – UN + ⊜ – BUTT     ✋ – H

_ _ _     _ _ _

🐴 – RSE + 🌿 – HOL

_ _ _ _

🥄 – OON + 🔥 – FE + 🪁 – KE

_ _ _ _ _ _

**Matthew 28:19**

KATIE THOMPSON

Write the missing letter to find when Jesus is with us!

In BALL ⬤, but not in BILL _____

In LETTER ✉ but not in BETTER _____

In WELL but not in BELL 🔔, _____

In HAT 👒 but not in HOT _____

In SILLY but not in SILL _____

In STOP 🛑 but not in TOP 👕 _____

**Matthew 28:20**

KATIE THOMPSON

Matthew 28:16-20

**Father, Son and Holy Spirit**

The disciples set off for Galilee to meet Jesus as arranged

Use the grid references to help them find the mountain where they are to meet

## MAP REF

**BF, CG, CH, BH, BI, AI, AJ, AK, BL, CL, DL, DM.**

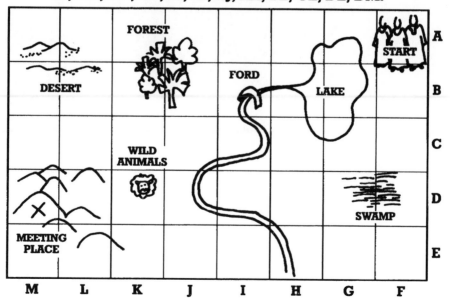

KATIE THOMPSON

## The Trinity

Ask the children and their leader to start us off by helping us understand what it means to be a community of faith. (They gradually unravel a ball of blue wool to surround the people in church.) Why did they choose blue? It looks a bit like water, and water reminds us of baptism. When we are baptised we are washed clean of our sins, and we are given new life in Christ. Just as we are all together inside this blue wool, we are all together in sharing our faith in God.

What is God like? We know God as the maker of our wonderful world; we know God as Jesus Christ who was born as a human baby, walked on this earth healing and teaching and showing God's love, died on a cross for love of us, and rose to new life so that he is alive for ever; and we know God as the powerful, energising Spirit who gives us God's life and strength. That's why we talk about God as 'Trinity' because 'tri' means 'three' and 'unity' means 'one'. So the nature of the one true God is *Father, Son and Holy Spirit*. (Everyone can repeat this whenever you mention it.) We aren't asked or expected to understand God's nature completely, but we are asked to put our faith and trust in him. And we know that God's nature is to be completely good and loving and faithful, so putting our faith in him is about the wisest and most sensible thing we can ever do.

We are the community of those who put their faith and trust in God – *Father, Son and Holy Spirit*.

SUSAN SAYERS

SUSAN SAYERS

Can you find:
AFRICA ☐
EAST ASIA ☐
SOUTH ASIA ☐
FORMER USSR ☐

The church is growing fastest in these places.

The biggest number of Christians is aged 22 years ...

... and most Christians are black.

Where are your contacts with them?

Go and baptise all the nations in the name of the Father and of the Son and of the Holy Spirit.
Matthew 28:19-20

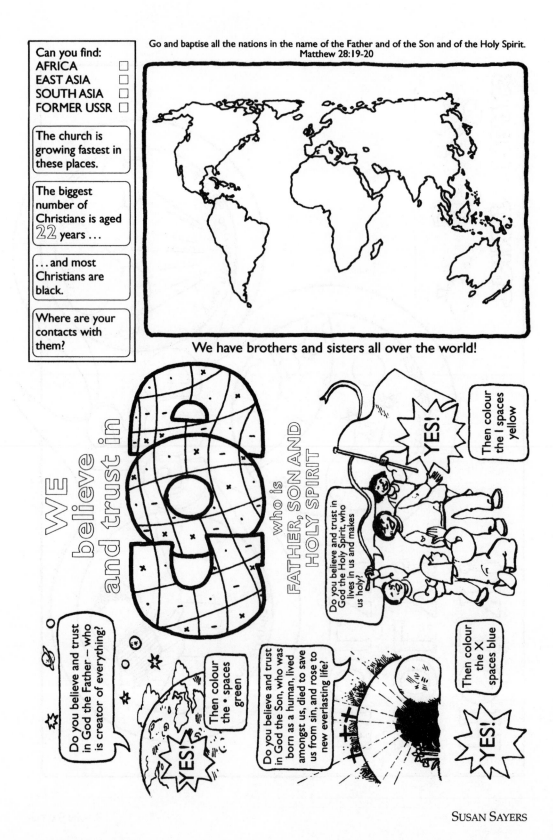

We have brothers and sisters all over the world!

WE believe and trust in

who is FATHER, SON AND HOLY SPIRIT

Do you believe and trust in God the Father – who is creator of everything?

YES!

Then colour the • spaces green

Do you believe and trust in God the Son, who was born as a human, lived amongst us, died to save us from sin, and rose to new everlasting life?

YES!

Then colour the X spaces blue

Do you believe and trust in God the Holy Spirit, who lives in us and makes us holy?

YES!

Then colour the I spaces yellow

SUSAN SAYERS

# Baptised in the name of the Father, Son and Holy Spirit

## Thought for the day

Each person in the Christian community is baptised in the name of the Father, the Son and the Holy Spirit.

## Reflection on the readings

Isaiah 40:12-17, 27-31
Psalm 8
2 Corinthians 13:11-13
Matthew 28:16-20

As Christians we are a community of people bound together by our baptism. The Church of God consists of all who are baptised in the name of the Father, the Son and the Holy Spirit. That means we are brothers and sisters in Christ with every person throughout the whole world who has been baptised – whatever their culture, whatever their age or status, whatever their denomination. This is world Church we are talking about, and of which we are members – it's all a lot wider and bigger than our local parish church, the Church of England or even the Anglican Communion. We have Christian relatives who worship in their thousands under the sky in the growing churches of Africa and Asia; others who worship in the simplicity of isolated chapels on windswept islands. What we all share is our declared faith in the amazing God who is Creator, Redeemer and Sanctifier all at once – community yet unity. Together it is we who are the Body of Christ, alive and available in this time zone, to live out God's love.

Thinking like this reminds us, too, of all who are members of the Church through baptism, but whose faith is barely a glimmer, and who rarely give God a thought. They, too, are our brothers and sisters in Christ, and that raises hard questions about our outreach to them, or even our local knowledge of who they are.

It also raises our awareness of what it means, in terms of privilege and responsibility, to be a baptised member of the Church of God. No one can ever become more of a member than they are by baptism; the youngest baptised baby is as fully a member of the Church as the most venerated archbishop, pope or evangelist. The great commission in today's Gospel was to make disciples of all nations, baptising them, and through baptism we are made into disciples – learners or students. We are to remain disciples – which means being willingly discipled – helping one another along in the faith, and living up to the reality of being God's community of love. Every time we receive Communion we are being fed Jesus' life and strength for this calling.

## Discussion starters

1. We are baptised in the name of God who is community in unity – three in one. What does that say about the model of living which we, as church, should show?

2. Baptism is full membership of the church. How does that affect our attitude to and nurture of the children in our church?

3. Being disciples means wearing L-plates. What aspects of being discipled do we gratefully accept, and which do we kick against?

SUSAN SAYERS

# Reflective material
## (sketches, meditations and poems)

### Praise

*Revelation 4:11*

*(This could be read by up to six people.)*

Lord God, we praise you for your light,
    which gleams and shines in distant stars,
    and streams forth from our neighbour sun,
    bathing in warmth this earth of ours.

Lord God, we praise you for your power,
    which holds the floating worlds in space,
    and lifts the mountains to the sky,
    and keeps the restless sea in place.

Lord God, we praise you for your truth,
    inspiring science, faith and art;
    for every prophet, every saint,
    who stirred the mind or pierced the heart.

Lord God, we praise you for your love,
    which caused this universe to be;
    for true compassion, friendship, care,
    and Christ who died on Calvary.

Lord God, we cannot plumb your depth;
    your height and breadth outstrip our thought.
We bow in penitence and awe,
    for you are all, and we are nought.

Yet, Lord, your light, your power, your truth
    you offer to us for our good;
    and most amazing is your love,
    which Christ has shown us by his blood.

PETER DAINTY

# Order of service

The people and priest:

**greet each other in the Lord's name**
(part of the welcome is an introduction to this teaching Eucharist, including the practical details concerning the children)

**confess their sins and are assured of God's forgiveness**
(everyone is gathered around the font for this)

**keep silence and pray a Collect**

**proclaim and respond to the Word of God**

- Isaiah 40:12-17, 27-31 – this is a communal reading, involving everyone
- Psalm 8 – use a metrical or responsorial version of Psalm 8, or a children's song
- 2 Corinthians 13:11-13 – this includes the Grace which everyone joins in
- Matthew 28:16-20 – gather everyone round the font for the Gospel
- After the Gospel, the children and adults engage in their own exploration of the Word
- All-age talk draws everyone's insights together

**renew their baptismal vows around the font**
(and there may be a baptism)

**pray for the Church and the world**

**exchange the Peace**

**prepare the table**

**pray the Eucharistic Prayer**

**break the bread**

**receive Communion**

**depart with God's blessing**
(with the words from Matthew 28 and the sounds of the ocean)

(During some of the hymns the children wave streamers of three strands – white, blue and green. The final hymn is accompanied by shakers and other percussion instruments.)

SUSAN SAYERS

## Time of Confession and Forgiveness

Everyone gathers around the font, with the children at the front or on adult shoulders so that they can see. Water is being scooped up and splashed down throughout.

Leader      We gather here around the font to remind ourselves that our loving God can wash us clean of all our sinfulness.

All         **As we begin our worship together,**
            **we want to tell God that we are very sorry**
            **for all our selfishness and lack of love.**

Leader      Lord, we know that you are the only one who can forgive sin.

All         **Please forgive us and cleanse us of all our sin.**
            **Amen.**

As a sign of God's cleansing forgiveness, invite everyone to dip their hands in the water and trace the shape of the cross on their foreheads before returning to their seats. (If there are large numbers of people, pour water into several bowls for this.)

## Psalm 8

Use a responsorial version. Hymns based on this Psalm include 'O Lord my God, when I in awesome wonder', 'Fishes of the ocean' and the children's song 'Our God is so great' (all in *Complete Anglican Hymns Old & New*).

If you make constellation-shaped pinpricks in black paper and place this on an OHP it can be projected upwards to cover the walls or roof with stars during the Psalm or song.

## The sending out

Play a CD or tape of ocean waves – such as *Ocean surf* (Music Collection International) – and then speak over it.

President   Thefore go and make disciples of all nations,
            baptising them in the name of the Father
            and of the Son and of the Holy Spirit
            and teaching them to obey
            everything I have commanded you.
            And surely I am with you always,
            to the very end of time.
            (Matthew 28:19-20)

All         **Thanks be to God.**                                    SUSAN SAYERS

# All Saints

# All Saints' Day

*The great company of heaven and the blessings of heaven*

### Revelation 7:9-17
*(also Psalm 34:1-10; 1 John 3:1-3; Matthew 5:1-12)*

## A reading from the Gospel of Matthew (5:1-12)

A crowd of disciples gathered around, and Jesus sat down and began to preach to them:

Happy are the poor in spirit, for the kingdom of heaven is theirs.

Happy are the broken-hearted, for they will be comforted.

Happy are the meek and gentle, for the earth will belong to them.

Happy are those who hunger and thirst for what is right, for justice will be theirs.

Happy are those who show forgiveness, because they will receive forgiveness in return.

Happy are those with a pure heart, for they shall see the face of God.

Happy are the peace-makers; God will call them his children.

Happy are those who suffer because they stand up for what is right; the kingdom of heaven belongs to them.

Be happy when people harass and mistreat you, and tell lies about you because you are my disciples. All this was suffered by the prophets who came before you. Be glad because when the time comes you will be richly rewarded in heaven.

This is the Gospel of the Lord
**Praise to you, Lord Jesus Christ**

KATIE THOMPSON

## Who's the lucky one?

*Matthew 5:3-10*

*The Beatitudes, as these lines are commonly known, are often misunderstood. It is not as if, 'come the Revolution', the tables will be turned and the unfortunates of this world will lord it over their oppressors. On the contrary, God's favourites will remain poor, unimportant, heartbroken, gentle and hungry. But it is they who are the really fortunate ones, because nothing stands between them and God. In fact, they are just like Jesus, who identified himself with the marginalised, and in whom they were therefore able to see the face of God himself. How much luckier can you get?*

How lucky you are if you are poor!
God will make you rich!

How lucky you are if you're not very important!
God will make you great!

How lucky you are if your heart has been broken!
It will mend even stronger!

How lucky you are if you're starving!
You'll get all you want and more!

How lucky you are if you're tender with others!
You know how tender God really is!

How lucky you are if you're straight with people!
You see God very clearly indeed!

How lucky you are if you make friends with people!
You've brought a bit of heaven to earth!

How lucky you are if people hate you
for standing up for what is right!
A new world can be built on people like you!

*The Beatitudes for Children* © McCrimmons. Used with permission.

H. J. RICHARDS

# Prayers

## Our Christian heritage

Lord God of history,
   we thank you for the way you have been with your people
      across the years –
      the way you called Abraham to leave everything
      and venture out into the unknown,
      the way you chose Moses to lead the people of Israel
      out of slavery and through the wilderness
      into the Promised Land,
      the way you called judges and priests,
      rulers and prophets,
      writers and thinkers,
      to guide and challenge your people,
      teaching them more of your will
      and constantly seeking to draw them closer to you.
   One generation shall laud your works to another,
      **and shall declare your mighty acts.**

Lord God of history,
  we thank you for the way Jesus called twelve ordinary people
    to be his apostles,
    how through their faith and witness
    you chose countless others to become your Church,
    and how through the years since then,
    despite all its faults and weaknesses,
    its errors and misunderstandings,
    you have spoken through your Church
    to countless generations,
    ever more people day by day coming
    to living and saving faith in Christ.
  One generation shall laud your works to another,
    **and shall declare your mighty acts.**

Lord God of history,
  we thank you for the way
    you called our own church into being –
    the way you led various individuals
    to begin a new initiative in this area,
    the way you guided them to this place,
    the way you inspired them to persevere
    despite the obstacles they faced.
  One generation shall laud your works to another,
    **and shall declare your mighty acts.**

We thank you for the way you have spoken
    through those who have been part of this church,
    the way you have taught and inspired
    through pastors and teachers,
    the way you made yourself known
    through the life, witness, and example
    of those who have gone before us,
    running their race and keeping the faith,
    and the way you continue to speak to us
    through one another.
  One generation shall laud your works to another,
    **and shall declare your mighty acts.**

Lord God of history,
  we thank you for the tradition of faith in which we stand –
    the great multitude of witnesses
    that surround us in past and present,
    and we thank you for the history of this church
    of which we are a part,
    the privilege of belonging to it,
    to one another and to you.

Help us, we pray, to learn from all that has gone before,
    to contribute meaningfully
    to this present chapter in our church's life,
    and to work faithfully so that those who come after us
    may be inspired by the legacy they inherit
    to continue your work and further your cause.
One generation shall laud your works to another,
    **and shall declare your mighty acts.**

Thanks be to God through Jesus Christ our Lord,
    the same yesterday, today and forever.
    **Amen.**

NICK FAWCETT

## Thanksgiving and petition – the people of God

Eternal God,
    we thank you for your hand at work throughout history,
        bringing order out of chaos,
        shaping the universe
        and creating the world we live in.
    But especially today, we thank you for men and women of faith,
        all those who, across the years and in our own lifetime,
        have given us an example to follow.
    For the great company of your people,
        and for our place within it,
        **Lord, we thank you.**

We thank you for the commitment of Abraham –
    his willingness to step out into the unknown,
    to walk in faith,
    to trust in your promise.
For the great company of your people,
    and for our place within it,
    **Lord, we thank you.**

We thank you for the dedication of Moses –
    the way you used him to lead your people out of slavery,
    guide them through the wilderness
    and bring them to the Promised Land.
For the great company of your people,
    and for our place within it,
    **Lord, we thank you.**

We thank you for the prophets –
    those who had the vision and courage to speak your word,
    to pronounce your judgement,
    to make known your mercy
    and to proclaim your love.

For the great company of your people,
  and for our place within it,
    **Lord, we thank you.**

We thank you for the Apostles –
  for their willingness to leave everything and follow Jesus,
  their witness to his death and resurrection,
  their courage in the face of hostility and persecution.
For the great company of your people,
  and for our place within it,
    **Lord, we thank you.**

We thank you for the great saints of the Church –
  those whose commitment to you has been self-evident,
  whose devotion to you has shone from their lives,
  who have given heart, mind and soul to the service of Christ.
For the great company of your people,
  and for our place within it,
    **Lord, we thank you.**

We thank you for those who have made known the gospel to us –
  those who have encouraged and instructed us in faith,
  who have been a source of inspiration,
  who have walked with us on our journey of discipleship.
For the great company of your people,
  and for our place within it,
    **Lord, we thank you.**

We thank you for one another –
  for our share in the inheritance of your people,
  for our unity in the body of Christ,
  for the comfort, strength and support we are able to give
    one to another.
For the great company of your people,
  and for our place within it,
    **Lord, we thank you.**

And so we pray finally for ourselves –
  that you will help us to continue
  in the footsteps of those before us,
  keeping the faith,
  running the race with perseverance,
  offering to future generations an example in turn.
For the great company of your people,
  and for our place within it,
    **Lord, we thank you.**

In the name of Christ.
**Amen.**                                               NICK FAWCETT

## Intercession

Loving God,
    we remember today all who have gone ahead of us
        in the journey of faith,
        running the race set before them,
        and holding firm to the end.
**Grant to them and to us your eternal blessing.**

We remember those you called at the beginning –
    like Abraham, Isaac and Jacob –
    examples of faith who have been an inspiration
    to generations since.
**Grant to them and to us your eternal blessing.**

We remember those you called to lead your people
    through adversity –
    like Moses, Joshua, Gideon –
    examples of commitment and determination
    against all odds.
**Grant to them and to us your eternal blessing.**

We remember those you called to speak your word –
    like Samuel, Elijah, Elisha –
    examples of wisdom and insight into your will.
**Grant to them and to us your eternal blessing.**

We remember those you called to rule your chosen nation –
    like Saul, David, Solomon –
    examples of human greatness and human fallibility.
**Grant to them and to us your eternal blessing.**

We remember those you called
    to proclaim judgement and renewal –
    like Isaiah, Ezekiel, Jeremiah –
    examples of openness to your word
    and courage in proclaiming it.
**Grant to them and to us your eternal blessing.**

We remember these and so many more
    leading up to the coming of Christ,
    and we remember also your servants
    who were a part of his ministry,
    or a part of his Church.
**Grant to them and to us your eternal blessing.**

We remember John the Baptist, the voice in the wilderness,
    Mary, the mother of Jesus,
    the twelve apostles, his friends and confidantes,

the women at the empty tomb, looking in vain for his body,
and all those countless individuals
who were touched by his earthly ministry.
**Grant to them and to us your eternal blessing.**

We remember Peter, the Rock of the Church,
Paul, apostle to the Gentiles,
and those who have followed in their footsteps,
saints known and unknown, near and far,
yet each a part of the great company of your people
in heaven and on earth.
**Grant to them and to us your eternal blessing.**

We remember those we have known,
those who have been part of our own church,
who have influenced our lives,
who have inspired and encouraged us through their lives.
**Grant to them and to us your eternal blessing.**

We remember those around us,
the churches of our town,
Christians across the country,
fellow-believers throughout the world.
**Grant to them and to us your eternal blessing.**

And we pray finally for those who will come after us,
all who will come to faith,
offer their service,
and live for Christ.
**Grant to them and to us your eternal blessing.**

Loving God,
we remember today all who have gone before us
in the journey of faith.
Help us and all who follow to run the race as they did,
holding firm to the end.
**Grant to them and to us your eternal blessing,**
**through Jesus Christ our Lord.**
**Amen.**

NICK FAWCETT

# All-age-talk material

## All saints?

### Aim

To show that All Saints' Day is not simply about exceptional examples of disciple-ship, but about anybody and everybody who follows the way of Christ.

### Preparation

No preparation is needed for this talk, but, to include a visual dimension, you may like to display the list of names given below.

### Talk

Begin by asking what special day it is. Explain that this is a day when tradition-ally the Church recalls the great saints and martyrs who have kept the faith before us. Ask if anyone can tell you what makes a saint. Invite suggestions and respond appropriately. Then tell the congregation you have found what seem to be the names of some unusual saints, and you need their help in deciding if any truly are. Read out the list, below, asking if anyone can identify who or what they are:

| | |
|---|---|
| St John's Wort | A flowering shrub |
| St Moritz | A ski resort in Switzerland |
| Saint-Saëns | A French composer |
| St Christopher | A saint associated with good luck |
| St Helena | A mountainous island in the South Atlantic |
| Saint (and Greavsie) | A football pundit |
| St Luke | Writer of Luke's Gospel |
| St Elsewhere | A television programme |
| St Andrew | The patron saint of Scotland |
| The Saint | A book and TV character |
| St David | The patron saint of Wales |
| St Leger | The name of a classic horse race |
| Saint-Laurent | A celebrated French fashion designer |
| The Saints | The nickname of Southampton Football Club |
| St George | The patron saint of England who, according to legend, killed a dragon |
| St Bernard | A breed of dog, and also the name of a medieval theologian |
| St Ives | A holiday resort in Cornwall |
| St Patrick | The patron saint of Ireland |
| St Ivel | A brand of dairy products |
| St Nicholas | The saint associated with Christmas |

Although they all have the word 'saint' as part of their name, clearly some are saints and some are not. It is not, then, the word 'saint' that's important, but what it represents. We remember people like St Andrew, St David, St Patrick and St George, and give them the title 'saint' because of the quality of their lives and the faith they showed. But they are not the only saints, at least not according to the Bible, for what we read there is that anybody and everybody who accepts and follows Jesus is part of the great company of saints in heaven and on earth. So it was that Paul wrote to the Colossians:

> May you be made strong with all the strength that comes from his glorious power . . . giving thanks to the Father, who has enabled you to share in the inheritance of the saints in the light. *(Colossians 1:11a, 12)*

We are all called to be saints of God, each one of us. This day, then, reminds us of those who have gone before us and kept the faith – the well-known and the not so well-known – and it challenges us to learn from their example so that we may inspire and encourage others in turn.

Finish with the hymn *I sing a song of the saints of God.*                    NICK FAWCETT

Like the saints
we can offer everything
we do as an act of
love for God

Think of three ordinary things which you could do as
an act of love for God and draw yourself doing them

ACTS OF LOVE

KATIE THOMPSON

Today's Gospel is sometimes called 'The Sermon on the Mount'. What other name is given to these words of Jesus?

Write the next letter of the alphabet above the letters given.
For example, E will be written above D

$\overline{\text{S}}$ $\overline{\text{G}}$ $\overline{\text{D}}$

$\overline{\text{A}}$ $\overline{\text{D}}$ $\overline{\text{Z}}$ $\overline{\text{S}}$ $\overline{\text{H}}$ $\overline{\text{S}}$ $\overline{\text{T}}$ $\overline{\text{C}}$ $\overline{\text{D}}$ $\overline{\text{R}}$

KATIE THOMPSON

## The saints in heaven

## Matthew 5:1-12

Someone who has lived a life of outstanding goodness, and who is already with God in heaven, is called a saint

### Match each patron saint with his country

| A | B | C | D |
|---|---|---|---|
| **Saint David** | **Saint George** | **Saint Patrick** | **Saint Andrew** |

**A and** _____   **B and** _____   **C and** _____   **D and** _____

| E | F | G | H |
|---|---|---|---|
| **Ireland** | **Scotland** | **England** | **Wales** |

KATIE THOMPSON

# Reflective material
## (sketches, meditations and poems)

## People of faith

I walked in the evening stillness
  and I saw wheat standing
  at the edges of fields
  already harvested,
  and I remembered Ruth,
  gleaning in the fields of Boaz –

and I reached out
  and touched her hand.

I walked in the evening stillness
  and I heard a breath of wind
  whispering in the trees,
  and I remembered Nicodemus
  coming to Jesus by night
  and how Jesus turned to the wind and said,
  'So is everyone
  that is born of the Spirit' –

and I bent my head
  to catch the sound of his voice.

I walked in the evening stillness
  and I saw clouds in the sky,
  so many shapes and colours,
  and I remembered Elijah
  praying on Mount Carmel
  and the little cloud
  that arose out of the sea
  no bigger than a man's hand –

and I stood beside him
  gazing over the waters.

I walked in the evening stillness
  and I remembered that we are surrounded
  by a great cloud of witnesses,
  a multitude that no man can number,
  people of faith from every generation,
  and as I reached out my hands to them,
  I did not feel alone any more.

Today I walked in the evening stillness
  and was comforted by God.

MARY HATHAWAY

## The Beatitudes

*Matthew 5:1-12*

*(Suitable for up to nine readers.)*

In the kingdom of Mammon they firmly believe
    that happiness is a cigar,
      an expensive meal, a successful deal,
      or a luxury motor car.
But the Kingdom of heaven belongs to the poor
    who want no more.

In the kingdom of Mammon they laugh and they sing
    to the promptings of pleasure machines;
      they are grimly resolved to enjoy every hour
      and perpetuate youth by all means.
But God gives true comfort to all those who mourn
    and are reborn.

In the kingdom of Mammon they know how to rule
    with arrogant metallic powers;
      they scan the horizon with violent eyes
      from distant electronic towers.
But God has apportioned this earth to the meek,
    who gently seek.

In the kingdom of Mammon they hunger and thirst
    for possessions and pleasure and power;
      and though the first taste may be sweet to the tongue,
      their increase is putrid and sour.
But those who crave good are eternally filled,
    as God has willed.

In the kingdom of Mammon the law of the state
    is enforced with an iron intent;
      the offender is crushed with the harshest revenge
      that justice's slaves can invent.
But God reserves mercy for those who forgive,
    glad to let live.

In the kingdom of Mammon they search for the truth
    in a million mystical ways:
      from magic and trances to dangerous drugs,
      and the latest nonsensible craze.
But God shines on those who combine a pure heart
    with childlike art.

In the kingdom of Mammon they're masters of war
    with their missiles and bombers and guns;
      they are always prepared for surprising attacks
      and the blazing of nuclear suns.
But the children of God are the ones who make peace;
    may they increase.

In the kingdom of Mammon they torture and kill
    for the sake of the popular good;
      any threat to the state will be jailed without trial
      or nailed to a blunt cross of wood.
But God's Kingdom belongs to all those who endure,
    faithful and sure.

The kingdom of Mammon looks noble and grand
    in the glare of technology's day,
      but its concrete foundations are rooted in sand
      and are ready to crumble away.
The Kingdom of Heaven is founded on rock;
    proof against shock.

PETER DAINTY

# Sources of Material

Bower, Tony:
*Buried Treasure*
*The Word that Changed the World*

Butler, Barbara: *Sharing Ways and Wisdoms*

Castle, Tony: *So Much To Celebrate*

Dainty, Peter: *The Electric Gospel*

Dale, Alan: *The Alan Dale Bible*

Fawcett, Nick:
*Getting it Across*
*No Ordinary Man*
*No Ordinary Man*, Book 2
*Prayers for All Seasons*
*Prayers for All Seasons*, Book 2
*To Put It Another Way*

Forster, Michael:
*Act One*
*The Big G Interviews*
*Three + One – A Book of Beginnings*
*Three + One – Festivals One*
*Three + One – From Trouble to Triumph*
*Three + One – Great Kings*

Forster, Michael and Simon Smith:
*A New Start in All-age Worship*

Fuller, Jill: *Looking Beyond*

Harding, Nick: *All-age Everything*

Hardwick, John: *Children's Talks with Puppet Sketches*

Hardwick, Susan: *Retreat and Quiet-day Resource*

Hathaway, Mary: *A Word for All Seasons*

Lomax, Tim: *Freedom Within a Framework*

O'Mahony, Gerald: *100 Ways To Hear the Good News*

Richards, H. J.: *Plain English Bible*

Rundle, Elizabeth: *You're Never Alone*

Sayers, Susan:
*100 Talks for All-age Worship*
*Bread and Wine People*
*Children Too*
*First Fruits*
*Including Children*
*Intercessions for the Church Year*
*New Intercessions for the Church Year*

Thomas, Stuart: *One Lord, One Faith*

Thompson, Katie:
*Celebrations for Young People*
*Footprints in Faith*
*Hear the Good News*
*Step by Step*

Townsend, Pete:
*Café Logos, Year A*
*Touch Wood*

Walker, David: *Sketches for the Church Year*

Woodhouse, Patrick: *Beyond Words*